Bad Form

BAD FORM

Social Mistakes and the Nineteenth-Century Novel

Kent Puckett

2008

OXFORD
UNIVERSITY PRESS

Oxford   New York
Auckland   Cape Town   Dar es Salaam   Hong Kong   Karachi
Kuala Lumpur   Madrid   Melbourne   Mexico City   Nairobi
New Delhi   Shanghai   Taipei   Toronto

With offices in
Argentina   Austria   Brazil   Chile   Czech Republic   France   Greece
Guatemala   Hungary   Italy   Japan   Poland   Portugal   Singapore
South Korea   Switzerland   Thailand   Turkey   Ukraine   Vietnam

Published by Oxford University Press, Inc.
198 Madison Avenue, New York, New York 10016
www.oup.com

Library of Congress Cataloging-in-Publication Data

Puckett, Kent.
  Bad form : social mistakes and the nineteenth century novel / by Kent Puckett.
      p. cm.
   ISBN 978-0-19-533275-9
   1. Fiction—19th century—History and criticism—Theory, etc.   2. Manners and
customs in literature.   3. Flaubert, Gustave, 1821–1880—Knowledge—Manners
and customs.   4. Eliot, George, 1819–1880—Knowledge—Manners and customs.
5. James, Henry, 1843–1916—Knowledge—Manners and customs.   6. English
fiction—19th century—History and criticism.   7. Literature and society—Great
Britain—History—19th century.   8. French fiction—19th century—History
and criticism.   9. Literature and society—France—History—19th century.   I. Title.
PN3499.P75 2008
809.3—dc22   2008003644

9 8 7 6 5 4 3 2 1

Printed in the United States of America
on acid-free paper

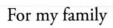
For my family

Acknowledgments

I've racked up a lot of debt while writing *Bad Form*, and if I can't repay it, I can at least (and with pleasure) acknowledge it. First, special thanks to David Miller, my marvelous friend, colleague, and critic. Talking with him about this book has made every one of its pages better and sharper than it could have been otherwise. Thanks, too, to Nick Dames, who responded to my work at several stages with terrific subtlety and intelligence. I owe more than I can say to a few who have—in different ways—kept me sane over the years: Eric Bulson, Bryan Wagner, and Adam Zucker. Graduate school was made great, as great as it could be, by the presence of a number of unusually brilliant and brilliantly unusual people: Dohra Ahmad, Chris Brown, Aman Garcha, Judith Goldman, Joe Keith, David Kurnick, Mike Malouf, Ana Mitrić, Derek Nystrom, Geoff Rector, Ben Robinson, Danny Siegel, and Robin Varghese. More recently, I have benefited from the advice and example of my colleagues at U.C. Berkeley. Particular thanks go to those who have generously read and commented on my work: Elizabeth Abel, Janet Adelman, Ann Banfield, John Bishop,

Mitch Breitwieser, Ian Duncan, Anne-Lise François, Catherine Gallagher, Steve Goldsmith, Kevis Goodman, Dori Hale, Celeste Langan, Sharon Marcus, Sam Otter, Mike Rubenstein, Scott Saul, and Alex Zwerdling. Many thanks go to Shannon McLachlan at Oxford University Press. She has made what is necessarily an anxious process into something both edifying and enjoyable. Thanks, too, to Alex Woloch and to other press readers for their insightful, sharp, and generous readings. It is a better book because of their advice. Susan Ecklund's judicious copyediting helped me to avoid (or at least to disguise) my own bad form. Thanks to Susan M. Griffin, editor of *The Henry James Review*; a part of chapter 3 has appeared in its pages. And, what can I say about my best friend, Kara Wittman? Her patience, imagination, and intelligence are only some of the wonders she brings with her everywhere she goes. I owe much, much more than this book to her. Finally, I would like to dedicate this book to my family, to my parents Kent and Franceen Puckett—they are generous, brilliant, hilarious—and to my sister Nora Puckett: counselor, rhythm section, pal.

Contents

Bad Form

Introduction: Making Mistakes

*He sacrifices his identity for a moment, and sometimes
the encounter, but the principles are preserved. He may be
ground between opposing assumptions, thereby preventing
direct friction between them, or he may be almost pulled
apart, so that principles with little relation to one another
may operate together. Social structure gains elasticity; the
individual merely loses composure.*
> —Erving Goffman, "Embarrassment and
> Social Organization"[1]

Verbal slips and tics, fashion failures, lapses, gaffes, and blunders: these are, we learn the hard way, what life is all about. Tough to anticipate but easy to recognize, mistakes happen; and, if they are an unavoidable aspect of life with other people, so are they bound up with an itch to narrate that life and to hear it narrated in turn. Mistakes make us embarrassed, and embarrassment, it seems, can make us talk. A truly comprehensive book about all the different mistakes we make would be a very big book: a shadow history of the social, an endless chronicle of the bungled, the forgotten, and the excessive, a theory of what ugly little things make history happen in the first place. Although *Bad Form* is about the mistake, it cannot in that case be about every mistake. It is, instead, an argument about the relationship between the social mistake, the omnisciently narrated nineteenth-century novel, and a bourgeois social order for which that novel held what authority it did.

1. Erving Goffman, *Interaction Ritual: Essays in Face-to-Face Behavior* (Chicago: Aldine, 1967), 112.

Insofar as this book argues for a relation between the novel and an etiquette system that came into existence in the form of etiquette books, advice columns, and other literary ephemera in the second quarter of the nineteenth century, it focuses not only on a certain kind of novel but also on a certain kind of mistake, a represented social mistake that falls short of scene-shattering intensity and, as it makes visible the space between what is and isn't done, produces a range of coherence effects within the novel at the related levels of character, plot, and narration.

I focus on a number of novels—by Elizabeth Gaskell, William Makepeace Thackeray, Honoré de Balzac, George Eliot, Gustave Flaubert, and Henry James—in order to account for relations between the social mistake and the nineteenth-century novel as well as between social form and literary form more generally. Still, even this work might come in many colors: if, for instance, *Bad Form* were a literary history of the nuts and bolts of how manners worked, it might begin with Caxton, Erasmus, or Castiglione and make its way, while thinking about relations between domestic privacy, psychological interiority, and the practice of etiquette, through Chesterfield, the conduct book, *Evelina,* and *Les liaisons dangereuses. Bad Form* is, however, less interested in the material details of that history (who did what with which fork when?) than it is in the fact that the tenuous difference between good and bad is an index of the context-specific ways in which forms of social and literary coherence are structurally embodied, understood, and valued at particular moments.[2] If it were a book on the assorted efforts to perfect and to produce the self through fraught attempts at perfect and perfectly productive manners in the nineteenth century, a book on the dandies, flâneurs, and other artists of modern life, it might look at Brummell, Baudelaire, or Wilde. This book is, however, less interested in the self-conscious management of self than it is in the represented experience of an upwardly mobile and increasingly literate middle class faced with social rules tethered to the shifting and antiteleological forms of fashion.[3] And, if it were a book about transgression, about

---

2. For more on the relation between the civilizing process and the rise of the novel, see Nancy Armstrong, *Desire and Domestic Fiction: A Political History of the Novel* (New York: Oxford University Press, 1987); Norbert Elias, *The Civilizing Process: Sociogenetic and Psychogenetic Investigations,* ed. Eric Dunning, Johan Goudsblom, and Stephen Mennel, trans. Edmund Jephcott (Oxford: Blackwell, 1994); John E. Mason, *Gentlefolk in the Making: Studies in the History of English Courtesy Literature and Related Topics from 1531–1774* (New York: Octagon Books, 1971); Philippe Perrot, *Fashioning the Bourgeoisie: A History of Clothing in the Nineteenth Century,* trans. Richard Bienvenu (Princeton, NJ: Princeton University Press, 1994); Margaret Visser, *The Rituals of Dinner: The Origins, Evolution, Eccentricities, and Meaning of Table Manners* (London: Penguin, 1991); and Ian Watt, *The Rise of the Novel* (Berkeley: University of California Press, 1957).

3. In this, *Bad Form* differs from recent work that aligns itself with, as Amanda Anderson puts it, "the late Foucault enacting the embrace of aesthetic modernity via his turn to ethos and practices of the self." Although the period I write about is significantly bookended by more or less successful

passions strong enough to shatter the self, the social, and the very structure of the literary, it might address novels by Thomas Hardy, Emily Brontë, or Fyodor Dostoyevsky.[4] This book is, however, less interested in the shameless, shattering abandon of the happy vulgarian—moments let wonderfully loose in Dickens, Turgenev, or Trollope—than it is in softer but still embarrassing kinds of error that it refers to as bad form, livable (but just barely!) lapses that help us to see the limits both of bourgeois social convention and of a novel form that did much to codify and to represent those conventions to subjects of a modernity increasingly and necessarily unsure of the rules of the game.[5]

I begin in the second quarter of the nineteenth century, a time in Europe marked by the proliferation of many and mutating social anxieties. In England, France, and elsewhere fraught relations between tradition, revolution, and reform had effects on the ways in which the importance of social convention was understood at both the most and the least abstract levels of experience; as I describe in the next chapter, these years witnessed the emergence both of etiquette as an autonomous quasi-ethical discourse and of the etiquette book as a key representative of that discourse. Where earlier kinds of writing about manners (conduct books, courtesy manuals, etc.) subordinated advice about what to do to a distinct and autonomous ethical ideal, the etiquette book followed the fluid and antifoundational forms of fashion: like the length of trouser legs and hemlines, etiquette's imperatives

---

efforts aesthetically to manage the self—with Regency dandies like Brummell at one end and Wilde at the other—good form remains in my argument and for the figures I discuss more a structurally determining and often maddening ideal than a strategically posited ethos. Amanda Anderson, "Victorian Studies and the Two Modernities," *Victorian Studies*, no. 2 (Winter 2005): 198.

4. In this, I both own a debt to and mark a distance from Leo Bersani. Although his work (*Balzac to Beckett: Center and Circumference in French Fiction* and *A Future for Astyanax* in particular), to which I refer regularly in what follows, offers an important model of what it means to talk about the social and its limits, the difference between his object of analysis and my own is something like the difference represented in Durkheim's distinction between the consequences that follow from breaking "rules of law" and other, less violent expressions of social constraint: "If I do not conform to ordinary conventions, if in my mode of dress I pay no heed to what is customary in my country and in my social class, the laughter I provoke, the social distance at which I am kept, produce, although in a more mitigated form, the same results as any real penalty." Émile Durkheim, *The Rules of the Sociological Method* (New York: Free Press, 1982), 50.

5. This distinction is one that animates some of Žižek's thinking on the relation between the individual and the "big Other" in a nontotalitarian but nevertheless determinate social field: "This nonknowledge of the Other opens up a certain distance that, so to speak, gives us breathing space, i.e., that allows us to confer upon our actions a supplementary meaning beyond the one that is socially acknowledged. For this very reason, the social game (the rules of etiquette, etc.), in the very stupidity of its ritual, is never simply superficial. We can indulge in our secret wars only as long as the Other does not take cognizance of them, for the moment the Other can no longer ignore them, the social bond dissolves itself. A catastrophe ensues, similar to the one instigated by the child's observation that the emperor is naked." Secret wars and social mistakes: both exist, both make waves, both make *form* without calling irreparably damaging attention to the systematicity of the social field. Slavoj Žižek, *Looking Awry: An Introduction to Jacques Lacan through Popular Culture* (Cambridge, MA: MIT Press, 1992), 72–73.

rose and fell routinely and without much reason.[6] Of course, this change
in the way the codes of everyday life were imagined by and presented to
a public was coincident with the sharpening of other anxieties about the
nature and sources of social authority. In England, etiquette's rise follows
a more general drift toward and anxiety about a reform movement best
represented by the several Reform Acts (1832, 1867, 1884). There were rules,
but rules, once reform is admitted as a structurally necessary alternative to
revolution, are always in flux: "We have discarded," wrote John Stuart Mill,
"the fixed costumes of our forefathers; everyone must still dress like other
people, but the fashion may change once or twice a year."[7] In France, an increasingly and oddly familiar oscillation between revolution and restoration
pushed the paradox of a political authority both potent and hollow to the
foreground: "The nineteenth-century political scene was sometimes tumul-
tuous, it is true, punctuated by revolutionary ruptures in 1830, 1848, 1871.
Nonetheless, Napoleon's great work of consolidation, represented by the
law codes, the judicial system, and the administrative bureaucracy, survived
all the surface tumult intact."[8] If these political plate shifts led to variously
conceived schemes to re-center the social, they were also managed locally
in the form of shifting social rules and fickle forms of fashion that were a
source of greater and greater nervousness because their self-conscious triviality was nonetheless motivated with all the force of an imperative.

Of course, this same stretch of time saw both the European novel and
an omniscient narration whose voice was the voice of that novel's cultural
authority come into their own, and *Bad Form* is above all else a theory of
that novel; it is, however, a theory that arrives at its claims about character,
plot, and narration through close analyses of the scene of the represented
social mistake. Why, though, look to the mistake as the basis for a theory
of the novel? For starters, the mistake, because we associate its contingency
with psychological depth and interiority, produces an especially convincing
character effect: to err, the saying goes, is human.[9] And, the mistake stands

6. One exceptionally well-placed commentator looking back from 1870 captured exactly this blend of
triviality, anxiety, and change: "Who can now record the degrees by which the custom prevalent in my
youth of asking each other to take wine together at dinner became obsolete? Who will be able to fix, twenty
years hence, the date when our dinners began to be carved and handed round by servants, instead of smo-
king before our eyes and noses on the table? To record such little matters would indeed be 'to chronicle
small beer.'" James Edward Austen-Leigh, *A Memoir of Jane Austen: And Other Family Recollections* (New
York: Oxford University Press, 2002), 30.

7. John Stuart Mill, *On Liberty and Other Essays* (Oxford: Oxford University Press, 1998), 79.

8. William M. Reddy, *The Navigation of Feeling: A Framework for the History of Emotions* (Cambridge:
Cambridge University Press, 2001), 215.

9. On the subject of character, see Diana Knight, *Flaubert's Characters* (Cambridge: Cambridge University Press, 1985); Watt, *The Rise of the Novel*; Ann Jefferson, *The Nouveau Roman and the Poetics of Fiction*

as the most concentrated instance of plot in a genre known for its plotted-ness and as a powerful source of formal coherence and narrative desire. Mistakes not only happen but also make us want things to be different, and the desire for the end to differ from the beginning is also the novel's desire.[10] And, what's more, if we follow Audrey Jaffe's *Vanishing Points: Dickens, Narrative, and the Subject of Omniscience* (as I often do over the course of *Bad Form*) and imagine omniscient narration as securing its authority on the basis of its structuring "refusal of" the embodied, marked character, *Bad Form* shows that an uneasy relation between a specifically omniscient narration and the literary character emerges forcefully at the site of the represented social mistake.[11] In other words, the novel's efforts to differentiate structurally and socially between character and narration with the help of the mistake tend to collapse in an identification that gives omniscient narration its own threatened character.

It must, of course, be admitted that narrative omniscience is a weird concept and that to rely on it is to risk seeming obsessed or out of touch. The term is tough in part because it is often made to do an unreasonable amount of work: it can seem incoherently to name both an act of narrating and the person of the narrator, both a loose cluster of literary devices and something like a single human consciousness. Jonathan Culler has recently argued that, because of this incoherence, few of the critics who rely on the concept "express much confidence in it."[12] It is not, however, just the questionable descriptive value of the concept that troubles Culler: it is instead "the *idea* of omniscient narrative rather than the diverse practices to which the name applies, that should sadden or outrage us."[13] The idea of omniscience is outrageous because it reproduces in the field of the literary a damaging theological error and as a result sustains an illusion against which no ordinary life could measure up. Omniscience is, in other words, an insult. And because the idea of omniscience is an insult both to readers and to the characters who live under

---

(Cambridge: Cambridge University Press, 1980); Deidre Shauna Lynch, *The Economy of Character: Novels, Market Culture, and the Business of Inner Meaning* (Chicago: University of Chicago Press, 1998); Alex Woloch, *The One vs. the Many: Minor Characters and the Space of the Protagonist in the Novel* (Princeton, NJ: Princeton University Press, 2003).

10. The notion of "narrative desire" is, of course, a central concern of Peter Brooks's *Reading for the Plot: Design and Intention in Narrative* (Cambridge, MA: Harvard University Press, 1992).

11. Audrey Jaffe, *Vanishing Points: Dickens, Narrative, and the Subject of Omniscience* (Berkeley: University of California Press, 1991), 13. First-person narratives (*Great Expectations, Cranford, The Sacred Fount, Henry Esmond*, etc.) do occasionally appear in the pages that follow, but they appear as limit cases both in the sense that they at moments approach omniscience in significant if oblique ways and in the sense that they allow my argument about the mistake and omniscience to gain greater clarity through implicit opposition.

12. Jonathan Culler, "Omniscience," *Narrative* 12, no. 1 (2004): 22.

13. Ibid., 32.

its fantastic thumb, because it is a degrading fantasy that "oppresses at the same time that it obfuscates," it should, in his view, be abandoned.[14] Culler is right, I think, to call attention to the bad feelings attached to the idea of omniscience in the classic realist novel; because it manages to mix the varied effects of structural perfection and social authority, the idea of omniscience is especially suited to produce feelings of inferiority, guilt, and aggression in characters and readers alike. Culler is wrong, however, to take this as reason to abandon the concept. On the contrary, the idea of omniscience is important to my account of the novel's organization because it functions as a motivating if necessarily impossible ideal, an ideal that figures prominently within a novel form built on the difference between the limitations of consciousness and the promise of something less limited. If thinking about characters caught in a world structured around a difference so essentially unfair is cause for dismay, that dismay turns to outrage precisely because it is so familiar:

> Patients of this sort complain that all their thoughts are known and their actions watched and supervised; they are informed of the functioning of this agency by voices which characteristically speak to them in the third person ("Now she's thinking of that again," "now he's going out"). This complaint is justified; it describes the truth. A power of this kind, watching, discovering, and criticizing all our intentions, does really exist. Indeed, it exists in every one of us in normal life.[15]

Like the bad conscience that won't leave us alone, omniscience is an insult: the complaint is indeed justified. This is exactly why the concept—the fantasy—of omniscience ought not to be abandoned.

As a result of its interest in the play between feeling and form, *Bad Form* is in closest conversation with varieties of novel theory that have been differently attentive to the ways in which literary form can stand by itself as a source of identification, anxiety, and aggression. I am thinking of moments in Adorno, Barthes, and Genette, as well as works like Leo Bersani's *A Future for Astyanax: Character and Desire in Literature*, Jaffe's *Vanishing Points*, Joseph Litvak's *Strange Gourmets: Sophistication, Theory, and the Novel*, D. A. Miller's *Jane Austen, or The Secret of Style*, Franco Moretti's *The Way of the World: The Bildungsroman in European Culture*, Mary Ann O'Farrell's *Telling Complexions: The Nineteenth-Century English Novel and the Blush*, and Alex Woloch's *The One vs. the Many: Minor Characters and the Space of the Protagonist in the Novel*. In each of these cases, literary form is understood not only as a

14. Ibid.

15. Sigmund Freud, "On Narcissism," in *The Standard Edition of the Complete Psychological Works of Sigmund Freud*, ed. James Strachey, 24 vols. (London: Hogarth Press, 1966), 14:95.

reflection of fraught social or psychic conditions but also as a point at which social, psychic, and literary effects cannot be told cleanly apart. To understand literary form is, in other words, to understand how it is both generally and at particular moments coincident with or identical to social form. Insofar as its subject is the mistake and the mistake is a point at which the workings, effects, and affects of social and literary form are practically identical, *Bad Form* is a contribution to a strand in the theory of the novel especially sensitive to the affective and to the social force of literary form.

Bad Form is first a theory of the novel. Because, however, the mistake and the novel are equally points at which the social, the affective, and the formal come together, this particular theory of the novel has had from time to time to moonlight both as sociology and as psychoanalysis. In terms of the former: the oscillation between social and literary analysis that the represented social mistake demands has led me to wonder what the sociology of form (differently represented in what follows by Georg Simmel, Erving Goffman, Johan Huizinga, and Pierre Bourdieu) might have yet to offer. What would a novel reading supple enough to allow for regular slides between the social and the literary look like? What would enable us to capture an alchemical process that turns social content into aesthetic form and aesthetic form into something that moves people and things as effectively as a good shove? "How, in a particular case, a content of experience becomes a form, an event becomes an image, boredom becomes its representation, despair becomes *spleen*: these are the problems."[16] A claim of this book is that the mistake helps us to see that a methodological opposition between social content and literary form is neither as useful nor as descriptive as it has sometimes seemed. Bringing an attention to literary form into close and constant contact with the mistake as a *social fact* helps us to recognize that, if worked properly, narratology might emerge as a productive kind of sociology.[17]

In terms of psychoanalysis: I return in this book to the language of psychoanalysis regularly and for a number of reasons. Of all the explanatory systems we have, none has been as careful as psychoanalysis in its consideration of the significance of the slip; and, if Freud sees the parapraxis as in every case meaningful, so does the nineteenth-century novel. Also, psychoanalysis is in

16. T. J. Clark, *Image of the People: Gustave Courbet and the 1848 Revolution* (Princeton, NJ: Princeton University Press, 1982), 13.

17. Put another way, this book takes the moment of the represented social mistake as a moment that allows the novel itself to emerge as a species of sociology: "We might say, then, that Balzac is sociological novelistically in the sense that he is able to use the novel to encapsulate a knowledge of social practice, of the ways a habitus functions, especially in moments of social crisis when that habitus no longer necessarily serves its agent well." This in the context of my project is to entertain the pleasing possibility that we are all novelistic sociologists when we are embarrassed. Michael Lucey, *The Misfit of the Family: Balzac and the Social Forms of Sexuality* (Durham, NC: Duke University Press, 2003), xxvii.

many of its Freudian and post-Freudian forms a system designed to account for ways in which and at what cost forms of psychic and structural coherence in egos, in novels, and in life are simultaneously threatened and secured.[18] Finally, psychoanalysis offers the beginnings of a vocabulary, one developed by those working after and in some cases against Freud, with which to talk about the relation between identification and a number of specific feelings—embarrassment, shame, and guilt—associated with the social mistake. More than any other, embarrassment is a feeling we can catch, and that contagiousness facilitates identifications between reader and writer as well as between narrator and character that give the novel much of its force.[19] That we can identify with a character is a strange psychic fact for which we need to account in terms of both literary effect and literary form.[20] Bad form, insofar as it affects

18. I am, in particular, interested in the structural play in Freud between the ego, the ego ideal, and the drives as an example of and allegory for the complicated negotiations that need to take place in order for effects of coherence to be produced. "We shall avoid a lack of clarity if we make our contrast not between the conscious and the unconscious but between the coherent *ego* and the *repressed*." The idea that formal coherence is constantly and tenuously secured against the force of self-destructive drives that both predate and undermine the ego's coherence emerges as central to psychoanalysis in "On Narcissism" (1914) and continues to be reworked in texts like *Beyond the Pleasure Principle* (1920), *Group Psychology and the Analysis of the Ego* (1921), and *The Ego and the Id* (1923). This turn can be understood in three ways: as a late return to concepts that had lain dormant since Freud's *Project for a Scientific Psychology* (1895); as a local structural clarification that resulted in the more general shift from the first to the second topography; and as a response to a question that haunted Freud's later years: why, if coherence feels good, are we drawn to feelings, acts, and varieties of violence that threaten coherence? Why, to put it in the terms of this study, does bad form feel good? Sigmund Freud, *Beyond the Pleasure Principle*, in *The Standard Edition of the Complete Psychological Works of Sigmund Freud*, ed. James Strachey, 24 vols. (London: Hogarth Press, 1966), 18:19.

19. Shame and embarrassment are key terms throughout this book. On the one hand, as the psychologist Silvan Tomkins suggests, shame is an affect pivotal to the developmental process; it is a feeling, as Eve Sedgwick writes, "both individuating and disindividuating." Shame has a similar role, I argue, in the production of sense in the novel form. And embarrassment (a related but not always identical feeling) is useful not only because it is the most social of feelings, requiring the presence or at least the idea of the presence of others to be activated, but also because it is one of the easiest to produce. Clinical psychologists writing about embarrassment have noted that "the good news about embarrassment research is that it is one of the few emotions, positive or negative, that can be quickly produced, in full flower, through laboratory manipulations." This is something that the novel, a form built around the production of feeling, recognizes and exploits. Silvan Tomkins, *Shame and Its Sisters: A Silvan Tomkins Reader*, ed. Eve Kosofsky Sedgwick and Adam Frank (Durham, NC: Duke University Press, 1998); Goffman, *Interaction Ritual*; Rowland S. Miller, *Embarrassment: Poise and Peril in Everyday Life* (New York: Guilford Press, 1996).

20. Again, I follow the language of psychoanalysis in seeing identification as an identity-forming "process whereby the subject assimilates an aspect, property or attribute of the other and is transformed, wholly or partially, after the mode the other provides." Each of the following chapters considers different aspects of and problems associated with identification in the novel: in chapter 2, how do novels show us identification at work? In chapter 3, what happens when an omniscient narration "falls" into creaturely identification? And in chapter 4, is there character without identification? What would a character fully free of the need to identify look like: a genius or a monster? J. Laplanche and J.-B. Pontalis, *The Language of Psychoanalysis*, trans. Donald Nicholson-Smith (New York: Norton, 1973), 205. For more on identification see Diana Fuss, *Identification Papers: Readings on Psychoanalysis, Sexuality, and Culture* (New York: Routledge, 1995).

psyches, societies, and literary structure, has much to tell us about an art that similarly counts on the simultaneous and jostling presence of those three: the nineteenth-century novel.

My first chapter examines a reciprocity (already mentioned) between the development of the nineteenth-century novel of manners and the emergence in the 1830s of etiquette as an increasingly autonomous social and, in fact, literary field. If good manners worked at earlier moments as a humanist or ethical buffer between different status groups, they become for the etiquette book, which appears rather suddenly as an autonomous genre in the 1830s, a cheerfully amoral set of conventions mastered in order simply to "get on" in the world. I argue, looking at British and French etiquette books published over the course of about fifty years, as well as at novels by Elizabeth Gaskell, W. M. Thackeray, Honoré de Balzac, and others, that as a means of disseminating good manners in the process of moving away from the explicitly ethical imperatives of conduct and courtesy, the etiquette book adopts a set of representational strategies that exploit oddly novelistic forms to introduce its readers to "good form." When good manners cease to stand as an index of the moral self, the social mistake (I focus in this chapter on the exemplary case of eating peas with your knife) ceases to stand as a merely local transgression and instead becomes a structuring imperative within a modernity struggling to reproduce itself. Because etiquette aims not at any fixed point but rather at the necessarily unfixed forms of a fashion system always already in motion, all that once seemed solid about being good threatens to melt into air. As a result, embarrassment, that most social of feelings, becomes a figure for the period's many social anxieties and takes on a crucial role in the nineteenth-century novel.

I argue in chapter 2, "Embarrassing *Bovary*," that *Madame Bovary* offers a theory of coherence in character and omniscient narration that counts on the individuating power of the mistake. The beautiful, ridiculous description of Charles's cap at the beginning of *Madame Bovary* stands both as a fashion mistake that is the measure of Charles's particular abjection and as a mistake—*overdoing it*—on the part of narration that is at once social and formal. I argue that this mistake explains the jarring shift from the first-person plural voice with which the novel begins to the impersonal narrative style for which Flaubert is famous (a shift that has remained largely unaccounted for within work on Flaubert), and that the odd formal retreat of the locatable first-person narrative voice in the novel resembles structurally the strategic absence of agency that Eve Kosofsky Sedgwick has suggested is built into the performative utterance "Shame on you." And if the shame that follows from bad form can account for so important a narrative shift, so can it form the basis of a theory both of the larger structure of *Madame Bovary* and, perhaps, of narrative omniscience as such.

I then offer a reading of George Eliot's oeuvre that takes a sense of style rarely associated with Eliot as central both to her ethics and to her narrative form. There is, in other words, a surprising relation between being good and looking good in novels that critics have tended to see as fashion-blind. I argue that Eliot's hitherto neglected concern for style, although at work in all of her novels, is most visible in a complicated relationship of identification and disavowal that exists between Eliot's voice and a character who tends, because of her style, not to receive much attention: Rosamond Vincy. This identification appears most clearly at a moment when Rosamond engages in a flavor of bad form we know was particularly distasteful to Eliot, an indulgence in aggressive, "infantine" talk that stands in the novel as both a bad thing and a distinct narrative style. Eliot tells us that Rosamond tells only to "evoke effects," a somatic strategy that stands opposed to Eliot's intellectual balance and that resembles both the sensation genre of the 1860s and, I suggest, a version of physical sensation central to G. H. Lewes's more controversial arguments about the human nervous system. I then offer readings of moments at which *Middlemarch* also "evokes effects" and as a result blurs the ethical distinction between competing styles of narration. This intense and sometimes aggressive play between styles is, I argue, a key aspect of the Eliot system.

Although chapter 4, "Hanging Together in Henry James," addresses a number of James's novels, I focus on *The Princess Casamassima* because its principal character, Hyacinth Robinson, is said never to make a mistake. If mistakes are, as I suggest, an important source of coherence in character, what would it mean to be really free of them? To take Hyacinth's character seriously is, in other words, to imagine a subject in whom the relation between the local slip and an identity-forming repression would not hold; if mistakes are, as psychoanalysis would have it, a significant manifestation of the unconscious, where would one be without them? In Hyacinth freedom from error produces a social invisibility that not only prepares him for the terrorist work for which he is recruited but also undermines an argument about social surveillance—that the novel's thematic engagement with spying points to a disciplinary resolution of seeing and power in its narrative form—that has become a critical commonplace in James studies. Because Hyacinth is an oddly charming blank in *The Princess Casamassima*, his presence marks a point at which surveillance, which claims to see everything, fails. While the Princess is embarrassingly conspicuous when she goes slumming, Hyacinth can pass imperceptibly from class to class, a fact that ruins the naturalist logic often supposed to organize *The Princess Casamassima*. I suggest that this ambiguity in Hyacinth's character gives James an opportunity to offer, in a book criticized for having a bad eye for historical detail, an account of history that, because it can make sense of the force of what we *don't* know, surpasses literary naturalism in its ability to describe the relation between blindness, bad form, and the political act.

Finally, in an afterword called "J'ai envie d'foutre le camp," I turn briefly to Jean Renoir's film *The Rules of the Game* as a self-consciously untimely meditation on bourgeois bad form that in this context doubles as a theory of a novelistic mode in decline. In the afterword's three main sections, "Games," "Rules," and "Quits," I show how Renoir's film stages a central paradox of bad form, one that has returned throughout this book: how can we reconcile the related facts that narration in the novel of manners secures its authority on the basis of others' mistakes and that pointing out another's mistake is itself a particularly egregious kind of social mistake? Octave, a character played by Renoir himself, says at one point in the film: "J'ai envie d'foutre le camp. . . . J'ai envie de . . . de disparaître, dans un trou!" That so self-destructive a sentiment comes from filmmaker and character at once makes our paradox especially palpable. Because Renoir's film, understood not as a novel but as a commentary on the ultimate failure of the novelistic, represents a moment just prior to the felt extinction of both good and bad form, it offers us a last opportunity to consider the structure and consequence of bourgeois sociability. This chapter, like Renoir's film, presents in condensed and late form a set of questions central to understanding the social mistake: what gives form to the formlessness of social life? Is life with others, no matter how tragic, ever more than a game? And what would it at last mean to call it quits?

CHAPTER I

Some Blunders

*Most disquieting reflection of all, was it not bad form to
think about good form?*

—*J. M. Barrie,* Peter Pan[1]

I.

Wouldn't it be nice if the above line worked as well in reverse?
If it were good form to think about bad form? Still, even if the
deceptively easy flip from bad to good could lend what follows a
hint of the authority good form always has to give, it could not
take away all that is "disquieting" about bad form. To know anything about bad form, which I take to refer to the assorted slips,
failures of style, and other sources of social anxiety that plague high
school dances, dinner parties, and novels of manners, is to know
the feeling that comes with it, a sinking feeling that appears with
telling regularity in the pages of the nineteenth-century novel. We
are, of course, right to feel some anxiety about bad form; after all,
everybody knows that a social order sensitive to its appearance "effectively polices itself, since any violation of propriety, any attempt

---

1. Hook, who, it turns out, "had been at a famous public school," retains as a pirate
both a schoolboy's "passion for good form" and that which we will come to recognize as
its structurally necessary sibling: anxiety about the bad. J. M. Barrie, *Peter Pan* (London:
Bloomsbury Books, 1994), 122–23.

to break out of the code, to express something not foreseen by the vocabulary of *mondanité*, immediately and fatally calls attention to itself."[2] If, however, it is true that "calling attention to oneself" encourages in novels as well as in life that feeling we call social anxiety, the "fear of situations where one may be scrutinized by others," one of the claims of this book is that bad form also works to produce coherence in social and textual systems.[3] More than just embarrassing, bad form is a source of related effects of social authority and narrative coherence as well as identifications between character, narrator, and reader without which the nineteenth-century novel could not be so eminently readable. The social mistake is not only a common occurrence in but also a constitutive formal aspect of the omnisciently narrated nineteenth-century novel, an aspect that helps give character its depth, narrative its desire, and narration its authority: without the mistake, novels would neither make the sense nor do the work that they so seductively do.

But why look for bad form in the nineteenth-century novel? Couldn't one look to tragedy for the essence of error, to Romantic poetry for the compulsively missed chance, or to the novel of sensibility for as many scenes of sick-making social discomfort as a body could stand? Indeed, the mistake is in general an exquisitely condensed instance of the necessary dissatisfaction, the necessary disquiet that separates the humdrum stasis of "once upon a time" from its equally dull twin, "happily ever after." As such, the mistake could stand as just another of narratology's widgets, one more term ready to make available not only a novel form long enough to resist close and comprehensive formal analysis but also any narrative artifact. The mistake is in these terms an especially portable, especially naked expression of narrative at work, a moment when the sometimes clumsy fact of plotting discloses itself at an atomic level. It is also a figure that demands from its reader special attention to the fact of form; the mistake as social fact and narrative function exceeds any particular content and thus tends to mark points at which differences between form and content as well as between the properly social and the properly literary are least stable and most visible. The mistake, so good at making us feel things, also makes us *feel* narrative form at work.[4]

2. Susan Winnett, *Terrible Sociability: The Text of Manners in Laclos, Goethe, and James* (Stanford, CA: Stanford University Press, 1999), 9.

3. Rick E. Ingram, Wiveka Ramel, Denise Chavira, and Christine Scher, "Social Anxiety and Depression," in *International Handbook of Social Anxiety: Concepts, Research and Interventions Relating to the Self and Shyness*, ed. W. Ray Crozier and Lynn E. Alden (New York: Wiley, 2001), 367.

4. A couple of books have recently appeared that deal with other aspects of error. Seth Lerer's *Error and the Academic Self* examines "the origins of error—as an ideology, a practice, a defining mode of scholarly identity" through a genealogy of the "academic self" that begins with errata sheets that made material the relation between humanist self-definition and early print culture in Renaissance England and that then looks at the consolidation of Anglo-Saxon studies as an especially prickly, error-sensitive discipline;

Although the mistake is inescapable in and necessary to any narrative system, I mean by bad form something more specific, something, as we will see, peculiar to the structure of an omnisciently narrated nineteenth-century European novel bound up with a characteristic self-consciousness, a characteristic anxiety about the significance of life with other people. Bad form is, this book argues, inextricably linked with formal literary developments—the "round" character, narrative desire, omniscient narration—that come to full flower in that novel and that find different but related expression in self-consciously novelistic scenes of a bourgeois sociability increasingly and popularly discussed in terms of its own good and bad form in types of writing proximate to the novel (etiquette books, burlesques, periodical literature, popular science, etc.). "Bad form" will thus both name a particular kind of mistake and refer to the fact that that mistake's appearance tends to coincide with moments where the social authority and the formal coherence of the nineteenth-century novel (thought of in relation to character, plot, and narration) are paradoxically and sometimes elaborately secured.

2.

Let's start with the following definition taken from the *OED*'s longish entry under "form":

> 15b. *good (or bad) form:* said of behaviour, manners, etc. which satisfy (or offend) the current ideals of "Society"; (good or bad) manners. *colloq.*

Although the definition sticks to a tact typical of the *OED*, something here means more than it says. The definition, although syntactically straitlaced, wants to insinuate as much as define: scare quotes, differently deployed parentheses, and a single capital letter all show, while maintaining the reserve appropriate to the disinterestedness of a dictionary, something more about bad form than can be said. For, although one can see how it is that good form

---

the anxious life of the Victorian philologist as imagined in the person of *Middlemarch's* Edward Casaubon; Erich Auerbach's *Mimesis* as a coded narrative of the "errant life" of the émigré intellectual; and even the science fiction film *Forbidden Planet* as "a fantastic allegory" of that same condition of academic exile. Julian Yates's *Error, Misuse, Failure: Object Lessons from the English Renaissance* works to reimagine the subject's experience of the early modern object world through its "dirtier" moments, points at which things that fail to do what they are supposed to do create "breaches in [the] settlement" between subject and object and that thus force us to reconsider in the most material of terms just what "Renaissance self-fashioning" might have meant to the subject/objects of that same Renaissance. Seth Lerer, *Error and the Academic Self: The Scholarly Imagination, Medieval to Modern* (New York: Columbia University Press, 2002), 2; Julian Yates, *Error, Misuse, Failure: Object Lessons from the English Renaissance* (Minneapolis: University of Minnesota Press, 2003), 8.

"satisfies" social convention, the parenthetical shrug with which the bad is dealt acts out even as it contains an anxiety about bad form; where the *OED* imagines good form as identical to one or more of the many rules and conventions that together make up society, bad form's position within the system isn't strictly and simply opposed to those conventions. Bad form isn't the thing that society could not imagine or allow; rather, these moments, these mistakes are always close enough to the good thing to require a specialist's social expertise to sort them out.[5] Indeed, one of the *OED*'s examples claims, "Happily it is not good form even to purchase the Bacchanalian handkerchiefs of the Burlington-arcade."[6] The alliterative fusion of the classical and the commercial, of "Bacchanalian" and "Burlington" performs both a definitional instability and what we will come to recognize as a tension within the social mistake: the vulgarity of the thing appears as legible not when it stands simply opposed to style or elegance. Rather, it is the messy, sumptuous mix of the two that makes bad form speak.

We might look, for example, to *The Egoist*. George Meredith's novel is filled with hard-to-distinguish moments of good and bad form. Immediately after a brief and hostile social exchange with a rival in which he tries hard—maybe too hard—to score a point, Sir Willoughby Patterne experiences a pleasure that shades subtly into pain: "He had refreshed himself. At the back of his mind there was a suspicion that his adversary would not have yielded so flatly without an assurance of practically triumphing, secretly getting the better of him."[7] Willoughby has *spoken sharply* and, as a result, has given himself away as conceited, bitter, and scared. Although it eventually becomes clear to him, to his neighbors, and to us readers that he has made a mistake, an interval of something like a whole page separates the act from its final interpretation, leaving him and us suspended between an experience and the understanding needed to give that experience its meaning. To tell the difference between success and failure here is a matter of finesse, and the sharp syntactical juxtaposition of pleasure ("He had refreshed himself . . . ") and headachy pain ("At the back of his mind there was a suspicion . . . ") figures the close and unnerving proximity of right and wrong. Meredith's novel models for us the process that converts the potentially neutral event into a mistake only after the fact; with that conversion comes a narrative coherence that both allows

5. It is with something like this in mind that Quentin Bell writes, "In 'good society' it is not however sheer lunatic eccentricity such as the absence of trousers or a wig worn back to front which excites the strongest censure; far worse are those subtler forms of incorrect attire: the 'wrong' tie, the 'loud' shirt, the 'cheap' scent, or the flamboyant checks of the overdressed vulgarian." Quentin Bell, *On Human Finery* (New York: Schocken Books, 1978), 13.

6. From the *Daily News*, December 24, 1868.

7. George Meredith, *The Egoist* (New York: Norton, 1979), 247.

us to see and relies on the contingent but nonetheless sense-making force of the social mistake.[8]

Another example: when, toward the end of *Peter Pan,* the perfectly poised Peter knocks Captain Hook finally and fatally overboard, the latter makes a last, desperate grab at dignity:

> He had one last triumph, which I think we need not grudge him. As he stood on the bulwark looking over his shoulder at Peter gliding through the air, he invited him with a gesture to use his foot. It made Peter kick instead of stab.
>   At last Hook had got the boon for which he craved.
>   "Bad form," he cried jeeringly, and went content to the crocodile.
> Thus perished James Hook.[9]

The affective intensity of the moment, its life-and-death content, and its position as narrative climax: all these at this moment turn on an ever-so-slight difference between a "stab" and a "kick," a difference the subtlety, the arbitrariness of which is registered in the fact that these short, sharp words are, at least on the page, both practically and prosodically interchangeable. The final cry, "Bad form," has as much a performative as descriptive function here—it is the cry that makes the difference between stabbing and kicking. After all, what other than their respective relations to ephemeral, context-specific social codes could make meaningful a difference between two gestures that lead to exactly the same grisly result? What, other than this relation, could encourage Hook to subordinate the fear of death to his feeling for the difference between good and bad form? This is not to say that a difference that almost isn't one is reason to doubt the intensity of the moment; it is, rather, the felt closeness of the alternatives—good and bad form—that can make a matter of form outweigh a matter of life and death.

Analogous to the fluctuating social scenes in which they are recognized as mistakes, handling a bad handkerchief, speaking sharply, and kicking where one should have stabbed are only really registered as mistakes after they have appeared and thus cannot be considered mistakes simply in terms of any fixed principle or prior rule. As such, the social mistake reproduces an ontological instability internal to etiquette and its close relation, fashion.[10] This instability is in turn an aspect of a modernity visible in the novel form, as well as in the

---

8. Thanks to Jami Bartlett, whose work on *The Egoist* got me thinking about that novel.

9. Barrie, *Peter Pan,* 135.

10. This was clear enough to Kant, whose take on fashion Gadamer sums up in this way: "The very word 'fashion' (Mode) implies that the concept involves a changeable law (modus) within a constant whole of sociable demeanor. What is merely a matter of mode has no other norm than that given by what everybody does. Fashion regulates as it likes only those things that can equally well be one way or another."

distinctly nineteenth-century etiquette system that helped give shape to the novel of manners and that was variously codified in the many etiquette books and *manuels de savoir-vivre* that began to appear in England and France in the second quarter of the century.[11] Although other kinds of texts had offered advice on etiquette—conduct books, courtesy manuals, and so forth—the etiquette book differed from these earlier genres in its smiling indifference to ethics:[12]

> The courtesy genre died because the conditions that sustained its difficult compromise between manners and morals did not themselves endure. When it became incongruous to think of fine manners as an essential element of civilized life, the courtesy book was doomed, and the etiquette book, a genre that cheerfully preached manners in a desecrated temple, became the appropriate vehicle for instruction in that diminished kind of manners that we call "etiquette."[13]

Kant describes fashion in this way so as to differentiate it from a faculty of *taste* that is not subservient to "what everybody does." I will return to the opposition between the contingency of fashion and the dreamed-of universality of "taste" in chapter 3. Hans-Georg Gadamer, *Truth and Method*, trans. Joel Weinsheimer and Donald G. Marshall (New York: Continuum, 2000), 37.

11. The circuits of exchange that connect these related traditions are complicated and by no means unidirectional. On the one hand, Philippe Perrot can write that in terms of the "ideals of self-control, self-possession, and the constant mastery of affect" associated with etiquette, "Victorian England, embodying these in the highest degree, served the various European bourgeoisies as a supreme reference for middle-class sociability." On the other hand, a British essayist could say in 1837 that the French example "has evidently suggested the best of those that stand after it; and we are not at all surprised to find a mania of the kind originating in a country where society presents one great hotbed of vanity, and the master of all-pervading passion is to pass for something greater than you are...." That exactly the same content can be seen shuttling between English, American, and French etiquette texts points to not only a strange relation between etiquette and theft but also a surprising international coherence to these traditions. Philippe Perrot, *Fashioning the Bourgeoisie: A History of Clothing in the Nineteenth Century*, trans. Richard Bienvenu (Princeton, NJ: Princeton University Press, 1994), 136; Abraham Hayward, "Codes of Manners and Etiquette," *Quarterly Review* 59 (1837): 397. For a related argument about the international moves that fashion, etiquette's close sibling, made in the period, see Sharon Marcus, "Same Difference? Transnationalism, Comparative Literature, and Victorian Studies," *Victorian Studies* 45 (2003): 683. And for more on the relation between the 1830s and the emergence of the etiquette book as a distinct literary and pedagogical form, see Curtin, "A Question of Manners: Status and Gender in Etiquette and Courtesy," *Journal of Modern History* 57 (September 1985): 395–423.

12. On courtesy, see John E. Mason, *Gentlefolk in the Making: Studies in the History of English Courtesy Literature and Related Topics from 1531–1774* (New York: Octagon Books, 1971); Frank Whigham, *Ambition and Privilege: The Social Tropes of Elizabethan Courtesy Theory* (Berkeley: University of California Press, 1984). On conduct, see Nancy Armstrong, *Desire and Domestic Fiction: A Political History of the Novel* (New York: Oxford University Press, 1987); Sarah E. Newton, *Learning to Behave: A Guide to American Conduct Books before 1900* (Westport, CT: Greenwood Press, 1994); Stephen H. Gregg, "'A Truly Christian Hero': Religion, Effeminacy, and Nation in the Writings of the Societies for Reformation of Manners," *Eighteenth-Century Life* 25 (Winter 2001): 17–28. See also Elias's sampling of different kinds of advice "On Behaviour at Table," taken from German, French, English, and other national contexts. Nobert Elias, *The Civilizing Process: Sociogenetic and Psychogenetic Investigations*, ed. Eric Dunning, Johan Goudsblom, and Stephen Mennel, trans. Edmund Jephcott (Oxford: Blackwell, 1994), 72–85.

13. Curtin, "A Question of Manners," 411.

The etiquette book was characterized by its distinct lack of a distinct ethical end. Never bothering to ask what it would mean at last to be good, the genre replaces particular ends (moral perfection, civic virtue, likeness to Christ, etc.) with the flow of protean fashion, a phenomenon defined by its necessary resistance to closure and by what Georg Simmel identified as its need for "feverish change."[14] An anonymous poet, writing in 1867, imagined a fashion system structurally resistant to closure as a figure hovering eerily between life and death: "But this Fashion died,—as it couldn't survive, / And like other Fashions—was buried—alive."[15] Similarly, Herbert Spencer could worry in the *Westminster Review* that with the shifting forms of etiquette "we have a reign of mere whim, of unreason, of change for the sake of change, of wanton oscillations from whither extreme to the other."[16] These are just a few representatives of what Walter Pater famously saw as the spirit of the age: "To regard all things and principles of things as inconstant modes or fashions has more and more become the tendency of modern thought."[17] Where bad form or its equivalent in another kind of advice book might measure a potentially reducible distance between one's behavior and a fixed point of perfection (even likeness to Christ, hard as it might be to achieve, is a fixed ideal), the indefinite deferral that characterizes fashion makes distance, anxiety, and the threat of losing one's edge permanent features of one's relation to the social world. Until fashion stopped moving—which it would not do—there would be bad form.[18]

These conceptual problems are reflected in the material form of the etiquette book, its Heraclitean tendency toward obsolescence made perfectly apparent in prefatory materials that acknowledged that the advice one held in

14. Georg Simmel, "Fashion," in *On Individuality and Social Forms*, ed. Donald N. Levine (Chicago: University of Chicago Press, 1971), 319.

15. Kortoxylon, *Phases of Fashion: and The Follies of the Age. A Satire* (London: Simpkin, Marshall, 1867), 15.

16. Herbert Spencer, "Manners and Fashion," in *Essays: Scientific, Political, and Speculative* (London: Willimas and Norgate, 1891), 29.

17. Walter Pater, "Conclusion" to *The Renaissance: Studies in Art and Poetry*, in *Selected Writings of Walter Pater*, ed. Harold Bloom (New York: Columbia University Press, 1974), 58.

18. We could, in other words, take the structural inevitability of "bad form" in the etiquette system as another quality of a modernity that, as Michael Warner sees it, "had already made [the social ideal of] virtuous self-unity archaic. In the bourgeois public sphere, talk of the citizen's virtue was already partly wishful." The fact that we "make a necessarily imaginary reference to the public *as opposed to* other individuals," that there is a difference internal to the very form of bourgeois citizenship, is given a local, everyday expression in social mistakes that are, in these terms, inevitable. I will also argue, throughout the book but especially in chapter 4, that not to make mistakes would result in something other than the sublime reward of virtue realized; it would result rather in a manic self-unity that the novel form identifies as pathological. Michael Warner, "The Mass Public and the Mass Subject," in *The Phantom Public Sphere*, ed. Bruce Robbins (Minneapolis: University of Minnesota Press, 1993), 235, 236.

one's hand was not only sure to be wrong in a year but also always palpably in the process of falling out of date. As Eliza Cheadle writes at the outset of her *Manners of Modern Society*:

> It may be said that the books already published on the subject of "manners" are sufficiently numerous for the wants of the community; but to this remark we would reply, that although the broad principles of manners remain the same, yet the *minutiae* are continually altering and varying, and modes of speech and action which were considered the height of politeness a few years ago, would be pronounced at any rate *very old-fashioned* if used and exhibited in the present day.[19]

Or, as one of her Parisian contemporaries put it, when it comes to the rules of *savoir-vivre*, "tout change, tout se renouvelle."[20] The restless social consequence of these statements found expression both in the sudden and sharp increase in the number of etiquette books published in the second quarter of the nineteenth century and in the surprising number of editions into which they ran, facts that suggest a reciprocity between an ever-accelerating literary marketplace and social anxieties that were the result of increased social mobility and fashion's ruthless rush forward. One grumpy reviewer could complain in 1837:

> Judging from the heap of publications on our table, and the numerous editions they are stated (we believe without much exaggeration) to have gone through, it would seem that the principal European nations, as well as America, are in a fair way to rival China in this particular department of letters and legislation.[21]

19. Eliza Cheadle, *Manners of Modern Society: Being a Book of Etiquette* (London: Cassell, Petter, and Galpin, 1872), vii. And Leonore Davidoff writes that although "the system of etiquette was highly formalized, its details were constantly changing." Leonore Davidoff, *The Best Circles* (London: Cresset Library, 1986), 45.

20. Louise d'Alq, *Le nouveau savoir-vivre universel* (Paris: Bureau des Causeries Familieres, 1881), 5.

21. Hayward, "Codes of Manners and Etiquette." Hayward considers a range of books from England, Italy, Germany, France, and America: *Nouvo Galateo* (Milan, 1827); *Die Regel von Hoflichkeit* (Vienna, 1832) *Code Civil, Manuel Complet de la Politesse, du Ton, des Manières de la Bonne Compagnie* (Paris, 1832); *L'Art de Briller en Société, ou Manuel de l'Homme du Monde* (Paris, 1829); *The Laws of Etiquette* (Philadelphia, 1836); *Hints on Etiquette and the Usages of Society; with a Glance at Bad Habits* (London, 1837); *Instructions in Etiquette* (London, 1836); *The Philosophy of Manner* (Glasgow, 1836); *The Science of Etiquette* (Glasgow, 1837); *The True Science of Etiquette* (Glasgow, 1836); *The Book of Etiquette* (London, 1837); *Chesterfield Modernized* (London 1837); *Kidd's Practical Hints on Etiquette* (London, 1837); *The Book of Fashion* (London, 1837); *The Book of Refinement* (London 1837); *The Pocket-Book of Etiquette and Vade Mecum of the Observances of Society* (Liverpool, 1837).

And, although *Le nouveau savoir-vivre universel* could boast that "cet ou-
vrage a déjà eu *trente et une* editions, quoiqu'il remonte à peine à sept années
d'existence,"[22] its success was not in its context unique: "There were numerous
manuals published between 1840 and 1875—the *Catalogue général de la librairie française* listed more than sixty not counting numerous reprints—which
implies an enormous readership."[23] The widespread idea that a jittery and
accelerated production of knowledge about how to behave—new rules, new
techniques, new prohibitions for an upwardly mobile, international, socially
anxious, and book-buying middle class—was under way both demanded and
supported an increasingly efficient mode of literary production, a fact that
again aligned etiquette with the nervous form and temporality of its sibling,
fashion: "Accelerated fashion created ephemera, profit, social wear and tear,
and thus inequality. Fashion's cycles—which made and unmade prices—sub-
stituted 'temporal' for physical scarcity."[24] Like everything else au courant, an
etiquette book would remain only this year's model.

    In all this as well as in its occasional use of narrated set pieces and stock
characters (one example, called *Good Form,* omnisciently narrates the exemplary social adventures of Mrs. Blank, Captain Plunger, Mr. Mahlstick,
Lady Townmouse, and Mrs. Highflier), the etiquette book closely resembled
another vigorously flogged market commodity: the novel.[25] Just as etiquette
drew on aspects of the novel form, so in turn did the novel exploit the structure of an especially fluid etiquette system. In the novel a necessarily indefinite distance between an individual and his or her ideally socialized self (a
distance indexed by the mistake) not only became an ubiquitous theme (differently figured but nonetheless present in both the bildungsroman and the
marriage plot) but also found formal expression in plot's resistance to closure
and in "character effects" that counted on a difference between what a person

---

22. d'Alq, *Le nouveau savoir-vivre universel,* 1.

23. Perrot, *Fashioning the Bourgeoisie,* 88.

24. Ibid., 184.

25. This is especially true of the silver-fork novel, alongside which the etiquette book grew up. Like the
etiquette book, the silver-fork novel, which also rose to prominence in the second quarter of the century,
coupled the pleasures of the novel form with exemplary lessons in navigating the rougher waters of upward
mobility. The "silver-fork school" names a cluster of fashionable best sellers written by authors like Theo-
dore Hook, T. H. Lister, Catherine Gore, and the young Bulwer-Lytton and Disraeli and almost all published by the firm of Henry Colburn; they enjoyed their greatest popularity between 1825 and 1845. Certain
of these novels, like those of Lady Catherine Gore, made their pedagogical zeal lucrative with a willing-
ness to mention explicitly tradesmen who produced different kinds of fashionable goods, a practice that
Thackeray lampooned to great effect in his burlesques "Lords and Liveries" and "Plan for a Prize Novel." If
the etiquette book was entertainment in the guise of pedagogy, the silver-fork novel was pedagogy in the
guise of entertainment. The most comprehensive work on the silver-fork novel remains Matthew Whiting
Rosa, *The Silver-Fork School: Novels of Fashion Preceding* Vanity Fair (New York: Columbia University Press,
1936). Lucie Heaton Armstrong, *Good Form. A Book of Every Day Etiquette* (London: F. V. White, 1889).

was and wanted to be in order to suggest depth, interiority, and moral authenticity. To make mistakes is to be or at least is to look human. A character impossibly without a structuring social anxiety would in that case stand as an equivalent to Kleist's perfectly graceful because perfectly empty marionette or to Carlyle's "true peptician," that "country man" who, when asked to say something about the state of his digestive system, "answered that, 'for his part, he had no system.'"[26]

We could think also of poor Pip's constitutive distance from what he would be in *Great Expectations*. The motivating desire to become a gentleman is born out of an early moment of shame: "I had never thought of being ashamed of my hands before; but I began to consider them a very indifferent pair. [Estella's] contempt was so strong, that it became infectious, and I caught it."[27] If Pip's two hands seem an "indifferent pair," that might be because they are in tacit competition with a pair that is as different as can be: the pair made up of the young, "coarse and common" narrated Pip and Pip, the older, smoother, narrating gentleman. That there is a shaming difference between these two is both what gives Pip an interior filled with pathos and desire and what gives *Great Expectations* its form. Its story is the story of a long approach toward structural dedifferentiation that Gérard Genette calls "temporal isotopy": by the time old narrating Pip and young narrated Pip are at last one and the same, both *Great Expectations* as a novel and Pip as a literary character (the character who had made the mistakes of which the novel is a record) are already over.[28] With the meeting of narrated and narrating Pip, both the subject and the object of narration disappear; without the desire that separates those figures (and the mistakes that generate that desire), Pip would be necessarily unnarratable. If to be human is, in that case, to desire, and to desire is to feel the difference between what we are and what we want to be, the mistake is an especially accessible and economical proof of that human-making desire. It is, in that case, for the impossible, for the nonnarratable, for the nonnovelistic that Captain Hook longs when he longs paradoxically to be in "good form without knowing it, which is the best form of all."[29]

We might, in that case, take bad form as a sociable, a *novelistic* version of Romanticism's "problematic self-consciousness,"[30] an alienation registered as the distance from a socially constituted ideal that, as it sits between the

---

26. Thomas Carlyle, *Characteristics* (Boston: James R. Osgood, 1877), 4.

27. Charles Dickens, *Great Expectations* (London: Penguin, 1996), 60.

28. Gérard Genette, *Narrative Discourse: An Essay in Method* (Ithaca, NY: Cornell University Press, 1980), 221.

29. Barrie, *Peter Pan*, 125.

30. See Geoffrey H. Hartman, "Romanticism and Anti-Self-Consciousness," in *Beyond Formalism: Literary Essays 1958–1970* (New Haven, CT: Yale University Press, 1970), 298–311.

equally nonnarratable states of prehistorical naïveté and end-of-history synthesis, gives the novel the material with which it has to work. What we find in
the etiquette book and the novel of manners is, in that case, a drama of alienation, familiar to us in the poet's strained relationship to the natural world
but played out in distinctly social terms. An internal division that Lukács
saw as "the deepest melancholy of every great and genuine novel" both gives
the novel its shape and finds local expression in what I am calling bad form:
gestures that at once reflect and produce the melancholy of form.[31] Spilled
drinks, poor timing, slips of the tongue: all these are minor infractions against
convention that nevertheless share with the most tragic failures of consciousness a structure that indicates and encourages a desire that in turn produces
in character, plot, and narration the effect of coherence.

3.

If distance, if anxiety is figured in bad form, then "good form" would name a
proximity or even an identity between an individual and the world of social
convention, between individuals and what Hans-Georg Gadamer, situating
himself within the long humanist tradition he describes in *Truth and Method*,
calls *sensus communis,* a felt collection of traditions and conventions constituted through habitual experience of the social. *Sensus communis* is "the sense
of what is right and of the common good that is to be found in all men[,] a
sense that is acquired through living in the community and is determined by
its structures and aims."[32] Good form, taken in this antifoundational sense,
would name a reciprocal relation to *sensus communis* and would stand as the
perfect fit, as the ability to remain locked snugly within a hermeneutic circle
of the particular and the general that would not require propping up by one
or another external or a priori principle; bad form would in that case stand
as the index of one's particular inability to embody that normative common

31. Georg Lukács, *The Theory of the Novel*, trans. Anna Bostock (Cambridge, MA: MIT Press, 1971),
85.

32. Gadamer, *Truth and Method*, 22. Gadamer traces over the course of a few pages (19–35) the development of this idea from Vico, whose privileging of the social "probable" over the metaphysical "true"
had its basis in the august opposition between rhetoric and philosophy, through Shaftesbury's gently anti-
foundationalist feeling for the polite and Thomas Reid's Scottish "common sense," up to Henri Bergson,
who spoke in 1895 of *le bon sens*, a "way of acting" as opposed to a method that "governs our relations with
persons." Gadamer opposes these to Kant, who replaces the immanent force of *sensus communis* with the
transcendental philosophical basis of taste and thus emerges as the foil to Gadamer's own antifoundational
hermeneutic. For a more recent discussion of the relation between ethics, politics, and *sensus communis*
in Kant, see Alan Singer, "Aesthetic Community: Recognition as an Other Sense of Sensus Communis,"
Boundary 2 24.1 (Spring 1997): 205–36.

sense, an inability that, as we have seen, becomes inescapable with the appearance of an etiquette that is always in flux.

It is to something like good form in this sense that Pierre Bourdieu refers when he describes the "feel for the game":

> The habitus as the feel for the game is the social game embodied and turned into a second nature. Nothing is simultaneously freer and more constrained than the action of the good player. He quite naturally materializes at just the place the ball is about to fall, as if the ball were in command of him—but by that very fact, he is in command of the ball.[33]

Unwilling to speak in terms of autonomous social rules that one could internalize and mechanically reproduce, Bourdieu opts instead for a hermeneutic reciprocity (the player both controls and is controlled by the ball) between the "good player" who does not need consciously to know the rules and rules that, because they are contingent to a specific set of social circumstances, cannot be learned anyway. The perfect complementarity of the good player and the social field is, Bourdieu suggests, the result of the way in which his or her cultural competence came about; where "the supposedly pleasureless thought of the petit bourgeois and the 'parvenu'" follows from hard work, the "connoisseur" achieves competence through a "slow familiarization" with social convention that results in an easy identity between a bourgeois social world and the bourgeois individual.[34] Although the "naturalness" of this homology is, as Bourdieu recognizes, rigged, its practical result is nonetheless an unself-conscious and spontaneous display of good form. What, though, would it in fact mean to achieve, even within the limited ideological frame of bourgeois society, identity with those rules? What would it mean not simply to be "good," but never to make a mistake?[35] If, as I have suggested, only dis-

---

33. Pierre Bourdieu, *In Other Words: Essays towards a Reflexive Sociology*, trans. Matthew Adamson (Stanford, CA: Stanford University Press, 1990), 63.

34. Put differently, good form is a contradiction-free habitus, which is for Bourdieu an "objective relationship between two objectivities [that] enables an intelligible and necessary relation to be established between practices and a situation," that emerges from the encounter between bourgeois practice and the bourgeois sociable field. Pierre Bourdieu, *Distinction: A Social Critique of the Judgment of Taste*, trans. Richard Nice (Cambridge, MA: Harvard University Press, 1984), 67, 101.

35. We could supplement Gadamer and Bourdieu with Althusser's classic reading of subjection in "Ideology and Ideological State Apparatuses": "We observe that the structure of all ideology, interpellating individuals as subjects in the name of a Unique and Absolute Subject is *speculary*, i.e. a mirror-structure, and *doubly* speculary: this mirror duplication is constitutive of ideology and ensures its functioning. Which means that all ideology is *centred*, that the Absolute Subject occupies the unique place of the Centre, and

tance is narratable, the creature both in and out of the novel that would result from a manic proximity to good form would amount to something strange, disturbing, maybe a little awful. As we shall see, being too good, coming too close to convention can lead on the one hand to monstrosity (in James, the mannered violence of *The Portrait of a Lady*'s Gilbert Osmond) and on the other to a state too tragically good for this world (also in James, the untimely but structurally necessary suicide of *The Princess Casamassima*'s poor perfect Hyacinth Robinson).

Despite these dangers, sociability is still imagined as a "play form" of the social because it stands as a formalized, closed, coherent system removed from the incoherence of the everyday: "Into an imperfect world and into the confusion of life [play] brings a temporary, a limited perfection."[36] And for Bourdieu, to produce habitus is precisely to produce a closed social system as game. It is in just these terms that we can and will see social and narrative form meeting in the novel: just as I understand good form as a kind of social "coherence effect" bound up with the structuring fact of what I am calling bad form, so will I understand aesthetic form as another and analogous coherence effect that finds expression in a novel tradition central to the European nineteenth century, one that operates through the textual production of interiority, closure, and omniscience. It is at the site of the represented social mistake that correspondences between these two logics of coherence—the literary and the social—become most visible; their structural similarity gives both novel and critic special opportunity to reflect on the social force of aesthetic form and the aesthetic forms of social life. And because both "coherence" and "form" name in this book variously produced effects as opposed to essential qualities, what follows will map

---

interpellates around it the infinity of individuals into subjects in a double mirror-connexion such that it *subjects* the subjects to the Subject, while giving them in the Subject in which each subject can contemplate its own image." In these terms, the motivating fantasy of good form is the fantasy of the good subject, the individual who best (mis)recognizes himself or herself in the Absolute Subject of good form. The relation between the Absolute Subject of good form and the individual will return in this chapter in related discussions of the importance of the sovereign position within the structure of the etiquette system and of narrative omniscience and the ego ideal. Louis Althusser, *Lenin and Philosophy and Other Essays* (New York: Monthly Review Press, 1971), 180.

36. J. Huizinga, *Homo Ludens: A Study of the Play-Element in Culture* (Boston: Beacon Press, 1955), 10. Huizinga's sense of play as that which produces the temporary effect of "limited perfection" (a beautiful phrase) has been developed within the emerging field of video game theory (also known as *ludology*): "Building on Johan Huizinga, Katie Salen and Eric Zimmerman have used the term *magic circle* to describe the border between the context in which a game is played and what is outside that context: 'the term is used here as a shorthand for the idea of a special place in time and space crated by a game.... As a closed circle, the space it circumscribes is enclosed and separate from the real world.... In a very basic sense, the magic circle is where the game takes place." To understand sociability as a kind of "magic circle" is to understand both the coherence that it seeks to achieve and the considerable anxiety that accompanies the effort to secure and then to maintain that coherence. Jesper Juul, *Video Games between Real Rules and Fictional Worlds* (Cambridge, MA: MIT Press, 2005), 164.

out the different and often messy strategies, feints, and sleights of hand that together and apart produce those effects and the authority that comes with them
in the nineteenth-century novel and in social life. Central to both processes is
the structuring presence of the social mistake.

4.

Still, it will seem to some serious-minded readers that the slips I discuss are
minor enough: Charles Bovary does not handle his hat like other kids; Rosamond Vincy talks out of turn; Hyacinth Robinson overdresses. Why make a
big deal out of such little mistakes? Isn't time spent worrying about using the
wrong fork, waiting too long to put your napkin on your lap, or eating peas
with your knife simply time wasted? What, after all, could be more innocu-
ous, less heavy than the kind of mistake that would inspire this:

> I eat my peas with honey—
> I've done it all my life.
> It makes the peas taste funny
> But it keeps them on the knife.[37]

If, though, it at first seems minor, a mistake like eating peas with your knife
can in fact carry a strange and compelling symbolic weight, a significance
that, once considered, gives us a better sense of what is at stake when bad
form happens. Presented as an especially exemplary social mistake not only in
etiquette books but also in scraps of doggerel verse (like the one just quoted),
magazine puff pieces, fashionable novels, and every other out-of-the-way
place where the *thing to do* is thought over, eating peas with your knife acti-
vates and exposes a set of anxieties central to the very fact of sociability.[38]
    In Elizabeth Gaskell's manners-obsessed *Cranford*, eating peas with your
knife figures what the novel perceives as a troubling difference between the

37. An "anonymous English poet," quoted in Margaret Visser, *The Rituals of Dinner: The Origins, Evolution, Eccentricities, and Meaning of Table Manners* (London: Penguin, 1991), 191.
    38. A *material* history of the error would look at the move from a two- to a four-pronged fork, the
different shapes that knives have taken at different moments and in different contexts (from wide and
spoonlike to narrow and sharp), and very different ways in which peas are supposed to be eaten (even today
etiquette books disagree about whether one should squash the peas on the "back" of the fork, do one's
best to balance them there, or simply cave in and scoop them up). What I am interested in is the fact that
despite these shifts in the way in which the peas are in fact dealt with, eating peas with your knife was and
has remained an unusually stable and unusually *representative* social mistake. For a look into the nuts and
bolts of forks and knives, see Visser, *The Rituals of Dinner*, 183–96. See also Henry Petroski, *The Evolution
of Useful Things: How Everyday Artifacts—From Forks and Pins to Paper Clips and Zippers—Came to Be as
They Are* (New York: Vintage, 1994), 3–21.

old-fashioned and the newfangled, a panic-inducing limit that only Mary Smith, a narrator who hovers between the epistemological limitations of character and the pure comprehension of omniscience, who can move between different social worlds, and who, as a result, speaks from what Hilary Schor calls a radical "position of intentional mediation," can successfully discern or describe.[39] And if, as Schor suggests, "history (in the sense of events, change, and narrative) is the unconscious" of *Cranford*, eating peas with your knife is its parapraxis, the slip in the form of which that repressed historical content makes its untimely return.[40] While dining with Mr. Holbrook (the "old bachelor"), Mary, Miss Matty, and Miss Pole are confused when both those hard-to-handle peas and the historically residual form of the "two-pronged, black-handled" fork appear; a general historical incommensurability of past and present finds a local, physical expression in the specific failure of *that* fork to deal with *those* peas: they "*would* drop between the prongs." But, where her friends are understandably stumped and leave their peas "untasted," Mary, whose exceptional narratorial purchase on the historical drops *her* between the prongs of past and present, improvises: "I looked at my host: the peas were going into his capacious mouth, shoveled up by his large round-ended knife. I saw, I imitated, I survived! My friends, in spite of my precedent, could not muster up courage enough to do an ungenteel thing."[41] Although Mary gets both to know like no one else how one should not eat peas and to eat them that way too, we should not think that the prohibition against eating peas with your knife has lost any of its trenchancy; rather, her gesture's exceptional status is preserved in such a way as both to foreground narration's own exceptional resistance to history's pull in *Cranford* and to disclose this mistake's exemplary position within the novel's etiquette system.[42]

39. Schor also writes that while *Cranford* is "most often praised for its own quality of loving nostalgia," "what it in fact registers is panic about change." Hilary M. Schor, *Scheherazade in the Marketplace: Elizabeth Gaskell and the Victorian Novel* (Oxford: Oxford University Press, 1992), 118, 85.

40. Ibid., 85.

41. Elizabeth Gaskell, *Cranford* (Oxford: Oxford University Press, 1998), 33.

42. To look to a later, even apocalyptic, example: the revolutionary potential of eating peas with your knife returns in H. G. Wells's *The War of the Worlds*. In that novel, Wells explicitly equates the taboo against eating peas with your knife with the very coherence of Western civilization. In an attempt to imagine the extent to which a world entirely colonized by human-eating Martians would be different, a working-class survivor of the alien attack instructs the narrator: "If you've got any drawing room manners or a dislike to eating peas with a knife or dropping aitches, you'd better chuck 'em away. They ain't no further use." If, on the one hand, this is to give us tough, Nietzschean insight into the flimsiness of a world ordered around the most narcissistic of minor differences (you eat peas with your knife, and I don't), so, on the other, does it seem to lift that mistake out of the trivial as a strangely exemplary figure for the end of human history itself. The future we cannot know is eating peas with your knife. H. G. Wells, *The War of the Worlds* (New York: Tor Classics, 1988), 171.

The fullest working-through of the significance of eating peas with your knife appears in Thackeray's *Book of Snobs*, a series of "papers" on different kinds of snobs (clerical snobs, university snobs, country snobs, etc.) that appeared in *Punch* from February 1846 to that same month in 1847 and then in book form in 1848.[43] Thackeray, working early in the series to set limits to his study of the snob, treats eating peas with your knife as a snob's primal scene. He writes:

> I once knew a man who committed before me an [atrocious act]. I
> once, I say, knew a man who, dining in my company at the "Europa
> Coffee-House," (opposite the Grand Opera, and, as everybody knows,
> the only decent place for dining at Naples,) ate peas with the assistance
> of his knife. He was a person with whose society I was greatly pleased
> at first—indeed, we had met in the crater of Mount Vesuvius, and
> were subsequently robbed and held to ransom by brigands in Calabria,
> which nothing to the purpose—a man of great powers, excellent heart,
> and varied information; but I had never before seen him with a dish of
> peas, and his conduct in regard to them caused me the deepest pain.[44]

This mistake and the narrator's reaction to it are worth thinking about for a number of reasons. There is, on the one hand, a distinct lack of proportion between the error and the response it produces: why such repulsion in the face of so minor a thing? And, on the other, the offense not only disrupts this little scene of sociability but also tears at the already strained conventional fabric of Thackeray's text. It is a lapse apparently serious enough both to warrant the at least temporary estrangement of the pea eater from the narrator (who gives his friend "the cut direct that night at the Duchess of Monte Fiasco's ball") and to disrupt the finely woven web of generic conventions that supports this scene. The travel narrative, the adventure story, the silver-fork novel: these forms are all present and competing in Thackeray's short account and are subordinated suddenly to the apparently painful sight of another eating peas with his knife.

43. The international success of Thackeray's snob papers marks another point at which bad form transcends a particular national context. Phillipe du Puy de Clinchamps writes in his "que sais-je?" volume on snobbery that though it was the very British Thackeray who made it what it still is, his snob was important not only in England "mais à travers toute l'Europe puis en Amérique. Chacun, en effet, dut constater que, s'il atteignait alors une sorte de perfection à Londres, le snob était de tous les pays et de toutes les civilizations. En France, *The Book of Snobs* fut traduit dès 1857 par G. Guiffrey avec, pour exergue, cette phrase malheureuse: <<*Béotien à l'état parfait*>>, qui montre que l'écrivain n'avait sans doute pas compris toute la profondeur du livre qu'il avait traduit." Phillipe du Puy de Clinchamps, *Le Snobisme* (Paris: Presses Universitaires de France, 1948), 40.

44. William Makepeace Thackeray, *The Book of Snobs* (Cologne: Könemann, 1999), 15. Subsequent references to this work will appear in the text.

Why does this particular act take on the symbolic value that it does for Thackeray? Why would the sight of another eating peas with his knife cause "the deepest pain"? For one, Thackeray is exploiting the figure's already codified presence within the etiquette system. We read, for instance, in the thirty-third edition of *Etiquette for the Ladies: Eighty Maxims on Dress, Manners, and Accomplishments* that "if you want to be thoroughly vulgar . . . make your knife do duty in the treble capacity of knife, fork, and spoon."[45] Too free a use of the knife often appears, along with occasional references to the specific transgression of eating peas with it, as an especially representative mistake, a social slip so legible, so familiar, but still so ghastly and possible that it could demonstrate not only the obvious utility of etiquette as a social strategy but also the authority of rules the bases of which are almost always obscure: why, after all, shouldn't I eat peas with my knife? Bertrand Russell for one recognized that "there may, for ought I know, be admirable reasons for eating peas with a knife, but the hypnotic effect of early persuasion has made me completely incapable of appreciating them."[46] This particular piece of advice about what not to do takes on a value exactly as a repetition of what you always already knew without knowing why you knew it, as a ritual and self-referential warning that works because it both grounds and foregrounds the logic that we find at the bottom of every social convention.[47] One of Thackeray's Parisian contemporaries, a woman writing from the position of

---

45. *Etiquette for the Ladies: Eighty Maxims on Dress, Manners, and Accomplishments* (London: David Bogue, 1846), 11. Nobert Elias mentions that the "imperative never to put a knife to one's mouth is one of the gravest and best known." And L'Abbe Th. G. Rouleau in his *Manuel des Biénseances: A l'usage des candidates aux brevets d'école primaire* (Quebec: Dussault Proulx, 1897) writes that "il est tout à fait impoli de porter son couteau à la bouche" (54).

46. Bertrand Russell, *Power: A New Social Analysis* (London: Routledge, 2004), 221.

47. George Bernard Shaw, who must have had *The Book of Snobs* in mind, brings out the arbitrary force of etiquette in *Getting Married* (1908). Hotchkiss, a self-proclaimed snob, explains how he understood that another man was *not* a gentleman:

> THE GENERAL: And pray, sir, on what ground do you dare allege that Major Billiter is not a gentleman?
>
> HOTCHKISS: By an infallible sign: one of those trifles that stamp a man. He eats rice pudding with a spoon.
>
> THE GENERAL: [very angry] Confound you, *I* eat rice pudding with a spoon. Now!
>
> HOTCHKISS: Oh, so do I, frequently. But there are ways of doing these things. Billiter's way was unmistakable.

In switching out the familiar "eating peas with your knife" in favor of the more ridiculous because more obviously benign "eating rice pudding with your spoon," Shaw points both to the fact that it is the snob's insight about modernity that one tautologically asserted minor difference is as good as another and to the logic of substitution and repetition native to etiquette that I have been describing. George Bernard Shaw, *The Doctor's Dilemma, Getting Married, and the Shewing-Up of Blanco Posnet* (New York: Brentano's, 1928), 243.

a father offering advice to his children, understood that mute acceptance of the irrational basis of etiquette's rules is itself etiquette's cardinal rule: "Convenons, mes enfants, que vous ne me demanderez point pourquoi tel usage subsiste, pourquoi telle expression est réputée de mauvais goût, et pourquoi la société même qui a fait ces lois, ne les a point motivés."[48] The fact that neither the particular genealogy nor the practical consequence of the prohibition against eating peas with your knife needs to be available to the pea eater gives that prohibition the appearance of "the pure form of law beyond its own content,"[49] a rule that "is sustained not by reason alone but also by the force/violence of a tautological enunciation—'The law is the law!'"[50] Why not eat peas with your knife? Because I said so.

Thackeray then goes on to convert the particular if exemplary act of eating peas with your knife into the etiquette system's general form of value: "If I should go to [a tea party] in a dressing-gown and slippers and not in the usual attire of a gentleman . . . I should be insulting society, and *eating peas with my knife*" (17). Eating peas with your knife has here the surprising ability to stand as equivalent to other social mistakes. We could thus extend Thackeray's claim indefinitely: "If I should *a*, I should be eating peas with my knife; and if I should *b*, I should be eating peas with my knife; and if I should *c*, I should be eating peas with my knife; and so on." That the mistake is exemplary should by now be clear; Thackeray, however, pushes that exemplarity to its limits and turns one thing among many into a term that is at once itself and every other thing within the system. Just as Marx's "general form of relative value, embracing the whole world of commodities, converts the single commodity that is excluded from the rest, and made to play the part of equivalent . . . into the universal equivalent," so does Thackeray convert eating peas with your knife into a social mistake curiously and universally equivalent to every other.[51]

48. Mme la Comtesse de Bradi, *Du savoir-vivre en France au dix-neuvième siècle, ou Instruction d'un père à ses enfants* (Paris: V. Berger-Levrault et Fils, 1858), 11.

49. Giorgio Agamben, *Homo Sacer: Sovereign Power and Bare Life* (Stanford, CA: Stanford University Press, 1998), 53.

50. Eric L. Santner, *On the Psychotheology of Everyday Life: Reflections on Freud and Rosenzweig* (Chicago: University of Chicago Press, 2001), 57. For another moment at which political authority, political violence, and *eating peas with your knife* come productively together, there is this probably apocryphal story about George Washington: "Fixing his eyes upon the guilty man, he put a spoonful of peas on his plate and asked him, 'Shall I eat of these?' 'I don't know,' stammered the man, turning deadly pale. *Washington took some on his knife*, and again asked, 'Shall I eat of these?' The man could not say a word, but raised his hand as if to prevent it." From G. P. Quackenbos, *Elementary History of the United States*, quoted in Minto, "Did Washington Eat Green Peas with a Knife?" *Magazine of American History with Notes and Queries* 16 (July–December 1886): 500.

51. Karl Marx, *Capital*, vol. 1, ed. Frederick Engels, trans. Samuel Moore and Edward Aveling (New York: International Publishers, 1967), 66.

I will leave aside Thackeray's peas for a moment to consider the essay "On Manners" that appeared in *Blackwood's Magazine* in 1861. Anne Mozley's essay, equal parts philosophical meditation and advice column, is like Thackeray's *Book of Snobs* insofar as it, too, is invested in the structure of a social order determined at least in part by the demands of the etiquette system.[52] A "good manner" is negatively defined in Mozley's essay not as a set of practices that could be imitated and finally mastered but rather as the absence of a kind of bad form that she identifies as affectation. You only need to be unself-consciously yourself to have a good manner. But, as becomes clear in her essay, being yourself is no easy thing. Indeed, in a way that anticipates Freud on the psychopathology of everyday life, Mozley imports into the quotidian world of etiquette the more exotic logic of the unhappy consciousness in order not only to define affectation but also to suggest why affectation is almost unavoidable:

> There is a constant little secret—the world is not to know the small shifts self is put to, which do not seem to matter while nobody knows. Now, this secret will always betray itself some way or another, and entirely stand in the way of the calm, easy, grand manner. The consciousness that everything about us will stand inspection, that the outside is an index of what is within, imparts ease, grace, and self-possession; while some touch—however faint, all but imperceptible—of sneaking or bluster will tinge the manner, conscious of something working out of sight.[53]

Affectation is the symptomatic "index" of a split within the self, and that split is one that everyone shares. There is, however, one figure necessarily without affectation in Mozley's system: the sovereign. She writes: "An affected king, or queen, or potentate of any kind would be a monster" (156). The sovereign position would escape affectation because it is by definition the position of perfect self-identity within the structure that Mozley describes. Where ordinary folk with ordinary things to hide will always show "some touch . . . of sneaking or bluster," the sovereign, personally identical to the rules of the game, is theoretically without secrets and is thus incapable of making a mistake. In a system otherwise so slippery, the sovereign occupies a position of fixed because tautological stability.

---

52. In addition to editing Cardinal Newman's posthumous papers (he chose her as a sympathetic, Anglican editor), Anne Mozley was a prolific journalist who wrote much for *Blackwood's*. Along with "On Manners," she wrote an equally remarkable essay titled "Dress": "'I think, therefore I am,' is the conclusion of the adult reason; the baby has leapt to a similar conclusion forty years sooner—'I have shoes and a red sash, therefore I am.'" Anne Mozley, "Dress," *Blackwood's Edinburgh Magazine* 97 (April 1865): 425–26.

53. Anne Mozley, "On Manners," *Blackwood's Edinburgh Magazine* 90 (August 1861): 157–58.

Mozley's argument is in this way a late elaboration of the logic of the "King's Two Bodies," the long-standing legal fiction that produced the sovereign as infallible (the king "is not only incapable of *doing* wrong, but even of *thinking* wrong") as well as structurally necessary and ubiquitous ("His Majesty in the eye of the law is always present in all his courts").[54] For this reason, the monstrosity of an affected king would be the monstrosity of a self-negating structural failure as opposed to the temporary result of any specific faux pas. Kantorowicz's reading of the key scene of Richard's personal and sovereignty's structural dissolution in *The Tragedy of King Richard II*—Richard "melts himself away" while looking and speaking into a looking glass—turns on the development of a certain kind of self-consciousness, one that, transplanted into the less tragic soil of the novel of manners, could stand as affectation in Mozley's sense: "The physical face which the mirror reflects, no longer is one with Richard's inner experience, his outer appearance, no longer identical with inner man. 'Was this the face?'"[55]

Affectation appears in Mozley's piece as the local performance of a structurally necessary problem. Although the absolute difference between the sovereign and everybody else is quite literally central to the system of the state, it is not the only difference at work; the almost infinite number of ways in which one could express one's bad form and thus one's individual distance from the sovereign position provides a totalizing, everyday, affective structuring support for a social order. The general fact of sovereign authority is experienced in and reinforced by the texture of an everyday life shot through with its particular lapses, gaffes, and embarrassments. The assorted local performances of good or bad form stand for Mozley both as an especially legible reflection of a structured social order and as a handy means of policing the boundaries of that structure; the social mistake, insofar as it stands for Mozley as an index of one's affectation, which is in its turn the index of one's structuring distance from the sovereign position, is in that case an expression at the molecular level of an efficient strategy of subjection, "the process of becoming subordinated by power as well as the process of becoming a subject."[56] Manners manage power by affectively tracing one's particular relation to that which would ground those manners.

Thackeray shares much with Mozley. To be a snob is for him also to be affected, to perform an awareness of one's structural difference from other posi-

---

54. Sir William Blackstone, *Commentaries on the Laws of England*, quoted in Ernst H. Kantorowicz, *The King's Two Bodies: A Study in Mediaeval Political Theology* (Princeton, NJ: Princeton University Press, 1997), 4–5.

55. Kantorowicz, *The King's Two Bodies*, 39.

56. Judith Butler, *The Psychic Life of Power: Essays in Subjection* (Stanford, CA: Stanford University Press, 1997), 2. I return to the subject of subjection in the following chapter.

tions within the social system: "Survey mankind, from Plimlico to Red Lion Square, and see how the Poor Snob is aping the Rich Snob; how the mean Snob is groveling at the feet of the proud Snob; and the Great Snob is lording it over his humble brother" (176). Snobbery is in these terms a relation: one can only be a snob with other people. And, as with Mozley, the only way out of snobbery is to achieve the kind of difference-dumb self-identity that she reserves for the sovereign position; the advice, always harder to follow than to give, is just to be yourself. There is, however, an important difference between Thackeray and Mozley: Thackeray does not grant any one figure sovereign self-identity within his social order. Where Mozely maintains the sovereign position of king as a position different in kind from every other, Thackeray collapses the social and structural difference between the king and his subjects. Rather than keep the sovereign safe, he offers a killing description of the "Snob Royal" early enough in the snob papers to invest in it the quality of the axiomatic: "To say of such and such a Gracious Sovereign that he is a Snob, is but to say that his Majesty is a man. Kings, too, are men and Snobs" (21).

The Book of Snobs is only one of several moments in Thackeray's career when he thought explicitly about sovereignty. *Barry Lyndon* is, among other things, a novel about the many ways in which genealogical claims to authority will always finally be found wanting; if Barry Lyndon's often asserted relation to the "kings of Ireland" is obviously ridiculous, Thackeray's structural critique of authority is far more general: whether the lie is located one or a hundred generations back, a hard foundation for social or political authority will in every case be found wanting. And *Henry Esmond* is, again among other things, a meditation on the consequences that the idea of the king's two bodies has for the political, the social, and the formal. After an oversexed James III, at this point a young "Old Pretender," attempts to seduce Beatrix, the woman and cousin Esmond loves, the opportunistic Bishop of Rochester cites the legal fiction of the body politic in an effort to smooth things over: "The Bishop was breaking out with some *banales* phrases about loyalty, and the sacredness of the Sovereign's person; but Esmond sternly bade him hold his tongue."[57] The felt split between the "sacred" person of the sovereign and his other body, a body that does its fair share of drinking and womanizing, finds an analogue in the relationship between Henry as extradiegetic narrator, a "sacred" and whole Esmond who has seen it all, and Henry as a diegetic character, a man-child almost always referred to by the implicit "I" of narration as a "he." That the novel's end coincides with the coming together of extradiegetic and diegetic levels, a coming together the political theology of the king's two bodies could not allow, suggests not that Thackeray believes in

---

57. William Makepeace Thackeray, *The History of Henry Esmond* (London: Penguin, 1985), 501.

the transubstantiation of earthly character into sovereign narration: rather, *Henry Esmond* points to the paradox of omniscience's sovereignty just as it pokes holes in the notion of juridical sovereignty through the ridiculous figure of James III.[58]

Thackeray's move—seeing the king as after all just another snob—puts him in a complicated position in *The Book of Snobs*. Without the stabilizing presence of the sovereign's exceptional body politic, the foundations of the social order threaten to dissipate; once the system's sovereign center is put into play, social positions that had defined themselves in relation to that center become unstable, endangered. Despite, however, the force of its critique of political theology and its appearance in book form in 1848, *The Book of Snobs* is no call to arms. Indeed, Thackeray both acknowledges and neutralizes the bloody potential of his idea by making a light joke about the resemblance between the publication of his Snob papers and other equally "world-historical" events like the French and American Revolutions: just as he was nominated by world-spirit to write about snobs, so was Robespierre found "to administer a corrective dose to the nation" (11). Thackeray wants to maintain a legible social order without the structuring social presence of the sovereign, but, once the stable sovereign center of Mozley's social structure is put into play, Thackeray is in turn put in the tight spot of finding a substitute for that lost term if order is to be preserved.

It is, as others have pointed out and as Thackeray never lets us forget, the fact that as soon as the term "snob," which names not a particular position within the social world but the inescapable fact of positionality itself, is let loose on the world, not a soul is safe from its taint; indeed, neither reader nor narrator of this strange text is safe from the fluid and contagious play of snobbery, a free play made all the freer by Thackeray's repudiation of a self-identical sovereign position.[59] How, though, does Thackeray resist the revolutionary consequence of his idea? How is the social world in *The Book of Snobs* kept from falling into disorder? What does that lost sovereign's work for Thackeray,

58. One might also look to Thackeray's *The Four Georges* or, even better, to his snide description of Becky Sharp's presentation at court in *Vanity Fair*: "What were the circumstances of the interview between Rebecca Crawley *nee* Sharp, and her Imperial Master, it does not become such a feeble and inexperienced pen as mine to attempt to relate. The dazzled eyes close before that Magnificent Idea. Loyal respect and decency tell even the imagination not to look too keenly and audaciously about the sacred audience chamber, but to back away rapidly, silently, and respectfully, making profound bows out of the August Presence." Thackeray, *Vanity Fair* (London: Penguin, 1985), 559–60.

59. For more on the fluid logic of *The Book of Snobs*, see René Girard, *Deceit, Desire, and the Novel: Self and Other in Literary Structure* (Baltimore, MD: Johns Hopkins University Press, 1976), J. Hillis Miller, "*Henry Esmond*: Repetition and Irony," in *Fiction and Repetition: Seven English Novels* (Cambridge: Harvard Univ. Press, 1982), 73–115; and Joseph Litvak, *Strange Gourmets: Sophistication, Theory, and the Novel* (Durham, NC: Duke University Press, 1997).

I would like to propose, is the social mistake. If it was the exceptional position of the sovereign in relation to social rules that kept Mozley's structure in
order, it is the mistake that allows Thackeray similarly to sort things out. As
trivial, as ephemeral, as minor as the particular mistake might seem, it stands
nevertheless as a stable, negative, exceptional point around which participants
in the social world might measure themselves. Where once a king embodied
the state of exception, now there is the mistake.

This is nowhere more apparent than in the case of eating peas with your
knife. That mistake not only stands as that which allows the narrator, who
is elsewhere a snob, to identify another as one and thus, if only for a moment, negatively to escape that designation, but also secures for narration
a tenuous authority that is everywhere threatened and that would evapo-
rate altogether without moments like this one.[60] Thackeray's text suffers, in
other words, from a generic instability similar to the social instability that
his critique has set in motion. I have already mentioned the layered character of the anecdote of the peas (is this an etiquette book, an adventure story,
a travel narrative, or all at once?). *The Book of Snobs* registers everywhere
in its form its position somewhere in between the ephemeral anatomies
and burlesques that filled the pages of *Punch* and the more recognizable
novel form that would occupy what we tend to remember of Thackeray's
career. More to the point, we feel that narration is itself caught between
two competing styles: the embodied, parasitic form characteristic of *Punch*'s
house style and a recognizably omniscient narration that combines in *The
Book of Snobs* a masterful view of a whole social world with the ability to
be anywhere and everywhere at once. Without pressing too hard, we might
say that *The Book of Snobs* initiates a structural consolidation of narrative
authority that brings into contact the particular form of this text, the arc
of Thackeray's career, and a social field that both is called upon to shore up
these other moves and also derives a surprising kind of definition from its
proximity to narration's structural gambit. What allows narration to emerge
for a moment as something other than just another snob and as something

---

60. Thackeray used the peas to make other, more familiar distinctions: "According to Mark Lemon
Thackeray once quarreled with Jerrold because he 'ate peas with his knife & therefore was not fit company
for him.'" The mistake is—by now predictably—doing double duty; on the one hand, there was a felt
difference in class origins between the two men, one that came to stand in for their political differences.
Thackeray is drawing on old associations between social class and the improper use of the knife. Davidoff
and Hall note that in "popular mythology, small farmers often embodied backward vulgarity. In 1816 a
local paper reported that an Essex farmer accidentally cut off a gentleman's finger in trying to carve the
wing of a fowl, the incident 'occasioned by the eagerness of the company who all had their hands in the
dish at the same time.'" Gordon N. Ray, *Thackeray: The Uses of Adversity, 1811–1846* (New York: McGraw-
Hill, 1955), 362; Leonore Davidoff and Catherine Hall, *Family Fortunes: Men and Women of the English
Middle Class* (London: Hutchinson, 1987), 399.

like omniscience is its identification and disavowal of another snob's mistake, the general form of which we could label, following Thackeray's lead, *eating peas with your knife.*

But still: although we can locate precedents in the etiquette system for the special position of eating peas with your knife, can see how this particular blunder has been converted into the general form of the social mistake, and can understand why one or another mistake would need thus to be converted into such a general form, we still have not accounted for why *this* mistake, eating peas with your knife, was elected to *this* position within Thackeray's *Book of Snobs.* Why not using the wrong fork, bolting your food, or depositing your napkin early or late? The question remains, what is it about this lapse that suits it to the task of standing in for the mistake in general? Perhaps we should look first to the peas. Tiny, smooth, soft, and perfectly round, peas might seem to offer the mouth a pleasure that Edmund Burke in his *Enquiry into the Sublime and Beautiful* called "sweetness" or "the beautiful of the taste": if a "single globe" is pleasant to the touch, "it is nothing near so pleasant . . . as several globes, where the hand gently rises to one and falls to another; and this pleasure is greatly increased if the globes are in motion and sliding over one another." It is, he goes on to argue, because particles of sugar are globular that they are sweet, and a dish of peas would have for the eyes, hands, and mouth a similar appeal. A knife that scores, that serrates, that makes rough would in that case stand as a threat to the smooth, continuous surface of the pea and would by extension stand as a particular threat to sweetness and thus to beauty itself.[61]

What's more, peas occupy an important place in the history of manners. Although dried peas had long been part of the European diet, the idea of fresh, shelled green peas as a special treat emerges in an oddly spectacular way in France towards the end of the seventeenth century: Maguelonne Toussaint-Samat writes that in 1660,

---

61. Edmund Burke, *A Philosophical Enquiry into the Sublime and the Beautiful and Other Pre-Revolutionary Writings* (London: Penguin Books, 1998), 180. This same tension between the benign pea and the threat of the blade encouraged a young Alfred Hitchcock to make a characteristically morbid joke. The following comes from "The History of Pea Eating," a short piece Hitchcock contributed to the *Henley Telegraph* in December 1920 (the *Telegraph* was the in-house newsletter published by and for the employees of W. T. Henley's Telegraph Works Company Ltd where Hitchcock worked in his teens and early twenties): "It appears that each competitor was required to balance a certain number of peas along the edge of a sword, from which he was to swallow the peas without spilling any. Of course, in very exciting matches the contestants' mouths and faces were often cut. It is believed that the performance of sword swallowing was evolved from this feat, and that very large-mouthed people of today are direct descendants from the champions of that period." This, a late theorization of a representative mistake, pushes it and its violence toward and even past a certain self-conscious limit. Late theorizations of the mistake are a subject of this book's afterword. Quoted in Partick McGilligan, *Alfred Hithcock: A Life in Darkness and Light* (New York: ReganBooks, 2003), 43.

. . . the Sieur Audiger brought a hamper of green peas back from
Genoa and presented it to Louis XIV in front of all his eminent
courtiers. "All declared in one voice," Audiger reported proudly, "that
nothing could be better or more of a novelty . . ." No sooner had news
of the green peas spread than they became a positive craze: everyone
wanted to eat them, at Versailles, in the outlying districts, in the
worlds of finance and the Church.[62]

While the craze begins at Versailles, the humble but delicious pea soon became both less exclusive and more widespread. William Cobbett's *The English
Gardener* (1827) helps us to appreciate the pea's ubiquity in early nineteenth-
century England:

This is one of those vegetables which all people like. From the greatest to the smallest of gardens, we always find peas, not to mention the
thousands of acres which are grown in fields for the purpose of being
eaten by the gardenless people of the towns. Where gardening is carried upon a royal, or almost royal scale, peas are raised by means of
artificial heat . . . [63]

We can take from this little history of the pea two possible reasons for its place
as part of the representative mistake, eating peas with your knife. First, the
fact that petits pois were associated at the outset with French courtly cuisine
gives them a key role to play in the history and the evolving and anxious
texture of an international etiquette system. The pea became a point around
which minor national differences between manners might be articulated and,
perhaps, exaggerated.[64] Second, because the pea went on to become, as Cobbett suggests, a food of both the large and the small, both the landless and the
royal, it also became available as an especially charged part of an especially
charged social mistake. If absolutely anyone can eat peas, it is how one eats
them that must make all the difference. The pea thus becomes a minor, everyday point at which social and national anxieties might come to the surface.

Now let's put the peas aside and take up the knife. Norbert Elias has considered the special place of the knife and its misuses in the long genealogy of
manners. He writes:

62. Maguelonne Toussaint-Samat, *History of Food*, trans. Anthea Bell (Oxford: Blackwell Publishing,
1992), 43–4.
63. William Cobbett, *The English Gardener* (London: A. Cobbett, 1845), 144.
64. "...*petits pois à la française* were accused of toxicity by Oliver Goldsmith in his letters. The French
way of cooking green peas, according to Goldsmith, made them practically inedible. Mere traveler's chau-
vinism, or a faithful reflection of contemporary British opinion?" Toussaint-Samat, 44.

Certainly the knife is a dangerous instrument in what may be called a rational sense. It is a weapon of attack. It inflicts wounds and cuts up animals that have been killed. But this obviously dangerous quality is beset with affects. [. . .] Fear, distaste, guilt, associations and emotions of the most disparate kinds exaggerate the probable danger. It is precisely this which anchors such prohibitions so firmly and deeply in the personality and which gives them their taboo character.[65]

Elias thus subordinates the various misuses of the knife—including pointing it toward the face—to "the general fear that the dangerous symbol arouses."[66] The negative affect associated with the use of the knife is tied to a general denial of instinct and a particular disavowal of violence associated with its other uses and with earlier, less "civilized" moments in the history of manners, an association embedded in a line Elias takes from William Caxton's *Book of Curtesye*: "Bear not your knife toward your face, for therein is peril and much dread." In this way, the misuse of the knife works well for Thackeray as the mistake's general equivalent because it bears the traces of the long history of the civilizing process and because its status as a mistake allows for the enacting of one's faith in a social order founded on but still wary of violence.[67]

Bearing a knife toward your face is not, however, an obvious danger to others; it is a danger to yourself. What is disavowed in the disavowal of eating peas with your knife is not the threat of violence that some take as the secret

---

65. Elias, *The Civilizing Process*, 104.

66. Ibid., 105.

67. Litvak has also seen that the scene of eating and the threat of violence go hand in hand in *The Book of Snobs*: reading a scene where a mild critique of "dinner-giving snobs" turns into a "rather startling genocidal fantasy," he writes that the "bloody-mindedness of this revolutionary fantasy might be attenuated by the evident irony with which Thackeray invokes the 'gentle shades' of Marat and Robespierre, were it not that this irony, so typical of what Sedgwick calls 'Thackeray's bitchy art,' with its 'feline gratuitousness of aggression,' functions rather clearly as a form of violence in its own right." One can also look elsewhere for associations of eating and violence in the nineteenth-century novel. Two other examples: Hindley terrorizes Nelly in *Wuthering Heights*: "'There, I've found it out at last!' cried Hindley, pulling me back by the skin of my neck, like a dog. 'By heaven and hell, you've sworn between you to murder that child! I know how it is, now, that he is always out of my way. But, with the help of Satan, I shall make you swallow the carving-knife, Nelly! You needn't laugh; for I've just crammed Kenneth, head-downmost, in the Blackhorse marsh; and two is the same as one—and I want to kill some of you: I shall have no rest till I do!'... 'Open your mouth.' He held the knife in his hand, and pushed its point between my teeth: but, for my part, I was never much afraid of his vagaries. I spat out, and affirmed it tasted detestably..." And Herbert gives Pip a lesson in *Great Expectations*: "'Let me introduce the topic, Handel, by mentioning that in London it is not the custom to put the knife in the mouth—for fear of accidents...'" Litvak, *Strange Gourmets*, 60; Emily Brontë, *Wuthering Heights (London: Penguin, 1995), 74*; Dickens, *Great Expecations*, 179.

engine of the "civilizing process," but self-destruction.[68] So here, at last, we get to the heart of the matter. The chief anxiety of *The Book of Snobs* is not that the narrator of that volume will from time to time get called a snob—that temporary identification is built into its system—but that the identification will stick, that we will never again be able to tell the difference between one snob and another, and that the loss of that ability will result in the total collapse of a narrative form expressed in that social order. Without a mistake to disavow, the difference between one snob and another, which is in this text also the difference between a narrator and what it narrates, would disappear. Not to disavow the mistake would be a mistake, which in turn would be to *eat peas with your knife,* a self-destructive gesture the consequences of which we begin to understand. The loss of the mistake would turn a structuring disavowal into an identification, and the novel form, which is only getting going in *The Book of Snobs,* would collapse in a manner final enough to justify the name self-destruction. Late in *The Book of Snobs,* Thackeray asks, "Do I wish all Snobs to perish? . . . Suicidal fool, art not thou, too, a Snob and a brother?" (177). Thackeray's narrator, a little nervous at where the question leads, never answers it. Insofar as the destruction of the snobs would not spare a soul—not even, maybe especially not the narrator—perhaps we can now see why *eating peas with your knife,* an act that has long carried with it "peril and much dread," is given pride of place in Thackeray's *Book of Snobs.* The mistake, however embarrassing, however threatening, produces social and formal coherence where otherwise there would be none.

What Thackeray's text gives us is not only a compressed account of different anxieties present at the site of bad form but also a description of the ways in which the mistake makes available different relations between social and narrative form in the novel. What had seemed like a relatively benign faux pas results in a social crisis internal to *The Book of Snobs* as well as a constitutive crisis of narrative form that, I will argue, is not unique to Thackeray. We will see again and again that bad form, along with its being a figure around which social distinctions are more or less successfully maintained, is bound up with efforts to produce and to secure narrative authority in the omnisciently nar-

---

68. The relation between the threat of self-destruction and eating peas with your knife is brought out in an anecdote related in James Edward Austen-Leigh's 1870 memoir of his famous aunt: "The celebrated Beau Brummel, who was so intimate with George IV as to be able to quarrel with him, was born in 1771. It is reported that when he was questioned about his parents, he replied that it was long since he had heard of them, but that he imagined the worthy couple must have cut their own throats by that time, because when he last saw them they were eating peas with their knives." Brummel's casually vicious joke about his parents' probable suicide blends perfectly the aggression toward the self and the aggression toward others that characterize this very representative social mistake. James Edward Austen-Leigh, *A Memoir of Jane Austen* (New York: Oxford University Press, 2002).

rated nineteenth-century novel. If, that is, we follow Audrey Jaffe's suggestion that narrative omniscience is not so much a presence we could ever describe as it is a negation of what we do know about the epistemologically limited literary character, the negation out of which narrative omniscience emerges is—in this case and in others—coincident with a specifically social negation.[69] If it was true in *The Book of Snobs* that the narrator could only just keep from falling forever into the world of the snobs he describes, that to resist *eating peas with your knife* requires a vigilance excessive enough, even vulgar enough to be its own kind of bad form, perhaps it is the case more generally that the narrator of the nineteenth-century novel must count on the social mistake to secure its authority and structural position. And yet if narration needs to point at another's bad form in order to secure its own good form, can it be said to be good form at all? Is it not, we again wonder, bad form to think about good form?

5.

If Thackeray's Mr. Snob, a marginal figure forced like Gaskell's Mary Smith to hover uneasily between embodiment and omniscience, is in some danger in *The Book of Snobs*, life must be something different for a narrative omniscience more fully realized, an omniscience absent and absolute enough to avoid contact with bad form's sticky residue. What, after all, could ruffle the angelic feathers of what Alain Robbe-Grillet refers to as "that omniscient, omnipresent narrator appearing everywhere at once, simultaneously seeing the outside and the inside of things, following both the movements of a face and the impulses of conscience, knowing the present, the past, and the future of every enterprise"?[70] Would it not amount simply to a contradiction to accuse an omniscience like this of bad form? And, indeed, it is with something very like God's own authority that Balzac's narrator—the "omniscient, omnipresent" figure to whom Robbe-Grillet refers—offers the following thoughts on the difference between good and bad form:

> The chief merit of fine manners and tone in high company is that they
> supply a harmonious effect in which everything is so well blended
> that there is no jarring note. Even those who through ignorance or by

69. See Audrey Jaffe, *Vanishing Points: Dickens, Narrative, and the Subject of Omniscience* (Berkeley: University of California Press, 1991).

70. Alain Robbe-Grillet, from *New Novel, New Man*, in Michael McKeon, *Theory of the Novel: A Critical Anthology* (Baltimore: Johns Hopkins University Press, 2000), 823.

blurting out their thoughts break the rules of this science, ought to realize that in this matter a single dissonance, as in music, is a complete
negation of the art itself, every canon of which must be meticulously
observed if it is to remain an art.[71]

Although the terms of Balzac's analogy have the ring of a received idea (a
manuel de savoir-vivre from 1861 tells us in similar terms that "Il est . . . es-
sentiel pour tout membre de la société d'être poli ou bienséant, comme pour
toute note de l'échelle musicale d'occuper un rang normal dans une relation
avec les autres notes"), it nevertheless gives us a sense of what is at stake with
a social mistake even as minor as the one to which the preceding narratorial
reflection is a response (the still-provincial Lucien de Rubempré is very nearly
done in when he sees an acquaintance at the theater and points at him: it
is, as everyone knows, impolite to point).[72] Balzac's narrator suggests in *Lost
Illusions* that the coherence of sociability relies on the resolution of many
parts into a closed whole.[73] Kept separate from the disorganized data of experience, sociability offers not only, we are to see, temporary refuge from the
hard knocks of everyday life but also, as Georg Simmel suggests, a distinctly
aesthetic pleasure:

> For "good form" is mutual self-definition, interaction of the elements,
> through which a unity is made; and since in sociability the concrete
> motives bound up with life-goals fade away, so must the pure form, the
> free-playing, interacting interdependence of individuals stand out so
> much the more strongly and operate with so much the greater effect.[74]

As a result, bad form is a source of more than merely temporary embarrassment; it is for Balzac a negative force that threatens to disarrange a coherence
that we would look for both in music's promise of pure aesthetic autonomy
and in an equivalent sociable play.

71. Honoré de Balzac, *Lost Illusions*, trans. Herbert J. Hunt (London: Penguin, 1971), 171–72.

72. E. Muller, *La politesse française: Traité des bienséances et du savoir-vivre* (Paris: Garnier Frères, 1861),
v–vi.

73. We can, I think, take Adorno's observation that "when the peasant [in Balzac] comes to the city,
everything says 'closed' to him" in a double sense: on the one hand, access to the good things of society is
denied to outsiders; on the other, the inscrutability of the city is the result of not only the affective relation
between those who are in and those who are out, but also the varieties of formal closure after which the
sociable system, like the traditional novel, seems to strive. Theodor W. Adorno, "Reading Balzac," in *Notes
to Literature*, 2 vols., ed. Rolf Tiedemann, trans. Shierry Weber Nicholsen (New York: Columbia University Press, 1991), 1:121.

74. Georg Simmel, "Sociability," in *On Individuality and Social Forms*, ed. Donald N. Levine (Chicago:
University of Chicago Press, 1971), 129.

It should, in that case, be clear what's in store for the young Eugène Rastignac when he makes a similar and famous faux pas toward the beginning of *Père Goriot*. While visiting the Count and the Countess de Restaud he mentions the name of his boardinghouse neighbor, "Père Goriot," not knowing that that name belongs to the father the countess has all but disowned. If, however, his form is bad, hers is beautiful: at first she flushes, "obviously embarrassed," but then recovers quickly and turns the conversation to music:

> She interrupted herself, stared for a moment at her piano, as if suddenly remembering something, and asked,
> "Do you care for music, monsieur?"
> "A great deal," replied Eugène, turning red and stunned to find that he'd committed some impossible stupidity, made some incredible mistake.[75]

She dexterously moves conversation away from a subject awkward to herself and to her husband, the count, toward the piano, an object especially available, we now know, as a musical metaphor for society's tonal complexities.[76] What's more, in turning to music, she aggressively and intentionally masters Eugène's own unintentional aggression:

> "Do you sing?" she cried, going over to the instrument and loudly striking key after key, from C in the bass clef all the way up to a high F. Rrrrah!
> "No, madame."
> The Count de Restaud was pacing up and down, back and forth, back and forth.
> "What a shame," she went on, "you've deprived yourself of a high road to success. *Ca-a-ro, ca-a-ro, ca-a-a-a-ro, non du-bita-re*," the countess sang. (49–50)

75. Honoré de Balzac, *Père Goriot*, trans. Burton Raffel, ed. Peter Brooks (New York: Norton, 1994), 49. Subsequent references to this work will appear in the text.

76. "'Society' is," as Emily Post says, "an ambiguous term; it may mean much or nothing." In this case I mean "society" in the restricted sense suggested by Georg Simmel but acknowledge productive dissonances between it and the less qualified object of sociology's interest: "It is...not without significance that in many, perhaps in all, European languages, the word 'society' [*Gesellschaft*] designates a sociable gathering. The political, the economic, the purposive society of any sort is, to be sure, always 'society.' But only the sociable gathering is 'society' without qualifying adjectives, because it alone presents the pure, abstract play of form, all the specific contents of the one-sided and qualified societies being dissolved away." Emily Post, *Etiquette in Society, in Business, in Politics and at Home* (New York: Funk and Wagnalls, 1922) 1; Simmel, "Sociability," 129.

While seeming to divert attention from the young man's blunder, she instead offers a performed Balzacian commentary on the nature of the social mistake. Eugène's inability to sing, to harmonize with the other players in this particular scene, threatens the whole complicated performance that is social life.

The countess's short song is a differently gendered performance of "Cara, non dubitar," a duet that begins Cimarosa's *Il matrimonio segreto* (1792), the two-part form of which demands from Rastignac a response that the countess already knows he is not at all up to. The relation between Balzac's novel and Cimarosa's opera also suggests a series of structural torsions: the countess sings "my love, don't doubt" when we know that it is doubt—self-doubt—that she looks to produce in Eugène; the strained phonetic rendering, *"ca-a-ro, ca-a-ro, ca-a-a-a-ro, non du-bita-re,"* shows us that for the countess the song is primarily a content to be worked and worked over; and, that she performs the part of Paolino, the capable young hero, places a necessarily silent Rastignac in what we are to take as the humiliating position of the piece's "youngest daughter," Carolina. What's more, the opera's comic plot—Geronimo, a wealthy but deaf and doddering merchant, seeks to marry his daughter, who has already secretly married for love, to a count in order to satisfy aristocratic pretensions—returns as tragedy in *Père Goriot*. Where the foolish Geronimo would have put fatherhood second to his social position but at last accepts his daughter's "matrimonio segreto," Goriot, a "Christ of fatherhood" whose devotion to his daughters eventually kills him, disinterestedly accepts his daughter's mercenary marriage even though it takes from him the pleasure of her company. As much as all this might threaten simply to derange the comic form of *Il matrimonio segreto,* the countess's ability to play the changes of genre, gender, and plot reinforces our sense of her as a gifted musician, one who can make an old tune sound new.

The success of the countess's performance solidifies a relation between aesthetic and social form that we have already seen at work in both Balzac and Thackeray, a relation that should hold not only for music but also for that most capacious of literary forms: the novel. It should come as no surprise that the novel, a genre especially able to represent the complex system of codes and relations that organize a society, would stand performatively as a metaphor for good social form; for the novel represents a specific social content and strives to reproduce society's ability to translate raw experience into intelligible form. It makes sense in that case that it would fall to the narrator to remind us that "the chief merit of fine manners and tone in high company is that they supply a harmonious effect." Even so, to take Balzac as representative of that ideal poses a problem: the ideal coherence that the Balzacian critique of bad form assumes as a model has, after all, little to do with the actual form of any novel of Balzac's.[77] Complex, unruly, inclusive to the point of breakdown, Balzac's novels, brilliant for other reasons, remain those on whose form we cannot count for the theoretically familiar if infrequently found pleasures of narrative economy or closure.[78] What's more, although narration in *Lost Illusions* argues that social mistakes are what threaten to burst the bubble of society's good form, bad form is on the contrary weirdly genetic in Balzac's novels. First, it is Eugène's slip that forces him out of the Restauds' drawing room and onto the battlefields of Paris and thus generates more and more narrative desire. In this way, the social mistake is an especially concentrated form of "narrative unhappiness," an instrumental bit of misery necessary to prolong the dilatory "arabesque or squiggle toward the end" that is plot.[79] It is also the case that Eugène later renarrates his own mistake, turning it to his advantage as the opening gambit in his seduction of the countess's sister, Madame de Nucingen: "Madame, my conscience bids me to tell you the truth [about her sister having shown him the door], but I must beg your indulgence in confiding such a secret to your ears. I live next door to your father. I had no idea that Madame de Restaud was his daughter. I was sufficiently incautious to speak of him, all innocently, which much angered both your sister and her husband" (98). Eugène's move, which of course works, leads us to wonder at the nature of a process that can so suddenly turn bad form into good, a process that, if we maintain Balzac's sense of the mistake as a "negation," amounts to a miraculous negation of the negation.

As well as prolonging narrative desire, Eugène's gaffe produces a bewildering set of structural correspondences and identifications. The music that follows the mistake ("Rrrrah!") complicates Balzac's analogy, giving us form

77. This in spite of the fact that it was against something "vaguely called the Balzacian novel," that the *nouveau roman*'s coherence-busting experiments were pitted. Ann Jefferson, *The Nouveau Roman and the Poetics of Fiction* (Cambridge: Cambridge University Press, 1980), 1.

78. Writing about Balzac asks with strange persistence whether the novels or the broader system of the *Comédie humaine* hang together. From Saint-Beuve, who felt that "the distortion and exaggeration of reality in Balzac's novels was unacceptable," to Leo Bersani, who asks at the outset of a long essay on Balzac, "Is Balzac, in fact, any good?," the structural and stylistic coherence of Balzac's work has been anything but taken for granted. We need only consider the unprecedented manner in which Balzac reintroduces Vautrin, who has had nothing to do with *Lost Illusions* for its first 600 pages and who appears disguised as the Abbé Carlos Herrera in order to save Lucien from suicide; marvelous as that famous sequence is, it has very little to do with what we expect from coherence in the traditional novel. David Bellos, *Balzac Criticism in France 1850–1900: The Making of a Reputation* (Oxford: Clarendon Press, 1976), 9; Leo Bersani, *Balzac to Beckett: Center and Circumference in French Fiction* (New York: Oxford University Press, 1970), 25.

79. D. A. Miller writes, "The narrative of happiness is inevitably frustrated by the fact that only insufficiencies, defaults, deferrals, can be 'told,'" a fact understood by Balzac, who calls one section of *A Harlot High and Low* "a boring chapter, since it describes four years of happiness." D. A. Miller, *Narrative and Its Discontents: Problems of Closure in the Traditional Novel* (Princeton, NJ: Princeton University Press, 1981), 3. The idea of plot as "arabesque" comes from Peter Brooks, *Reading for the Plot: Design and Intention in Narrative* (Cambridge, MA: Harvard University Press, 1992), 104.

where there should be none. The proliferating embarrassment that his faux pas generates (her husband is embarrassed, which embarrasses her, which in turn embarrasses Eugène) points to the Goffmanian role that embarrassment has in the affective organization of literary texts and social life (" . . . in these matters ego boundaries seem especially weak").[80] And, Balzac's metaphor for Eugène's particular embarrassment ("Il se trouvait dans la situation d'un homme introduit par faveur chez un amateur de curiosités, et qui, touchant par mégarde une armoire pleine de figures sculptées, fait tomber trois ou quatre têtes mal collées")[81] both reaffirms the sense of the sociable as an exquisitely organized and thus exceedingly fragile form and suggests a set of correspondences between the social, the affective, and the historical; for, even if Eugène does not at this moment know that Goriot, once a vermicelli maker, made the money on which the Restauds have lived using his influence as president of his revolutionary section to exploit the volatile grain market of 1793, his feeling that heads could roll points nonetheless to the Bourbon Restoration's anxiety about its own problematic paternity. The name Goriot thus both stands as an index of Eugène's immediate lack of experience with what everyone in Paris seems already to know and raises the nerve-wracking specter of revolution through the sensitive medium of the social mistake.

Indeed, the scene is brought to life by a tension always implicit in bad form. If we were to stick to the social logic that the Balzacian novel explicitly offers ("a single dissonance, as in music, is a complete negation of the art itself"), we would think that all form is good form, that condition of both literary texts and social events that renders them coherent and intelligible, and that bad form is, as Balzac suggests, not form but rather form's negation. As we have, however, begun to see, Eugène's moment of bad form is productive, engendering the sorts of relations—identifications, disavowals, correspondences—between people, ideas, and distinct aspects of the novel that make literary texts readable and that give them what we call and what we experience as their form.

And, as if to underscore the fact of bad form's productive contagiousness, the narrator of this scene seems, impossibly, to catch it. If it becomes clear that Eugène has made a bad move, it seems that, at least according to Peter Brooks, the writing that represents him might be just as bad:

> The crudity of Balzac's rendering—the excess of the comte's successive reactions, the rapidity of Rastignac's complete acceptance and complete rejection—make the labels comedy of manners and social real-

---

80. Erving Goffman, *Interaction Ritual: Essays in Face-to-Face Behavior* (Chicago: Aldine, 1967), 99.

81. Honoré de Balzac, *Père Goriot* (Paris: Flammarion, 1995), 102. The translation I use elsewhere fails to convey the passage's specific threat of decapitation.

ism inadequate and misleading. If we see the scene as such, we will be forced to conclude that it is bad social realism.[82]

If Balzac's writing is in this instance bad, we find ourselves employing terms more social than formal to describe why it is bad.[83] Balzac rushes his story where he should have lingered, showing a lack of restraint that could do as much drawing-room damage as Eugène's own unfortunate slip (Brooks calls this Balzac a "bull in the china closet"). Brooks goes on to suggest that the felt badness of the scene is the result of a category mistake on our part. For Brooks, the Balzacian text sees past etiquette's finer shades to the heart of what "is only on the surface a code of manners." To treat that text as if it were comedy instead of melodrama is to fail to describe our object: where civilized comedy can afford to be light, bright, and sparkling, Balzac, society's melo-dramatist, must rudely "push *through* manners to deeper sources of being," a style that is for Brooks characteristic of melodrama's "mode of excess."[84] While it is, however, no doubt the case that Balzac is more concerned with what manners hide than with producing a pious anatomy of those manners, Brooks's analytical shift from comedy to melodrama turns away too quickly, I think, from the odd overlap between narration's bad form and the bad form that it narrates. We should pause a moment with the discomfort that results from what looks like narration's mistake.

Balzac's is a distinctly social omniscience. Really to know something in Balzac is to know society not as an especially perceptive observer but as a subject identical to society's conventions and codes, a subject who, in the self-congratulatory words of *The Portrait of a Lady*'s Gilbert Osmond, is "not conventional but convention itself."[85] So if narrative omniscience is not so much a presence that we could ever describe as it is a negation of all the things we do know about literary character, the structural negation that engenders Balzac's narrative omniscience must be mixed up with a specifically social negation.[86] What character has that narration doesn't is a capacity for bad form;

82. Peter Brooks, *The Melodramatic Imagination: Balzac, Henry James, Melodrama, and the Mode of Excess* (New Haven, CT: Yale University Press, 1995), 131.

83. Early critics of Balzac looked to analogies between Balzac's writing style and his lifestyle to resolve the difficult formal contradictions in his work: "In the satirical *Charivari*, Balzac's mannerisms and eccen-tricities were derided by frequent short space-fillers throughout 1836 and 1837. The novelist's aristocratic pretensions, political ambitions, and use of neologisms provided the bulk of the material. Even his living quarters (presumably the Cassini flat) became the butt of ridicule: one journalist described them as resem-bling the home of some 'joueur subitement enrichi par un coup inespéré de bourse.'" Bad taste, in other words, offered a way to figure and thus to naturalize the complex form of Balzac's novels. Bellos, *Balzac Criticism in France*, 8.

84. Brooks, *The Melodramatic Imagination*, 131, 4.

85. Henry James, *The Portrait of a Lady*, ed. Robert D. Bamberg (New York: Norton, 1995), 265.

86. Again, see Jaffe, *Vanishing Points*.

the knowledge that young men from the provinces like Lucien and Eugène seek about what tailor to go to, where to get gloves without ready cash, and who is sleeping with whom is always already under the belt of a narration whose work is to lay bare those codes for the reader.[87] So why at this moment, a moment when Rastignac's bad form is represented, when we would most expect narration to look good, does it come so close to bad form?

We are perhaps better used to the opposite motion in Balzac; throughout the *Comédie humaine,* individual characters are temporarily possessed by the voice of narration. When Vautrin exposes the social lie to Eugène in *Père Goriot* or Etienne Lousteau introduces Lucien to journalism's black heart in *Lost Illusions,* what we experience is not the best that a character has to offer but moments when, in a strange inversion of free indirect style, characters speak narration and as a result are in better form and embody the law in a manner that cannot be reasonably sustained. Vautrin, in the scene alluded to, is able to speak not only for the social as a whole but also for Eugène, which he does with something like omniscience's view of the thoughts of the other: "And us, we're ambitious, we have a connection with the Beauséants but we still go around on foot, we want to be rich but we haven't got a cent, we eat boiled stew at Momma Vauquer's but we prefer fine dinners in the Faubourg Saint-Germain, we sleep on a straw bed and wish we had a mansion" (83). Vautrin's performance straddles the simple but shrewd perspicacity suggested by "his way of looking hard and searchingly at people" and a supernatural access to other minds that threatens to obliterate a difference between the diegetic and the extradiegetic on which the novel's form counts. And, to take another example from *Lost Illusions,* after Lousteau's tearful and uncharacteristic speech to Lucien, one in which he begs him not to become a journalist and in which he reaches an ethical register that *supersedes* his position in the novel, he snaps back into character with a tangible sense of relief: "'Well, well!' said the journalist. 'One more Christian going down into the arena to face the lions! My dear fellow, there's a first performance this evening at the Panorama-Dramatique'" (251). Lousteau's sharp return to his usual, urbane, and embodied tone is a relief to the reader and to poor Lousteau, who has seemed understandably uncomfortable shouldering the manic burden of omniscience for five or so pages: "Well, well!"

The case I have been describing is different but no less disturbing. At the moment when we would expect, given what we know about the novel, to see narration perform most definitively its structuring negation of character, the negation of the bad form that very nearly sinks Eugène Rastignac, we

---

87. Franco Moretti notices that in Balzac, "story and discourse undergo an inversely proportional relationship: the more unaware and bewildered the hero, the wiser and more farsighted the narrator." Franco Moretti, *The Way of the World: The* Bildungsroman *in European Culture* (London: Verso, 2000), 135.

instead catch narration identifying with that bad form and engaging in a narrative style that, if judged according to its own rules ("a single dissonance"), would no doubt result in a crazy sort of exile. Jaffe writes that, "what we call omniscience can be located . . . not in presence or absence, but in the tension between the two—between a voice that implies presence and the lack of any character to attach it to, between a narratorial configuration that refuses character and the characters it requires to define itself."[88] As I have suggested, one way to mark out that structuring difference is to draw attention to the mistakes that characters make and to the mistakes that make character. If the ability and inability to make mistakes offer one way for us to order the novel, narration's specifically social slip in Balzac not only upsets the order of the drawing room but also threatens as it secures the very coherence of the novel form: the possibility of narration's fall into the fraught social world it narrates both threatens to undo a distinction between diegetic and extradiegetic narrative levels on which the novel as a form counts and gives that distinction a social and affective significance it would not otherwise possess.

What we have seen in the loss of tone that narration exhibits in the preceding scene is the formal equivalent of psychoanalytic identification, the "process whereby the subject assimilates an aspect, property or attribute of the other and is transformed, wholly or partially, after the mode the other provides."[89] And although we can thus easily diagnose the sort of relation that emerges spontaneously between narration and character in *Père Goriot*, we must nevertheless ask why bad form is so particular a site of an identification that short-circuits the purity of narration's structural negation, an identification that, more than simply indexing a basic figural instability, counts on a strong reciprocity between the social and the formal.

Lingering too long with this question, however, threatens to become its own brand of bad form; for, if we know anything about narration, it is that narration isn't much of anything. If character is, as it is sometimes said, only smoke and mirrors, narration is nothing at all, and talk of its character can only reflect the critic's blind adherence to an ideology of the personal. Jonathan Culler calls the search for personality in narration a kind of "naturalization," an ideological project to resolve the inconsistencies of a narrative system around a structuring intention, a project, furthermore, that satisfies the critic's nostalgia for the good old days of bourgeois subjectivity. In other words, to align, as I have begun to do, a textual effect with the social and affective conditions activated by the social mistake they accompany risks

88. Jaffe, *Vanishing Points*, 4.

89. J. Laplanche and J.-B. Pontalis, *The Language of Psychoanalysis*, trans. Donald Nicholson-Smith (New York: Norton, 1973), 205.

reducing complex formal states of affairs to merely psychological "excesses which display the narrator's individuality [or] symptoms of his obsessions," a process that, at least in the case of the *nouveau roman,* turns an otherwise interesting novel into something "thoroughly banal."[90] It would be wrong, in that case, to talk too seriously of narration's identifications because to imagine that possibility is already to have naturalized a textual system into something like a coherent, intentional, and human being.

We have, however, already seen that at particular moments in Balzac, characters can seem for a moment to identify with narration, to borrow some quantity of the social power that narration displays in its capacity as a normative agency. Put differently, at moments when one character "disillusions" another, he or she realizes Balzacian narration's identity with the total system of rules, information, secrets, strategies, and prohibitions that structure the social. These moments of resemblance between character and narration problematically blur a clear opposition between identification and disidentification in the novel. While the practical value of this collapse is obvious (for the narrative to proceed, a character needs to learn something that narration knows, but because narration cannot talk to characters with its own voice, because it is, as Franco Moretti suggests, structurally "estranged" from the world of its characters, it needs temporarily to possess a character to speak to that world), that collapse disturbs a difference on which the novel form counts.

Although they command distinctly different amounts of social authority in Balzac, that authority—the same authority—stands nevertheless as a shared ideal for both character and narration. And because narration's conspicuous competence is only the best version of a competence that everybody wants, it reminds us, in its particular perfection and the manner in which it encourages identification, of the ego ideal, that perfectly lovable object which precedes and in fact produces the superego as a regulative force in the Freudian account of social and moral development.[91] And like the ego ideal,

90. Although this part of Culler's argument deals directly with the *nouveau roman,* it is clear from its context that it can be extended, in the way that the readerly seems to shift into the writerly when looked at long and hard enough, to narration in the traditional novel as well. Culler has, as we saw in the introduction, recently returned to this line of thinking. Jonathan Culler, *Structuralist Poetics: Structuralism, Linguistics, and the Study of Literature* (Ithaca, NY: Cornell University Press, 1975), 200; Culler, "Omniscience," *Narrative* 12, no. 1 (2004): 22–34.

91. The superego makes its early, unnamed appearance in "On Narcissism" as that agency which works to call attention to the structuring and sometimes maddening differences between the ego and the ego ideal. If the superego is a regulative agency, an *aspect* of the psyche that emerges as a result of the establishment of the ego ideal, the ego ideal itself is a perfect object that serves as a compensation for the lost object of primary narcissism. Two points need to be stressed here: (1) If, as Janine Chasseguet-Smirgel suggests, "the meeting of ego and ideal" would result in the dissolution of "the superego," so would it result in the dissolution of the socially recognizable because socially subjected ego. (2) This subjection results not only in the structuring of the self around the tension between ego and ego ideal but also in shared,

which is not only an object with which the ego longs to identify but also a "substitute for the lost narcissism of youth," a substitute for that constitutive primary identification with and libidinal investment in the self that makes later identifications and, indeed, identity itself possible, narration's authority is not an a priori category but is itself founded on a prior identification with what is maybe most lovable: bourgeois good form. Narration's is not, in other words, an abstract authority, but is rather one wrapped up in and dependent on a social world that is in turn dependent on in its own uneasy and never-ending production of ideals.

We could extend the analogy between narration at its unrealizable best and the ego ideal to see the distance between a narration and a character as another way to figure narrative desire. More than simply moving toward the quiescence of narrative closure, that desire could be read as a tension "experienced by the gap between the ego ideal and the actual ego [which] becomes an important motor for development."[92] And if that desire for identity is one form of narrative, too sustained an identification between narration and what it narrates would necessarily force the novel into nonnarratability; "too close a proximation to [one's ego ideal], not to mention its actual attainment, would result in the de-differentiation of manic psychosis."[93] The "dedifferentiation" of character and narration in the traditional novel would amount to something other than the traditional novel. As I will later argue, *The Sacred Fount* stages exactly the descent of a Jamesian narration whose social perspicuity we must identify as something like omniscience into the world of the novel, a descent that is explicitly registered in the novel as "crazy."

Narration's omniscience is thus caught between two kinds of relation: on the one hand, we have a disidentification with the limitations of character, a negation that helps to produce what we recognize as narrative authority; on the other, we have an identification with good form, that monstrous collection of codes, conventions, and *things to do*, the mastery of which produces authority as such and which the social climber looks to command. The knowledge that the protagonist of the social bildungsroman seeks, the authority that

---

circulating, and structuring aggressivity; Judith Butler, following Freud and the Lacan of "Aggressivity in Psychoanalysis," writes that "the aggression toward the ideal and its unfulfillability is turned inward, and this self-aggression becomes the primary structure of conscience" (142). This aggression both provides an affective circuit for figural exchanges between the different aspects of the self and their various projective stand-ins and, in terms of this argument, helps to give a novel form whose space is the space between narration and character its own structuring, affective character. Janine Chasseguet-Smirgel, *The Ego Ideal: A Psychoanalytic Essay on the Malady of the Ideal*, trans. Paul Barrows (New York: Norton, 1985), 78; Butler, *The Psychic Life of Power*, 142.

92. Joel Whitebook, *Perversion and Utopia: A Study in Psychoanalysis and Critical Theory* (Cambridge, MA: MIT Press, 1994), 65, 173.

93. Ibid., 173.

would represent his or her success in the world and which would, if achieved, result formally in narrative closure, stands, it seems, as a shared ideal for both narration and character in the nineteenth-century novel, a common desire that gives way to identification where disidentification was expected. This play between identification and disidentification is, as I have begun to argue, necessary to the structure and authority of the omnisciently narrated nineteenth-century novel; and that play—so crucial to the novel—relies, as I will continue to argue in the chapters to come, on the social mistake.

CHAPTER 2

Embarrassing *Bovary*

HATS: Complain about their shape.
　　—*Gustave Flaubert,* Dictionary of Received Ideas[1]

It is against *the thing to do* that poor Charles Bovary sins in the first pages of *Madame Bovary.* That sin, when read alongside Flaubert's many remarks on good style and good form in letters to Louise Colet and others, must stand as a perfect and particular signifier of the haplessness that is Bovary's lot in life.[2] Bovary, introduced simply as the new boy *(le nouveau),* does not, as his properly social peers do, toss his cap upon entering the classroom. While this is the kind of lapse that makes special sense to the very young, it is one that nevertheless exposes perfectly the structure of the most mature social mistake. The convention is appropriately arbitrary, the kind of rule that exists only to allow for the making

---

1. Gustave Flaubert, *Bouvard and Pécuchet with the Dictionary of Received Ideas,* trans. A. J. Krailsheimer (London: Penguin, 1976), 309.

2. Gustave Flaubert, *Madame Bovary,* trans. Geoffrey Wall (London: Penguin, 1992), 2; subsequent references to this work will appear in the text. "The thing to do" is Wall's translation of Flaubert's "le *genre."* Flaubert, *Madame Bovary* (Paris: Librarie Générale Française, 1999), 56.

of distinctions: "We had a custom, on coming back into the class-room, of throwing our caps on the ground, to leave our hands free; you had to fling them, all the way from the door, under the bench, so that they hit the wall and made lots of dust; it was *the thing to do*."[3] What makes throwing the hat an exemplary social convention is not in this case simply the fact that it is a custom with origins as cloudy as those of any social myth, but that it, like the hat that won't get tossed, is of "the Composite order"; the steps involved, steps that *it was necessary*—"il fallait"—to follow, are in themselves trivial but, as they add up to *the thing to do*, disclose the strange necessity and complex structure of social form.

The scene does not, however, end with the usual expulsion, temporary or otherwise, that should result from Charles's misunderstanding the rules of social play. Failing to do the done thing should, after all, be quite enough both for the purposes of schoolyard humiliation and for the scene's narrative demands. Instead, and in excess of the social logic expressed by the rule of the hat, Charles's cap is something *too* ridiculous, and it encourages narration on to this remarkable and often remarked upon performance:

> But, whether he had not noticed this maneuver or did not dare to attempt it, prayers were over and the new boy was still holding his cap on his knees. It was one of those hats of the Composite order, in which we find features of the military bear-skin, the Polish chapska, the bowler hat, the beaver and the cotton nightcap, one of those pathetic things, in fact, whose mute ugliness has a profundity of expression like the face of an imbecile. Ovoid and stiffened with whalebone, it began with three big circular sausages; then, separated by a red band, there alternated diamonds of velours and rabbit-fur; after that came a sort of bag terminating in a cardboard polygon, embroidered all over with complicated braid, and, hanging down at the end of a long cord that was too thin, a little cluster of gold threads, like a tassel. It looked new; the peak was gleaming. (2)

That one hardly knows where to begin is an essential effect of this passage: we understood prior to the preceding description how Charles's lapse works

3. Tony Tanner reads the toss of the hat in this way: "The fact that 'nous,' the boys already established within the school, like to throw their caps under their seats and against the wall—to leave their hands freer—may indicate some initial disinclination to rest easy under the allotted headgear of their society." I disagree: the gesture, because it is *the thing to do*, seems rather to be simply another example of socially recognized, socially regulated behavior, a transgression that is really transgression's opposite. The good boy knows both when to wear his hat and when to toss it. Tony Tanner, *Adultery and the Novel: Contract and Transgression* (Baltimore: Johns Hopkins University Press, 1981), 240.

within the particular social structure for which it is a lapse. This hat, however, seems not only to break the rules of the bounded social system that this first chapter works to represent but also to trouble the rules, codes, and conventions that structure the literary system that is *Madame Bovary*. The description is offered as a thing especially significant; its length, the specificity of its detail, and the exuberance with which a certain judgment is suggested but not articulated all go to suggest a literary object that is above all meaningful. But what does it mean?[4] The hat signifies the confusion of its wearer, but so overdoes it as to remove that act of signification from the realm of the socially legible. As Jonathan Culler suggests, we feel that the hat's extravagance cannot be translated into an idea, that the hat and the riot of interpretations it encourages might be a "trick" played on the reader by "the narrator or critic." For Culler, this condition points to and introduces into the reader the thing that he takes to be most especially Flaubert's: "an emptiness, in the guise of linguistic despair."[5]

Leaving aside for a moment the semiotic hollow that is or is not at the heart of *Madame Bovary*, it is clear that in terms of the social use to which it is put, the hat is a bigger mistake than was required by the novel. We saw right away that Charles was in rough shape; his shabby clothes and his stiff, embarrassed demeanor had already and in concert with the slip with which we began alerted the reader to Charles's not-so-secret clumsiness. The hat is, in that case, *too* good, it does *too* much. The description is, in other words, its own kind of mistake. The hat is embarrassing not only to its poor wearer but also potentially to the voice that describes it. Although that voice, represented in the opening pages of *Madame Bovary* in the first-person plural, speaks in the service of convention and with a potent social authority conferred upon it by the force of the "we," the narrator nevertheless *jumps the gun* and says a lot where only a little was required.[6] This slip might provide a reason for the

---

4. For some readings of the cap that count on its famously meaningful meaninglessness, see Jonathan Culler, *Flaubert: The Uses of Uncertainty* (Ithaca, NY: Cornell University Press, 1974), 92; Victor Brombert, *The Novels of Flaubert: A Study of Themes and Techniques* (Princeton, NJ: Princeton University Press, 1966); Tanner, *Adultery and the Novel*, 237–40; Dennis Porter, "*Madame Bovary* and the Question of Pleasure," in *Flaubert and Postmodernism*, ed. Naomi Schor and Henry F. Majewski (Lincoln: University of Nebraska Press, 1984), 120–21.

5. Culler, *Flaubert*, 92–93.

6. Figures like the hat reappear within the Flaubertian system: like certain images in *The Temptation of Saint Anthony*, the hat fantastically exceeds the imaginative powers of the reader. For all the distance between Flaubert's fantasy of Saint Anthony and the provincial world of the pharmacist Homais, there is something shared in the structure of Charles's remarkable cap and a vision that sees that "stones are similar to brains, stalactites to nipples, iron flower to tapestries ornate with figures." The feeling produced in each case is not merely a shock at the sometimes violent force of the imagination but embarrassment again: embarrassment at the limits of the imagination. The hat, like the visions of Saint Anthony, shames the imagination of a reader who would want to add those details up into some meaningful whole. We can take this as a kind of monstrous instance of the Barthesian opposition between the real and the operable. The hat does not function in the same way that other examples of the real could; that is, instead of guaranteeing

notable haste with which the "I" of that narratorial "we" departs. It is, of course, a well-known if poorly accounted for fact that the narrative voice of *Madame Bovary* shifts rather suddenly from the first-person plural of these first pages to the impersonal style for which Flaubert is famous. Like an embarrassed party guest who knows only enough to know when it's time to leave, that voice quits while it's ahead (if only just).

Critics have tended to look to Flaubert's meticulousness, his mastery of the novel form to recuperate what looks at first like a mistake. Victor Brombert writes: "[The first-person] point of view is not sustained, and very soon an anonymous author's perspective replaces this more personal voice. It seems hardly conceivable that so careful a craftsman as Flaubert should not have noticed the discrepancy, and that the curiously oblique approach should be the result of inadvertence."[7] This particular tautology—Flaubert's genius guarantees the subtle slip that in turn guarantees his genius—is a popular one.[8] If we take seriously, however, the idea that the hat is not only the masterful if absurd description for which it is usually taken but also an impropriety on the part of narration, what could provide better cover for an embarrassed voice that says more than it should than a retreat to an omniscience to which nothing could stick.

The "thing to do" is, after all, also "le genre," and the hat's description exists in as complicated a relation to literary convention as the hat does to sartorial convention: it is a bad figure, ekphrasis gone wrong.[9] It is conventionally allusive in ways that have short-circuited: the hat looks, on the one

---

the "realness" of the novel's realism, the hat points to the possible monstrosity of the real. Gustave Flaubert, *The Temptation of Saint Anthony*, trans. Kitty Mrosovsky (Ithaca, NY: Cornell University Press, 1981), 231.

7. Brombert, quoted in Culler, *Flaubert*, 101. About this "puzzlement," Culler writes that it "seems a result of the *seriousness* which incapacitates so much Flaubert criticism; an attitude which induces reverence before the work of art and a refusal to entertain the possibility that it may be engaged in parody . . . " Although this seems right in general, I will argue that, in this particular instance, neither wishing the mistake away nor taking it as managed part of parody can fully account for its constitutive relation to Flaubert's voice and to the novel as a whole. Culler, *Flaubert*, 101.

8. Along with Brombert, we can look to Enid Starkie, who gives up on the shift with something of a shrug; and Dacia Maraini takes it that "given the insane meticulousness of the writer," the mistake is present to "confuse the reader," which, because Flaubert is meticulous, constitutes the novel's "subtle originality." Enid Starkie, *Flaubert: The Making of the Master* (New York: Atheneum, 1967); Dacia Maraini, *Searching for Emma: Gustave Flaubert and* Madame Bovary, trans. Vincent J. Bertolini (Chicago: University of Chicago Press, 1998), 3.

9. Leo Bersani, following Proust's somewhat exaggerated claim "that he could not find a single beautiful metaphor in Flaubert's work," says that "Flaubert's metaphors are the 'fall' of his style, and they give the impression of a literary chore done conscientiously and unenthusiastically." These bad figures and the embarrassment they produce in Flaubert's critics will be a subject to which we will return. Let it be said for now that the shabby metaphor is a kind of crystallized version of the problem of economy that we find in Charles's famous, maybe too-famous, cap. Leo Bersani, *Balzac to Beckett: Center and Circumference in French Fiction* (New York: Oxford University Press, 1970), 190.

hand, like a fashion mistake in the Balzacian tradition, an error in dress that shows the young provincial's weak hand. Like Lucien's too-new green suit in *Lost Illusions*, a conspicuous aspect of the hat's failure is its tacky newness: "It looked new; the peak was gleaming" (2). On the other hand, unlike Lucien's unfortunate resemblance to a tailor's dummy, Charles's failure is not one that can be attributed to the difference between the provincial oaf and the Parisian dandy: new or not, the hat is just awful, an abuse of convention that looms larger than whatever convention could be invoked against it. The hat is in this way a double mistake, a mistake legible within the social system of *Madame Bovary* and a performed mistake on the part of the novel's narration; if Charles had known in that first moment how to do the done thing, the narrator could also have tossed away the embarrassing narrative error that is the hat's description. Insofar as Charles's embarrassment makes these events narratable, it appears that narration at once produces, attempts to dodge, feels, and needs the feeling of embarrassment in *Madame Bovary*.

Flaubert's first pages are embarrassing: they embarrass, as is absolutely clear, poor Charles; they embarrass, in a way that is only a little harder to see, an embodied narrative voice that gets gone before it can really get going; and, what's more, they embarrass their readers.[10] The critic or casual fan of the novel form cannot but feel familiar with the conventions that structure the story of Charles's first day at school. In this case, however, familiarity does not bring comfort but instead produces confusion and shame. The standard reading of this effect, standard anyway since the "Golden Age of Flaubert Studies,"[11] is that Flaubert revolutionized the form of the novel through a sadistic subversion of literary convention; the formal oddity of this scene is meant to teach a lesson to readers and critics too comfortable with the conventions of the bourgeois novel. The attractions of this reading are clear: the unconventional Flaubert's subversion secures his place both as literary terrorist and as father to a literary avant-garde. The critical quality of the unconventional or anticonventional style thus foregrounds Flaubert's relationship not only to other and later writers of experimental fiction but also to a literary critical establishment that would support them.

---

10. Of course, the conjugations of "ridiculus sum," which Charles is ordered to copy out as punishment on his first day of school, implicitly spreads the shame, both personally (you, they, we, etc.) and temporally (are ashamed, will be ashamed, have been ashamed, etc.).

11. Diana Knight coined the phrase "Golden Age of Flaubert Studies," which stands for a critical moment "inaugurated by the publication of *L'idiot de la famille* in 1971 and 1972, accompanied by the *Uses of Uncertainty* (1974) and *La production du sens chez Flaubert* (1975), culminating in 1980 with an avalanche of conference papers and the stimulating (re)birth of genetic criticism celebrated in *Flaubert à l'oeuvre*." Diana Knight, "Whatever Happened to Bouvard and Pécuchet?" in *New Approaches in Flaubert Studies*, ed. Tony Williams and Mary Orr (Lewiston, NY: E. Mellen Press, 1999), 170.

This approach must thus take some of its pleasure from the same impulse to shame the conventional bourgeois reader that Flaubert exhibits through-out his writing and in his letters.[12] Culler, whom we may take as an especially strong representative of the Golden Age, works in a particularly performative relation to his thesis; in the introduction to *The Uses of Uncertainty*, he de-scribes the feeling of first reading Flaubert:

> The reader who encounters Flaubert's works for the first time is likely
> to feel rather like Emma Bovary when, a few days after her marriage,
> she begins to suspect that she has been deceived and wonders what ex-
> actly in her brief experience is supposed to correspond to those grand
> words, "bliss," "passion," "ecstasy," that she has oft heard repeated. For
> like love, Flaubert has such an exalted literary reputation that disillu-
> sion almost inevitably falls hard upon one's first experience.[13]

Culler, the experienced critic, whose first time with Flaubert happened a long time ago, puts the reader in a necessarily awkward position; one has to con-sider, faced with this passage, whether or not reading Flaubert has offered, on the first or any reading, the special critical experience at which Culler hints. The force of the question comes from the degree to which it damns you whether you do or don't: saying that you really liked it, which would be a lie, and that you didn't, which would be weak, amount equally to embarrassing admissions of textual inexperience. What's more, the comparison of the first-timer to Emma herself suggests what kind of consequence comes with trying to "get it" in the first place. The first-timer who wants the thing to look and feel like everyone said it would labors stupidly under the weight of bourgeois illusion and convention; if, like Emma, you go looking for the real thing, you get punished. But, where Emma gets a fistful of arsenic and more than a little irony looking for love, the reader gets equal parts irony and shame looking for the familiar, for the conventional in *Madame Bovary*.

As, however, I suggested earlier, embarrassment is not for Flaubert a one-way street. The shaming gesture that opens *Madame Bovary*, the gesture that

---

12. "Bourgeois" is for Flaubert a necessarily ambiguous term, representative less of any particular class or social position than the general object of Flaubert's very active anger: "This way of using his favorite term of abuse with no regard for sociological rigor throws further doubts on Flaubert's reliability as a wit-ness. His loathsome bourgeoisie was a state of mind rather than a recognizable social class, and 'bourgeois' an all-purpose epithet. In the summer of 1861, shortly after completing his strange, sanguinary novel about Carthage, *Salammbô*, he professed to be looking forward to irritating the archaeologists and being unintel-ligible to the ladies. He hoped people would call him a pederast and a cannibal. *Salammbô*, he told Ernest Feydeau, 'will annoy the bourgeois, that is to say, everybody.'" Peter Gay, *Pleasure Wars: The Bourgeois Experience: Victoria to Freud* (New York: Norton, 1998), 31.
13. Culler, *Flaubert*, 11.

puts Charles down before he has a chance, carries with it a trace of shame not only for Charles and for the reader and for the novel's ephemeral first-person plural voice but also for him whom we expect to do all the shaming: even Flaubert is not free from the spread of shame. As he wrote it, Flaubert expressed an anxiety that his novel, which was to deride and to expose the banality of convention, would become corrupted by what was to be the target of its scorn: "This bourgeois subject brutalizes me. I feel the effects of my Homais" (June 2, 1853). Homais's unexpected autonomy is the result of his double relation to Flaubert's system: he is, as a figure for the bourgeois, at once the object of Flaubert's attack and the means by which that attack can be achieved. Flaubert needs Homais to destroy Homais, convention to destroy convention. This double bind suggests that embarrassment is not only fluid, flowing easily from one person to another, but also sticky, tending to leave a mark while on its way: embarrassment makes differences between one ego and another, between the social and the individual, between aggressor and aggressed hard to maintain. We will remember that *Madame Bovary*'s motto is not "You, stupid reader, are Emma Bovary," but "Madame Bovary, c'est moi." That is not to say that what will follow will simply reassert the familiar sense that sadism and masochism are sometimes hard to tell apart; rather, the complex identification of *embarrassing someone* and *being embarrassed* in Flaubert points to a problem with the social and formal conventions that allow for the differentiation of the two in the first place. Flaubert's novel stages an engagement with the troubling fact that its literary and social coherence depend on a bad form that is both a threat to and a guarantee of exactly that coherence.

In these terms, we can take the narrative shift at the beginning of *Madame Bovary* as an affective reaction to a narrative impropriety and an embodiment of shame's structure in narrative form. Eve Kosofsky Sedgwick, in an essay on the developmental logic of Henry James's prefaces, moves from J. L. Austin's famous reliance on the "I do" of the wedding ceremony to another more complicated performative utterance: "Shame on you." Unlike "I do,"

> its pronoun matrix begins with the second person. There is a "you" but there is no "I"—or rather, forms of the inexplicit "I" constantly remain to be evoked from the formulation "Shame on you." They can be evoked in different ways. The absence of an explicit verb from "Shame on you" records the place in which an I, in conferring shame, has effaced itself and its own agency. Of course the desire for self-effacement is the defining trait of—what else?—shame.[14]

---

14. Eve Kosofsky Sedgwick, "Queer Performativity: Henry James's *The Art of the Novel*," *GLQ* 1 (1993): 4.

What is the opening of *Madame Bovary* if not an elaboration of "shame on you"? Poor Charles is put in the corner, and we readers, another "you" to Flaubert's narrative "I," are left feeling equally out of place. It is in that case telling that the long performative utterance that is the opening section of *Madame Bovary* ends up realizing the desire for the effacement of the "I" that Sedgwick tells us is part of the structure of shame; the first person gives way to and seeks shelter in the facelessness of omniscience. Left there, we would have a peculiar psychogenesis of a key aspect of Flaubert's style; faced with the other side of the shame that Flaubert looks to pile upon his characters and his readers, the locatable, specific narrative voice with which the novel begins becomes untenable. The grammatical structure of shame will not allow, we see, for so concrete a figure for the shaming "I." Thus is produced the notably impersonal narrative voice that occupies such an important place in Flaubert's correspondence and in the criticism that surrounds his work. Instead of an always already impersonal mastery on which we can as readers religiously count, we find that the motive of Flaubert's famously negative narrative theology is shame, an embarrassment that is the result of the act of embarrassing.

But we ought not stop there. Sedgwick not only understands that the shame game is one that cuts both ways but also sees that the absence of the "I" in the structure of shame turns out after the fact to be a most personal kind of impersonality. The obliteration of identity that is the end result of shame is also necessary to the founding of an identity: "But in interrupting identification, shame, too, makes identity. In fact shame and identity remain in a very dynamic relation to one another, at once deconstituting and foundational, because shame is both particularly contagious and peculiarly individuating."[15] Shame makes as it unmakes, does as it undoes personality. This raises a problem for our Flaubert: if we take it that the impersonality of Flaubert's narrative presence is a product of shame, that the retreat of the narrative "I" (once part of a "we") in the first pages of the novel is a formal reaction to a feeling that is at once emotional, social, and formal, where should we look to find the "peculiarly individuated" subject that is the other structural result of Sedgwick's shame? Where should we look for the chastened person under the cover of *Madame Bovary*'s impersonality?

To answer this question is to run one's own risk of embarrassment. On the one hand, to look too hard for the mess that is the individual in the literary text has become something tacky in literary criticism; to talk about anything other than a bulletproof constitutive absence or an exemplary cultural-historical case is to risk the charge of caring too much for intention. This is especially true in relation to Flaubert, who, as the "novelist's novelist" (the

---

15. Ibid., 5.

phrase is Percy Lubbock's), occupies a particularly safe place in the good books of a novel theory little interested in the vexed presence of persons within narrative forms. On the other hand, its lack of an organizing intention is taken not only as a thing about *Madame Bovary* but also and more often as a determining aspect of the novel's system and its style:

> A number of other commentators, including Erich Auerbach and Tony Tanner, . . . have offered theories that take as their point of departure this sense of there somehow being a hole at the center of this book. Yet it seems the unavoidable tendency of such theories that begin with the perception of something missing in *Madame Bovary*, to find the meaning of the novel in precisely the fact of lack, to make coherence of incoherence.[16]

We will remember that Culler, along with Auerbach and Tanner, was interested in the degree to which a semiotic hollow was the determining element in Flaubert's work. The sense, however, that this lack makes does not stop at that linguistic truth; the "hole at its center" not only turns the novel into an allegory of an absence that is, we take it, always present in all language but also becomes the safe ground from which the terrorist Flaubert's attacks on bourgeois convention can be staged. In other words, for Flaubert's shaming of the conventional to work without any incidental embarrassment for Flaubert, there can be no intention, no individual, no Flaubert behind the gesture.

At the same time, however, the argument that demands that the affective center of the novel be evacuated rests on an implicit assumption that Sedgwick makes explicit: shame and thus a shaming that results in shame are individuating. They produce the person. The possible presence of an embarrassed intention in the economy of Flaubert's work troubles the received idea that a narration that can be both "everywhere and nowhere" is Flaubert's real contribution to the novel. Because the absence of intention or interest that we associate with Flaubert's narrative style is a negative effect secured at the expense of another, the purity of that absence is necessarily compromised. Too wrapped up in and dependent on the social world it describes to be really free from its pull, Flaubert's voice enacts an embarrassing problem related to bad form generally: to stake one's reputation on another's mistakes is, as everybody knows, itself a mistake.

Flaubert treats the conventional as something contaminating, something one would want at all costs to avoid; convention is, however, also the neces-

---

16. Bruce Fleming, "An Essay in Seduction, or The Trouble with *Bovary*," in *Emma Bovary*, ed. Harold Bloom (New York: Chelsea House, 1994), 164.

sary backdrop against which the shaming of others occurs. Shitting on convention, insofar as that act requires the prior digestion of a whole world of convention, must always make a mess. It will be my suggestion that Flaubert's style can be read both as a strategic position from which these contradictions can be managed and as a figure for those contradictions. Flaubert writes in a letter dated March 20, 1852: "The entire value of my book, if it has any, will consist of my having known how to walk straight ahead on a hair, balanced above the two abysses of lyricism and vulgarity (which I seek to fuse in analytical narrative)."[17] To steer clear of either abyss would be to keep clean. Because, however, the strand of style upon which Flaubert sits is stretched uneasily above the equally conventional messes of the merely eccentric and the brutally common, it cannot help but get at least a little dirty.

Discussions of narrative omniscience have tended to make a mess of novel theory because any engagement with the concept has been a walk on or fall from a thread as precarious as Flaubert's: a thread suspended above an all-too-human narratorial presence on one side and an absence pure enough to look like nothing much at all on the other. If these, however, have seemed to stand as the poles of omniscience, we must also see that the one makes little sense without the other. Audrey Jaffe has written, "What we call omniscience can be located . . . not in presence or absence, but in the tension between the two—between a voice that implies presence and the lack of any character to attach it to, between a narratorial configuration that refuses character and the characters it requires to define itself."[18] What Jaffe shows is that a division that has tended to organize critics of the novel—between those who look hard for the character in omniscient narration and those who just know nobody's home—is in fact a structuring opposition internal to omniscient narration as such.

The first sort of critic sees the ruling presence of the author within the work as a fact that need not be argued away; an early and influential proponent of Flaubert's uncomplicated authorial presence was Percy Lubbock:

> Flaubert is generally considered to be a very "impersonal" writer, one
> who keeps in the background and desires us to remain unaware of his
> presence; he places the story before us and suppresses any comment
> of his own. But this point has been over-laboured, I should say. . . .
> The famous "impersonality" of Flaubert and his kind lies only in the

---

17. Included in Gustave Flaubert, *Madame Bovary*, ed. Paul de Man (New York: Norton, 1965), 311.

18. Audrey Jaffe, *Vanishing Points: Dickens, Narrative, and the Subject of Omniscience* (Berkeley: University of California Press, 1991), 4.

greater tact with which they express their feelings—dramatizing them, embodying them in living form, instead of stating them directly.[19]

For Lubbock, the effect of impersonality or absence that characterizes Flaubert's narrator is merely an effect of that voice's feel for propriety, good manners in an aesthetic sense that brings together two different ways of hearing the phrase "good form." To call unnecessary attention to one's presence, to force one's opinions on an audience—the sign, surely, of a crank or a boor—is not in Lubbock's mind an error of technique but rather a lapse in taste, an instance of vulgarity that should be seen and described by the novel critic exactly as such. That *Madame Bovary* exhibits this tact is what makes it "perpetually the novel of all novels which the criticism of fiction cannot overlook."[20] The trouble with Lubbock's sense of things is of course clear: to identify a novel's narrator not only with the author but also with any consciousness at all is to count on the familiar fallacy of a unifying intention to resolve inconsistencies and to lend the literary object a cognitive coherence we like to reserve for persons.[21] What's more, the difference between crude interestedness and an interestedness tactful and tacit enough to *resemble* disinterestedness is in the end no difference at all. Finally, the good taste that Lubbock takes as *Madame Bovary*'s ruling note prevents him from taking into account the blunder with which we began: a potentially clumsy shift from the first to the third person that seems so spectacularly to obliterate, to disindividuate the novel's narratorial presence.

This is not, however, simply to argue for the opposite case: if the twists of Flaubert's narration in the opening pages of *Madame Bovary* make a mess of a tastefully present point of view, so do they manage to louse up the purity of perfect narrative absence. We are encouraged, for instance, by his use of Flaubert's line, "l'auteur, dans son oeuvre, doit être comme Dieu dans l'univers, présent partout et visible nulle part," to reconsider D. A. Miller's suggestion that "to even speak of a 'narrator' at all is to misunderstand a technique that, never identified with a *person*, institutes a faceless and multilateral regard."[22] Far from standing as the best example of that technique, narration in *Madame Bovary* is anything but faceless. There is not only a face here (obscure in its brief identification with the *nous*, but present all the same) but also an individuating shamefacedness. The bad feelings that it would appear to be the job of omniscient narration to dole out backfire, rendering the regulative force of social discipline into something contagious enough for a narration no longer coated with good form's Teflon surface to catch it. Insofar as narration

19. Percy Lubbock, *The Craft of Fiction* (New York: Peter Smith, 1947), 67–68.
20. Ibid., 60.
21. This is a point to which I will return in chapter 4.
22. D. A. Miller, *The Novel and the Police* (Berkeley: University of California Press, 1988), 24.

exploits an act of shaming in order to secure the authority of impersonality in the novel's opening pages, that voice cannot remain safe from the slips, falls, and humiliations we associate with the embodied individual.

Here, then, are two accounts of narrative omniscience that don't quite work for *Madame Bovary*: Flaubert's narrator—here today and gone tomorrow—is neither purely present nor purely absent. What the novel instead offers is a complicated and, in a sense, buried argument about the different kinds of work—formal, social, affective, and developmental—that go into the production of its own narrative design. What we need, in that case, is to unpack *Madame Bovary*'s own theory of narration's "subjection," a process that is already and by all accounts a deeply narrative one:

> The story by which subjection is told is, inevitably, circular, presupposing the very subject for which it seeks to give an account. On the one hand, the subject can refer to its own genesis only by taking a third-person perspective on itself, that is, by dispossessing its own perspective in the act of narrating its genesis. On the other hand, the narration of how the subject is constituted presupposes that the constitution has already taken place, and thus arrives after the fact. The subject loses itself to tell the story of itself, but in telling the story of itself seeks to give an account of what the narrative function has already made plain.[23]

Judith Butler uses the language of literary narration not only because it provides a useful and familiar technical vocabulary with which to describe a complicated set of psychic and social conditions but also because our efforts to get at the details of a process that necessarily predates cognition must depend on developmental fictions; we are, in other words, left in our efforts to account for the beginnings of the subject (the subject before the subject) to make do with a set of imaginative tools not different from those with which we make and interpret literary texts. And, because the scene of subjection is necessarily withheld from the subject, its narration becomes more productive than descriptive. In a moment of narrative sublation, the third-person perspective loses as it consumes a cognitively unavailable (because presymbolic or preideological) first person so as to make way for the emergence of the (symbolic, ideological) subject. And, that final version of the subject can exist only because it has overcome and preserved as it has constructed these earlier

23. Judith Butler, *The Psychic Life of Power: Theories in Subjection* (Stanford, CA: Stanford University Press, 1997), 11.

versions of itself.[24] The subject, in other words, emerges here as the story of its own development; it *is* its own story.[25]

Similarly, when we look for what remains of the early first-person narrator of *Madame Bovary*, we find that that first voice has disappeared *with* a trace; for, in the manner described in the first part of this chapter, a shame that at first seemed a local effect proved pervasive, a contagious element that touches Charles Bovary, the early first-person narrator that describes him, the reader, and—because, as I have argued, omniscience appears as a prophylactic response to that early shame—the novel's whole narrative system. The novel's omniscient narrator seems in the undermotivated shift from the first to the third person not only to replace but also to subordinate or to consume that earlier "we," placing those narratorial positions in a complicated developmental relation to one another. It also, however, comes away from that process not free from but marked with the traces of that individuating shame. What we cannot yet appreciate is the result of this process, the subject of a narration that emerges as a result of this developmental relation. It will be my suggestion that Flaubert's narration, a paradoxical subject that both wields power and is limited by it, that gets at different moments to be both here and nowhere, depends on the complicated network of effects that Flaubert calls "style." Before, however, tracing the final turn of *Madame Bovary's* narrative subjection, we must turn temporarily from narration back to character and consider that novel's object, surrogate, and—as I will argue—structural double: Emma Bovary.

24. For a neo-Nietzschean account of this same process, see Alenka Zupančič's reading of the temporality of subjection in Chris Marker's *La jetée*: "This configuration implies that, in terms of our schema subject—event—subject, the grown-up man (falling down) is the 'first' subject. The fact that, in this scene, we see him only via the 'interface' of the event (whereas, in the last shot, we are seeing the scene simultaneously from his perspective) is a good reminder of the fact that the place of subjectivity as involved in the event (one could even say the 'subjective condition' of the event) gets subjectivized only subsequently or retroactively in and by the event. The transformation we are dealing with on this level of the story is the transformation of the configuration 'X—event—subject' into 'subject—event—subject,' this being precisely what is involved in the Nietzschean formula 'to become what one is.'" Alenka Zupančič, *The Shortest Shadow: Nietzsche's Philosophy of the Two* (Cambridge, MA: MIT Press, 2003), 23.

25. In his work on psychoanalytic aesthetics, Nicolas Abraham makes the case not only that the work of art needs to be thought of in terms of the way in which it embodies its own "fictitious genesis" but also that it needs to be understood as something not *like* but in fact *as* an ego: "A work of art is an autonomous being insofar as it conveys a self-sufficient ego. According to what has just been said, the ego includes a bipolar unconscious (the wish and the superego) and, in the case of a work of art, the ego also denotes its own genesis as part of the fictional fabric of the work itself. The work of art is an original and symbolic form of coming to terms with a fictitious conflict between an id and a superego, themselves the timeless products of an equally fictitious genesis." Nicolas Abraham, *Rhythms: On the Work, Translation, and Psychoanalysis*, trans. Nicholas T. Rand (Stanford, CA: Stanford University Press, 1995), 118.

If it is true that omniscient narration is a fantasy built not out of what it is but out of what it is not—it is not, that is, a bounded, marked character whose necessarily limited epistemological position is a by-product of its status as a "psychological [entity], with identifiable patterns of speech and behavior"—then we have more reason to feel that there is something odd about narration in *Madame Bovary*.[26] If we take it that the "psychological" quality that limits character is both that thing which produces the effect of depth and that thing against which omniscient narration must define itself, then Emma Bovary seems especially ill suited to do the dialectical work that narration demands from her. Emma is, as many readers have felt, *thinner* than the kinds of character we expect either to embody or to produce conventional effects of novelistic interiority. Leo Bersani, for instance, notes:

> Flaubert's intention of giving a realistic and inclusive image of bourgeois provincial life—the book's subtitle is *Moeurs de province*—partly disguises a certain thinness and even disconnectedness in his psychological portraits. True, the portrait of Emma Bovary is eventually filled in with an abundance of psychological and social details, but, during much of the narrative, she is nothing more than bodily surfaces and intense sensations.[27]

Although the point is well taken, "thinness" is an infelicitous physical metaphor in the context of Bersani's account of Emma's character. While thinness does suggest shrinkage of the interior, a wasting away that threatens to collapse the difference between the outside and the insides of the thinning body, that threat, if it is to be meaningful, demands that the wasted, ravaged interior persist. A reading that would count on that kind of an interior, that kind of psychological guarantee, is exactly the sort that Bersani takes as a misreading:

> If we respond to what is most original in Flaubert, we are, I think, bound to see the inappropriateness of attempting to infer a biographical self from his work, or even of trying to construct a thematic self wholly within his work. For such critical procedures are irrelevant to what Flaubert's novels are most interestingly about: the arbitrary, insignificant, inexpressive nature of language.[28]

26. Jaffe, *Vanishing Points*, 13.

27. Leo Bersani, *A Future for Astyanax: Character and Desire in Literature* (Boston: Little, Brown, 1976), 90.

28. Bersani, *Balzac to Beckett*, 144.

If this is a general problem with selves in Flaubert, we should take it as doubly true in the case of Emma, who is most often apprehended as a collection of discrete and fragmentary physical details, a bundle of variously meaningful fetish objects conjured into coherence by the desires of the men with whom Emma comes in contact, and who also seems similarly to apprehend the world as if it were a disjointed field of isolated objects, sensations, and conventions. For Bersani, *Madame Bovary* is characterized by the absence of interiorities that would guarantee psychological coherence and persistence of character over time.

As persuasive as Bersani's reading is, we are left nevertheless to account for an interest in the development of character over time that appears in different forms in that novel. On the one hand, this means simply that *Madame Bovary* is a perverse (or reverse) bildungsroman; it is the developmental story of Emma Bovary's growth (or fall) as a character in relation to a defined set of social circumstances that gives the novel's subtitle, "*moeurs de province,*" its sense.[29] On the other hand, *Madame Bovary* offers a couple of discrete narratives that work to explain the manner in which a social character is determined by and can in turn determine her social conditions and to indicate what needs developmentally to happen in a novel in order to differentiate between characters we discuss in terms of the conventions of psychological realism (interiority, intention, depth) from those we never bother to consider in those terms at all.[30]

A key moment in the most important of these developmental narratives is offered in the eighth chapter of the novel's first book, in which Emma Bovary attends what might be the great event of her life: the ball at La Vaubyessard. Thrown by the politically ambitious Marquis d'Andervilliers as part of a general program to secure his influence among his constituency, the ball is a self-consciously constructed fantasy of social convention, a bounded social structure the autonomy of which is reflected in the self-contained quality of the chapter. Chapter 8 begins with Emma's arrival at the château, "recently built, in the Italian style," and ends with her poignant regret at having ever had to leave (36). The ball is offered as a sort of primal scene, a determining event that colors what content comes later and that provides a structuring center for Emma's character. Importantly, this process, the production of

---

29. *Bovary* differs from the traditional bildungsroman insofar as it persistently eschews the will toward the synthesis "between external and internal, between the 'best and most intimate' part of the soul and the 'public' aspect of existence" that Franco Moretti identifies as an essential aim of the form. Franco Moretti, *The Way of the World: The* Bildungsroman *in European Culture* (London: Verso, 2000), 30.

30. The maintenance of that line—the line between the major and the minor—is one subject of Alex Woloch's *The One vs. the Many: Minor Characters and the Space of the Protagonist in the Novel* (Princeton, NJ: Princeton University Press, 2003).

character, is understood in terms of the physical cultivation of the insides; psychic density and physical weight gain are aligned closely enough in chapter 8 to suggest that the easiest way to prove that you have an interior is to put food there.[31] My claim is that the novel opposes to the idea of character as an unmotivated bundle of details the case of Emma's formative experience at the ball, an experience that takes on a material significance that returns us in two senses to the idea of the "thin" character (thinness, taken seriously as a physical metaphor, at once diminishes and relies on the idea of a character's interior). In other words, given the proliferation of genetic narratives, figures of incorporation, and complications that character presents in *Madame Bovary*, "the arbitrary, insignificant, inexpressive nature of language" is itself a dish a little too thin to account for the whole of what that novel does.

Chapter 8 is stuffed with food: there are roast meats, truffles, "little oval loaves," and lobster claws; there are baskets of fruit, quails, and pomegranates; later, there are maraschino ices, "quantities of Spanish and German wines," Trafalgar puddings, and almond milk soup. We are told that, at dinner, "in silk stockings, knee-breeches, white cravat and frilled shirt, solemn as a judge, the butler, handing the dishes, each already carved, between the shoulders of the guests, would drop on to your plate with a sweep of his spoon the very morsel of your choice" (37). The butler has reason to look solemn; he, both agent and embodiment of the social system he serves, stands as a figure for sociability's bind. He is a regulatory presence insofar as he is there to satisfy "whims" ("le morceau qu'on choisissait") intelligible to the logic of the system he represents. Those desires that are not intelligible are passively forbidden, rendered impossible by the tacit, socially imposed limits of desire. What's more, eating is here a total experience, a practice that ensures the stability of class identity through symbolic cannibalism; if you are what you eat, the rich must eat as richly as possible in an effort to internalize so as to express the social system to which they belong.[32]

Emma, acting in the spirit of the evening, contributes to its regulatory force by combining her sartorial preparations with a shaming gesture that re-

---

31. Victor Brombert, following J. P. Richard, writes that "food plays an extraordinary role in [Flaubert's] novels: feasts, orgies, bourgeois meals, peasant revels. This concern for appetite and digestion corresponds unquestionably, as Richard suggests, to the larger themes of his work: the 'appetite' for the inaccessible, the voracious desire to *possess* experience, the preoccupation with metamorphoses, the tragedy of indigestion, and ultimately the almost metaphysical sense of nausea as the mind becomes aware that not to know everything is to know nothing." Brombert, *The Novels of Flaubert*, 49.

32. I am indebted here and in the pages that follow to Joseph Litvak's discussion of Thackeray's "mocking incorporation, what might be called his in(di)gestion, of both aristocratic and bourgeois tastes" in his chapter "Kiss Me, Stupid." Joseph Litvak, *Strange Gourmets: Sophistication, Theory, and the Novel* (Durham, NC: Duke University Press, 1991), 63.

minds us of the shaming of Charles with which we began, a fact that hints at some significant affective similarity between Emma's character and narration in *Madame Bovary*. After dinner, Emma dresses for the dance:

> Emma arrayed herself with the meticulous care of an actress making her debut. She did her hair in the style the hairdresser recommended, and she put on her muslin dress, laid out on the bed. Charles's trousers were too tight in the waist.
> -These ankle straps are going to be awkward for dancing, he said.
> -Dancing? said Emma.
> -Yes.
> -You must be out of your mind! They'd laugh at you. You stay sitting down. Anyway, it's more appropriate for a doctor, she added. (38)

Emma's total attention to her toilette coincides with the stagy, totalizing quality of the scene she is about to enter. Charles, ever *le nouveau*, can't manage his clothes and bursts out of the fancy dress that would allow him to enter into and identify with the social world of the ball; the ankle straps that cut into his foot and the "sigh of pleasure" he gives when pulling off his boots at the end of the evening display both Charles's unshakable clumsiness and a material poorness of fit that characterizes his relation to the social world. The embarrassment that Emma feels around Charles here takes the form of her embarrassing of Charles, a blurring of cause and effect that we saw at work in the novel's first pages; just as the shaming "we" of *Madame Bovary*'s first chapter performed the structural proximity of shaming and being shamed, Emma performs a complicity of composure and embarrassment that is necessary to the structure of social play, a complicity visible in the characteristic lack of transition between the description of Emma's toilette and its wonderfully blunt punch line: "Le pantalon de Charles le serrait au ventre."[33]

And if dinner adds embarrassing inches to Charles's middle, it gives Emma a bad case of indigestion:

> Her journey to La Vaubyessard had made a hole in her life, just like those great crevasses that a mountain storm will sometimes open up in a single night. She made no protest though; piously she folded away in the chest of drawers her lovely ballgown and even her satin slippers with their soles yellowed from the beeswax on the dance-floor. Her

---

33. Gustave Flaubert, *Madame Bovary* (Paris: Librarie Générale Française, 1999), 117.

heart was just like that: contact with the rich had left it smeared with something that would never fade away.

So it filled the time for Emma, remembering the ball. Every time Wednesday came around again, she said to herself when she awoke: "A week ago . . . two weeks ago . . . three weeks ago, I was there!" Slowly, slowly, the faces blurred in her memory, she forgot the tunes of the quadrille; no longer did she see so clearly the liveries and the apartments; certain details disappeared, but the regret remained. (44)

Given this hangover, we are right to ask what Emma ate and why it made her sick. As we shall see, it is the fact of the ball that Emma finds ultimately indigestible. Emma retains, she remembers no one thing about the ball; in fact, as the weeks following the ball pass, she loses exactly the details of the evening: "Slowly, slowly, the faces blurred in her memory, she forgot the tunes of the quadrille; no longer did she see so clearly the liveries and the apartments; certain details disappeared, but the regret remained." She does not long, in other words, for any special dish, any especially tasty detail. She regrets the loss not of any particular aspect of her marvelous night but of *the whole thing*. Emma, her eyes bigger than her stomach (no one can resist the size of Emma Bovary's eyes), seems to have bitten off more than she can chew or, better, more than she can digest insofar as the morsel of her choice is a whole social experience, which, because she cannot live in it, she swallows whole so that it might live in her. Because, however, totalizing regret takes the place of novelistic detail, preservation becomes a version of loss. Similarly, the structural identity of the ball and the chapter in which it appears encourages us to see that Emma has ingested not only the ball but also the chapter that describes the ball. She places, as she forgets them, the precisely rendered details of chapter 8 in a complicated position within the novel's epistemological economy. The details of the ball, so central to what follows, are bracketed off as the one mind for which they were meaningful loses track of them.

This play of loss and gain, forgetting and remembering, is typical of a melancholic process that Freud, in *The Ego and the Id*, associates with the formation of character in general:

We succeeded in explaining the painful disorder of melancholia by supposing that [in those suffering from it] an object which was lost has been set up again inside the ego—that is, that an object-cathexis has been replaced by an identification. At that time, however, we did not appreciate the full significance of this process and did not know how common and how typical it is. Since then we have come to understand that this kind of substitution has a great share in determining the form taken by the ego and that it makes an essential contribution towards building up what is called its "character."[34]

As a result of our innate reluctance to part with anything that once gave us pleasure, when an object or an experience is "lost," it is preserved *inside* the ego and *as* character; we become what we cannot have. Importantly, Freud's late revision of his concept makes what he once called melancholia not only into something more normal than pathological but also into a precondition for any character at all. Emma thus suffers from the *bad incorporation* of social convention, a structurally melancholic but necessary condition produced in her case by the unfortunate choice of something too rich for the provincial diet that she is both used to and stuck with.

Indeed, as subsequent chapters demonstrate, Emma's diet never gets back on track:

> But it was particularly at meal-times that she could not stand it anymore, in that little room on the ground floor, with its smoking stove, its creaking door, its sweating walls, its damp flagstones; it seemed as though all the bitterness of life was being served up on to her plate, and, with the steam off the stew, there came swirling up from the depths of her soul a kind of rancid staleness. Charles was a slow eater; she nibbled a few nuts, or else, leaning on one elbow, spent the time sketching lines on the oilcloth with the tip of her knife. (51)

In the food she cannot eat, Emma sees traces of the debilitating regret that followed the extravagance of her classy culinary experience at La Vaubyessard. Emma's eating disorder becomes more and more pronounced as pages pass. At first her eating habits are unpredictable, strange: "She would order different food for herself, and leave it untouched; one day drink only fresh milk, and, next day, cups of tea by the dozen" (52). Later, "she began drinking vinegar to make herself thinner, contracted a little dry cough and lost her appetite completely" (53).

Emma's eating is related to her experience at the château in a couple of ways. First, the extremity of her habits is an effort to reproduce in another form the effects of social distinction that she saw at work at the ball; just as truffles and Trafalgar puddings are opposed to a conventional middle-class diet, so are her capricious tastes and her unwillingness to eat set against the healthy, boring appetites of those around her. Charles is a slow but steady eater; Père Rouault,

---

34. Sigmund Freud, *The Ego and the Id*, in *The Standard Edition of the Complete Psychological Works of Sigmund Freud*, ed. James Strachey, 24 vols. (London: Hogarth Press, 1966), 19:28.

Emma's father, commemorates annually the cure of his broken leg, the accident that brought Charles and Emma together, with "a splendid turkey for his son-in-law" (52). Where for Charles and Emma's father, eating is the very index of healthy normality, Emma, because she cannot live forever at the ball, chooses to represent her desired difference from humdrum provincial experience through a cultivated and extreme dietary asceticism.[35]

What's more, Emma's unwillingness to eat is a response to the way in which she internalized the ball in the first place. Melanie Klein, in "A Contribution to the Psychogenesis of Manic-Depressive States," adds to Freud's understanding of the relation between anxieties about one's insides and the structure of melancholic incorporation: "The anxiety of absorbing dangerous substances destructive to one's inside will thus be paranoiac, while the anxiety of destroying the external good objects by biting and chewing, or of endangering the internal good object by introducing bad substances from outside into it will be depressive."[36] This is what is so upsetting about the same old stew: Emma's feeling that the food she is served in the cold comfort of home might be poisoned ("all the bitterness of life was being served up on to her plate") is not, within the structure of class incorporation described here, all that crazy. What Emma ate to preserve at La Vaubyessard was a whole class experience, an internally coherent system of conventions that gets inside Emma and also becomes her insides. The poisonous stew, in that case, would not stand as a threat to the body; rather, it is Emma's object—the memory of the ball (a memory, we remember, she has mostly forgotten) as the character-forming *thing*—that needs to be protected from the contaminating influence of the bad bourgeois object. Drinking vinegar to thin the body, to reduce the physical barrier that would separate her phantasmatic class experience from the exterior world of dull fact, privileges the preservation of the lost object over the body itself.

The novel's fascination with eating is, in other words, not only a meditation on the relation between melancholia and incorporation or the relation between class and symbolic cannibalism but also a representation of a particular literary method. The novel presents the reader with an elaborate allegory of the mechanism by which literary subjection—the production of imaginary

35. Lillian Furst sees Emma's eating habits as a way of exerting control over a social situation in which women had little opportunity for expression: "Her revulsion at the customary food of her time and place signifies her repudiation of the life apportioned to her. Always extreme and uncompromising, if she cannot have what she wants, she would rather opt for the drama of suicide as her final flamboyant protest." Lillian R. Furst, "The Power of the Powerless: A Trio of Nineteenth-Century French Disorderly Eaters," in *Disorderly Eaters: Texts in Self-Empowerment*, ed. Lillian R. Furst and Peter W. Graham (University Park: Pennsylvania State University Press, 1992), 160.

36. Melanie Klein, *The Selected Melanie Klein*, ed. Juliet Mitchell (New York: Free Press, 1986), 127.

people—works. As her experience at the ball traps her in a depressive oscillation between eating and thinning, Emma's character gains a coherence, a persistence, the effect of an intent that it did not have in the earlier parts of the novel. That is not to say that the character Emma Bovary really has an interior; rather, the novel offers in practice its own account of how psychological realism achieves one of its key conventional effects. Real people, we feel, have insides; so it is when we are given proof of the inside of a character—a proof that is necessarily only the account of its development—that the subjection effect can occur. The best demonstration that one has an inside is not to show it but to narrate the development of that inside in a way that refers to a time when things were different, a time that is, as we have seen, necessarily unavailable to cognition because it predates a character that is its result. What, in *Madame Bovary*, separates the times before and after that all-important developmental shift is a failed effort to incorporate a whole world of convention in the form of the delicacies that La Vaubyessard had to offer.

Another example: Charles, bungling and blind to a taste that is everything to Emma, does not initially share Emma's eating troubles. Riding away from the château, Charles finds and picks up "a cigar case edged in green silk with a coat of arms at the center" dropped by one of the fashionable guests. That night at home:

> Charles lit a cigar. He smoked it thrusting his lips forward, spitting repeatedly, flinching at every puff.
> -You'll make yourself ill, she said scornfully.
> He put his cigar down and ran to the pump for a glass of cold water.
> Emma, snatching the cigar-case, threw it forcibly to the back of the cupboard. (43)

Charles's attempt at class incorporation ends with the suggestion of what we take to be a healthy response: an urge to purge prevented only by the dual intercession of Emma and the pump. Charles's embarrassing reaction to the sick-making cigar is an involuntary act of judgment, a choice that is not one between the bad preservation of the incorporated thing and its good expulsion: "Expressed in the language of the oldest—the oral—instinctual impulses, the judgment is: 'I should like to eat this,' or 'I should like to spit this out'; and, put more generally: 'I should like to take this into myself and keep that out.' That is to say: 'It shall be inside me' or 'it shall be outside me.'"[37] Where Emma's condition reproduces the problematic blurring of the

---

37. Sigmund Freud, "Negation," in *The Standard Edition of the Complete Psychological Works of Sigmund Freud*, 668.

good and the bad or, to return to Flaubert's terms, the lyrical and the vulgar,
Charles's impulse to expel the traces of the ball allows him to occupy com-
fortably, although stupidly, silently, a position within a given social world, a
position that is itself the structural result of the expulsion of the bad from the
good and that marks out a healthy difference between inside and out, world
and self.

Indeed, as Charles goes crazy after Emma's suicide, we can see that as he
loses the ability to part with the lost loved object, he also gains a narratable
interior. Charles, who to that point has not shown the slightest trace of imagination, becomes after Emma's death quite as romantic as she had been in life,
as his funeral arrangements suggest:

> I wish her to be buried in her wedding-dress, with white shoes and a
> crown of flowers. Her hair is to be arranged loosely about her shoul-
> ders: three coffins, one of oak, one of mahogany, one of lead. Let no
> one speak to me and I shall manage. Cover everything with a large
> piece of green velvet. Such is my wish. Let it be done. (268)

Charles, whom readers are often content to view as simply stupid, has in the
last moments of the novel an idea. His requests are surprising not only to
the reader of *Madame Bovary* who has taken his character as a figure for slow
wits and familiar notions but also to the novel's other characters: Homais
and Bournisien "were greatly astonished at Bovary's romantic ideas" (268).
Charles's inability to part with Emma's body ("No, I don't think so. No. I
want to keep her") and the unusual length of his mourning culminate in
his effort to *become* Emma: "To please her, as though she were still alive, he
adopted her predilections, her ideas; he bought patent leather boots, he took
to wearing white cravats. He waxed his moustache, he signed bills just as she
had done. She was corrupting him from beyond the grave" (280). Charles,
who not only outlives Emma in the novel's story but also lingers on at the
level of narrative discourse for twenty pages after the novel's putative subject
has disappeared, develops through this melancholic incorporation a kind of
character, a kind of autonomy he could not approach in the earlier parts of
the novel. Like Emma's, Charles's character is offered as the result of the newly
possible presence of an interior, an interior that is itself the result of the melancholic process described earlier: "An object which was lost has been set up
again inside the ego—that is, that an object-cathexis has been replaced by an
identification."[38] What is different in this case is that where Emma's interior
is the index of her incorporation of an alien class experience, Charles, whose

38. Freud, *The Ego and the Id*, 19:28.

mourning has gone wrong, develops an interior that is Emma. The interminable period of Charles's mourning is marked by the constant appearance
of bills signed in Emma's lifetime and his own descent into something very
much like Emma's debt: "She was corrupting him from beyond the grave."
Charles, having incorporated Emma, incorporates another's experience of incorporation. Like the three caskets that Charles orders for Emma's funeral,
Charles's melancholia is marked by its box-within-a-box logic: inside Charles
is an Emma whose insides were an incorporated but undigested system of social conventions. What's more, the series of boxes covered in green velvet that
makes Emma's final resting place reminds us of the cigar box, "edged in green
silk," that Charles picks up after the ball. His response to that cigar, which I
suggested was related to Emma's culinary incorporation of the class experience of the rich, was to get rid of it. Now, after Emma's death, he preserves
Emma in a box, a crypt that not only represents some internal melancholic
space but also stands for that same box that in turn stood in for the previously
rejected possibility of incorporating a whole system of taste.

Emma's own last act incorporation is the ingestion of the arsenic from
Homais's lab. Emma, aware that her affairs and debts are at last becoming
public, cajoles Homais's young assistant, Justin, into letting her into his master's *Capharnaum*: "The key turned in the lock, and she went straight to the
third shelf, her memory serving her well, she got the blue jar, pulled out the
cork, stuck her hand inside, and, taking a fistful of white powder, she put
it straight into her mouth" (257). It is curious that Emma's memory would
serve her so well in this instance; it was, after all, precisely a *failure of memory*
that produced her determinate regret and its attendant, doomed search for
compensation. Regret, we remember, took the place of the ball after its details were lost to memory. Given, however, the importance of the ball in both
her life and the novel, it seems odd that she would so clearly remember the
minor details of how Homais arranges his workshop. Indeed, the scene in
which she first learns about the position of the arsenic does not seem all that
memorable. Emma, returning from her first adulterous encounter with Léon,
is stopped upon reentering Yonville by Felicité, who tells her mysteriously:
"Madame, you must go to Monsieur Homais's at once. For something ur-
gent" (200). Charles has for some reason entrusted Homais with the task of
informing Emma that his father has died. Upon her arrival at the laboratory,
however, Emma finds Homais screaming at the hapless Justin, who has taken
the key to the *Capharnaum*:

- Do you realize the risk you were taking? . . . Didn't you notice anything, on the left, on the third shelf? Speak up, reply, produce some
sound!

- I d-d-don't know, stammered the young boy.

- Oh you don't know! Well I do know! You saw a bottle, a blue one, sealed up with yellow wax, containing a white powder, one with Danger on it in my writing, do you know what was in it? Arsenic! And you were going to touch it! (201)

The scene is roughly handled. The narrative need to make Emma aware of the location of the arsenic produces a situation that doesn't make much narrative sense. Why should Homais break the news? Why does he go into such detail about the position of the arsenic when that is one of his secrets? Roger Huss suggests that "the implausibility of the whole elliptical motivating sequence . . . is here recuperated by a familiar topos readily available in this context (the cuckold's ignorance of his wife's desires and actions) and by our sense (established at the beginning of the novel and since repeatedly confirmed) of Charles as one who does not understand."[39] Although the scene does make this thematic sense, we are left still to wonder that Emma, fresh from her first sex with Léon and nervously awaiting bad news, would remember the position of a blue bottle that should have held little interest for her (she is not yet thinking of dying) when she is importantly unable to recall the great event of her life. Rather, though, than understand these facts as at odds, we should see that the one depends on the other. Insofar as the suicide is a late effect of her determinate regret (she regrets, she cheats, she is found out, she dies), remembering the arsenic is in fact a necessary narrative effect of forgetting the ball.

Character in *Madame Bovary* counts on the production of a kind of subjection effect, a narrative method that places an only implicit interior in a temporal and structural relation to the diverse exterior aspects of character, those aspects, that is, that are available to reading. As we saw in Butler's account of subjection, the subject's story is one based on the sublation of earlier, fictional forms of the self. The subject not only posits and naturalizes an anterior "I," which works as a guarantor of later stages, but also absorbs that earlier self, incorporates the structurally necessary first person into the later, publicly available self. Subjectivity is in these terms only the act of narrating the subject's coming into being, a coming into being that moves from a cognitively unavailable first person, through the productive attentions of a third person, to the final stage of a publicly available, socially *subjected* first person. Emma *becomes* a character by bringing together into relation ideas about what she was like before and after the social event at La Vaubyessard.

39. Roger Huss, "Flaubert and Realism: Paternity, Authority, and Sexual Difference," in *Spectacles of Realism: Gender, Body, Genre*, ed. Margaret Cohen and Christopher Prendergast (Minneapolis: University of Minnesota Press, 1995), 181.

This interiority effect thus has two roles to play in the constitution of character: first, it stands as the incorporated anterior self that naturalizes and thus makes possible a coherent interpretation of a character's behavior (Emma's desire exerts a legible narrative force only *after* the novel offers its account of her subjection at the ball); second, the exterior elements of character are given value in relation to an interior that is itself the phantasmatic effect of the narrative sequence I have described (the incorporated experience of the ball, the experience around which her character has taken shape, is a *forgotten memory*; just as the primal scene is for Freud *both* a "real" recollection *and* a productive act of the imagination, so is the most important event of Emma's life both real and almost entirely lost to consciousness). If Emma largely forgets the details of an event that had seemed all important, that is because interiority and the memory that would function as its index are at last effects of a larger process of narrative subjection at work.

As she shoves a fistful of arsenic into her mouth, Emma engages in a last repetition of the act of ingestion that was her journey to La Vaubyessard. Falling in the eighth chapter of the third part of *Madame Bovary*, the suicide not only answers the bad object choice of the eighth chapter of the first part but also offers that scene as a point at which formal correspondences between Emma and narration in *Madame Bovary* become especially clear. Emma, having taken the poison, waits for its effects to begin: "She was observing herself with a certain curiosity, to see if she felt any pain. No, nothing yet. She could hear the clock ticking, the noise of the fire, and Charles, standing there by her bed, breathing" (258). Emma's cool analysis of the beginning stages of her reaction to the arsenic reminds us of Flaubert's own narrative style; she exhibits indifference to the scale and relative importance of details; she exploits a provocative flatness of tone; she takes, insofar as she has any left, her time. At this moment, the difference between Emma's voice and the novel's voice amounts to no difference at all. If Emma's suicide is a repetition of her earlier act of incorporation, we can see that the novel is engaged in another kind of repetition: the eighth chapter of part 3 is a structural repetition of the same chapter in part 1. That these similar acts, the ingestion of a certain class experience and the ingestion of killing arsenic, fall in similar places in the novel suggests a *formal* relation between the novel and a character it contains: Madame Bovary and *Madame Bovary* are caught repeating at just the same moment. We are led by this structural identification to ask if—because the coherence of character is based on a performed act of incorporation—the coherence of a threatened omniscient narration is based in *Madame Bovary* on that incorporation's narrative equivalent. In other words, the possible identification of the novel *Madame Bovary* with the character Emma Bovary points toward another incorporation that we have yet fully to identify, an incorporation that returns us to our beginning: *Madame Bovary's* embarrassing subjection.

In a letter to Hippolyte Taine in which Flaubert answers his friend's questions about the nature of his great imaginative powers, he writes:

> My imaginary characters overwhelm me, pursue me—or rather it is
> I who find myself under their skins. When I was writing Madame
> Bovary's poisoning scene I had such a taste of arsenic in my mouth, I
> was so poisoned myself, that I had two bouts of indigestion one after
> the other, and they were quite real because I vomited up all of my
> dinner.[40]

Flaubert's discomfort suggests that he stands in a complicated digestive relation to his characters and in particular to his Emma. Flaubert claims that it is he who is *inside* the character, a figural turn which suggests not only that the relationship between narrator and character in Flaubert's *style indirect libre* is more reciprocal than is usually thought but also that there is in *Madame Bovary* another structure of incorporation that seems strange in the context of this visceral reaction to his writing. For, while he says that it is he who is under the skin of Emma Bovary, suggesting that Emma has eaten him, the bad taste in his mouth points to the opposite relation—he has also eaten Emma. The taste of arsenic suggests something more than an author's sympathy with the character he created. Just as Emma incorporated the system of convention that she found at La Vaubyessard, so does Flaubert need to incorporate Emma insofar as she represents the conventions he would shame. Purging, however, offers little relief to Flaubert; for, if Emma bites off a bigger portion of a class experience than she could possibly chew, Flaubert works in *Madame Bovary* to swallow something *more*. Where Emma's choice morsel is an exquisite dish, a rare taste of the high life, Flaubert, a man of appetites, gets sick on a bigger bite: the whole world of bourgeois convention that he needs to incorporate in order to deal with Emma Bovary (and, in time, Frédéric Moreau, Bouvard, and Pécuchet).[41] Léon, in his first conversation with Emma, uses language much the same as Flaubert's to describe what he likes about reading: "You melt into the characters; it seems as if your own heart is beating under their skin" (66). The similar sound of what Flaubert expects us to take as a piece of pseudo-aesthetic idiocy and Flaubert's own note to Taine reminds us of Proust's claim that "[Flaubert's] images are generally so weak

---

40. Gustave Flaubert, *Selected Letters*, trans. Geoffrey Wall (London: Penguin, 1997), 316.
    41. "I have probably damaged my brain quite seriously, to judge from my need for sleep, for I am having ten or twelve hours' every night. Is this the first sign of a pathological softening of that organ? Bouvard and Pécuchet occupy my thoughts to such an extent that I am turning into them! Their stupidity is mine and it is sinking me. That may be the explanation." From a letter to Edma Roger des Genettes, April 1875, Flaubert, *Selected Letters*, 391.

they scarcely rise above those that his most insignificant characters might have hit upon."[42] Although Proust's interest is in this case the quality of Flaubert's metaphors, we can see nevertheless that Flaubert's take on his imaginative relation to his characters stages his internalization of and his identification with convention.

The oddly physical blurring of boundaries that Flaubert's taste of arsenic suggests is importantly reproduced at the level of the text in the formal complications of Flaubert's liberal and innovative use of the free indirect style. For example, after receiving Rodolphe's good-bye letter and contemplating a jump out the window, Emma is called both to dinner and to her senses:

> - Where are you? Come on!
> The idea that she had just escaped death made her nearly swoon with terror; she closed her eyes, and she shuddered at the touch of a hand upon her sleeve: it was Félicité.
> - Monsieur is waiting for you, madame; the soup is served.
> And down she had to go! Down to sit at the table!
> She tried to eat. The food choked her. (166)

Just as it is hard to tell who tastes what when Flaubert thinks of Emma's arsenic, so is it hard, just prior to yet another scene of eating and not eating, to tell who is saying what when we read, "Down to sit at the table!" The intensity of the utterance (!) seems to come from two places at once and thus from nowhere, an awkward situation that we might see as one cause for the choking that so immediately follows.[43] What's more, Flaubert's free indirect style is not only a mode that makes it hard to tell one voice from another but also a mode that comes necessarily up against the danger implicit in writing *anything* once language as such has been judged stupid: "Irony in *Madame Bovary* manages to be at once rhetorical and self-directed, corrective and universal, because Flaubert's existential predicament is manifest in the common and commonplace language that he shares with his characters."[44] If the free indirect style is one mark of Flaubert's style (Ann Banfield reminds us that "Flaubert exploited its possibilities fully") and a means by which he is able effectively to criticize the bourgeoisie, we see that it is also a point at which the narrative voice of *Madame Bovary* becomes indistinguishable from the events it narrates. What, in the face of so blurred, so potentially

42. Marcel Proust, *Against Sainte-Beuve and Other Essays* (London: Penguin, 1988), 261.

43. For more on what is unspeakable about such sentences, see Ann Banfield, *Unspeakable Sentences: Narration and Representation in the Language of Fiction* (Boston: Routledge and Kegan Paul, 1982), 222.

44. Vaheed K. Ramazani, *The Free Indirect Mode: Flaubert and the Poetics of Irony* (Charlottesville: University Press of Virginia, 1988), 113.

embarrassing a situation, keeps the narrator separated from the narrated in *Madame Bovary*?

> It has become a critical commonplace to debunk Flaubert's doctrine of impersonality by identifying instances where his narrator overtly judges characters or events. Yet the Flaubertian narrator remains impersonal in the much more important sense that he eludes characterization. He may on occasion be dramatized (and such occasions are rare), but the sum of these dramatized moments is not a coherent personality.[45]

Ramazani's point seems strong at first: what saves the narrative presence of *Madame Bovary* from the force of its own attack is its lack of coherence. This is another expression of the prophylactic logic we saw at work in the novel's opening pages: if there is no coherent person behind a shaming gesture, that gesture remains safe from shame's backfire. Incoherence in the context of *Madame Bovary* is, however, like shame insofar as both are contagious. In a novel whose main character is alternately called conventional, unconventional, religious, irreligious, and so on, the relative coherence of its characters and its narrator is not a basis upon which distinctions between the two can be made or secured. If Emma's look of coherence is the result of what I have called a subjection effect, the result of the retroactive suggestion of a naturalized interior, then it becomes difficult to differentiate between the play of coherence and incoherence that is character and the narratorial figure that was the possible result of the similarly structured developmental drama with which we began.

The free indirect style is thus one more methodological expression of an effect everywhere at work in *Madame Bovary*: it is a narrative technique that stages one voice's incorporation of another, narration's incorporation of character. It might be for this reason that critics often discover the narrator's irony, an irony that suggests something like a locatable character, at the site of free indirect style; for, just as Emma's interior was what resolved the external aspects of her character into a "character," so would a previously incorporated voice—an interior only a narrator could possess—produce the subjection effect in omniscient narration.[46] If character figures the relation between the

---

45. Ibid., 35.

46. We might read this claim alongside Banfield's suggestion that the irony in novelistic episodes "resides nowhere in them but is rather a way of reading their intentionality." In other words, we need not assume the interpretive and always anterior *presence* of a narrator in order to hear irony in a moment of represented thought; on the other hand, the play of intentionality necessary to irony might nevertheless help to produce the subjection effect that I have begun to describe. If talk of a narrator cannot explain irony, the structure of irony might in its turn help us to understand why we would need to resist the force of that explanation in the first place. Banfield, *Unspeakable Sentences*, 222.

different developmental stages of subjection, then we have made a return to the turn of *Madame Bovary*'s subjection. For if that shamed move, the retreat from the first to the third person in the opening pages of *Madame Bovary*, was a version of the developmental shift away from the early particularity of character, and if that shift is, as we learned from Judith Butler and Eve Sedgwick, one of the preconditions for a later social individuation, we can see in Flaubert's incorporative style a formal equivalent to subjection's individuating work. What does the work, finally, of narrative individuation is a performative and developmental process that exchanges any particular narrative perspective or any particular content for the autonomy of a subject whose interior is neither the sublated prior self nor any particular incorporated content, but whose interior is instead a relation, another, different process of subjection. If character is the result of the subjection effect I have so far described, omniscient narration sublates that *process* insofar as Flaubert's style, always relationally dependent for its form on the presence of a character (whether swallowed, spoken, or shamed), is itself the incorporation of the whole process that produces character. We might see this narratorial subjection effect as an equivalent to the "double-game" that Pierre Bourdieu sees at work in the structure of *Sentimental Education*.[47] If the effect of social disinterestedness is produced through the "double refusal of opposed positions," so is the effect of omniscience's impersonality produced in *Madame Bovary* through the incorporation not of a particular position but of the relation between the positions that produce the effect of interiority in the literary character; true to the form of the shame with which we began, the play of individuation and disindividuation that characterizes narrative omniscience is the result of a developmental story that sees impersonality emerge out of the most personal of processes. Omniscience in Flaubert is the result of the simultaneous disavowal and incorporation of character, a dual process that not only resembles but also is in *Madame Bovary* structurally identical to the doubled form of a shame that is, as we have seen, both individuating and disindividuating.

In a letter composed while he was writing *Madame Bovary*, Flaubert relates the story of an old servant of his family who had what should by now be a familiar problem with his insides:

> We used to have a poor devil of a servant, a man who now drives a hackney-coach . . . anyway this wretched Louis had—or thought he had—a tapeworm. He talks about it as if it were a real person who

47. Pierre Bourdieu, *The Rules of Art: Genesis and Structure of the Literary Field*, trans. Susan Emanuel (Stanford, CA: Stanford University Press, 1996), 28–34.

talks to him and tells him what it wants, and he always refers to this
creature inside him as *he*. Sometimes he has cravings and he attributes
them to the tapeworm: "*He* wants it," and Louis immediately obliges.
Recently *he* wanted thirty sous worth of brioche; another time *he* had
to have some white wine, and the next day *he* would kick up a fuss if
he were given red wine (I quote). This poor man eventually sank in
his own estimation to the same level as the tapeworm; they are equals
and they are locked in a dreadful battle. "Madame (he said to my
sister-in-law recently), that scoundrel has got it in for me; we are dag-
gers drawn, you see; but I shall have my revenge. One of us will be
left standing." Well it's the man who will be left standing or should I
say the man who will step aside for the tapeworm. *So as to kill it and
get rid of it,* he has recently swallowed *a bottle of vitriol,* and he is now
dying as a result. I am not sure if you appreciate the profundity of
this story. Can you see this man finally believing in the almost human
existence of what was perhaps only an idea, becoming the slave of this
tapeworm?[48]

Louis's tapeworm stands as a weird precursor to the thing inside that Emma
Bovary ends up poisoning and as an illustration of shame's role in the constitution of narrative voice. The "profundity of this story" rests not only in
the man's decision to swallow poison but also in Louis's ability to believe that
his tapeworm, an only imaginary internal creature, could possess an "almost
human existence." This is the profundity of character and the profundity of
subjection; that characters whom we know to be too thin can possess the
qualities of persons and that they can in turn possess us is indeed something
profound.

48. Flaubert, *Selected Letters*, 207.

CHAPTER 3

Looking Good: Style and Its Absence in George Eliot

The reality principle is an insult.
    —*D. W. Winnicott,* Home Is Where We Start From[1]

What has George Eliot to do with bad form? While Eliot's works have everything in common with the traditional novel form with which this book is as a whole concerned, they couldn't seem to care less about specifically Jamesian shades of the social slip or Flaubertian feelings for the genetic potential of social embarrassment. Eliot is too big, somehow, too bright and brilliant to feel for long the smart of the social mistake. What after all could less rankle *Middlemarch's* narrator, a voice deeply and theoretically invested in an ethical point of view that might encompass and thus transcend any particular set of beliefs or any special code of behavior, than the risk of getting wrong the ephemeral and necessarily rule-bound forms of social play? That is not to say that a concern with society's rules is not present as content within Eliot's work; rather, that concern is there as a thing to negate, a thing against

1. D. W. Winnicott, *Home Is Where We Start From: Essays by a Psychoanalyst* (New York: Norton, 1986), 40.

which the ethical and social neutrality of Eliot's position might appear all the more transcendent: we need only think of the socially accomplished and supernaturally cruel Henleigh Grandcourt, the genial and insipid Arthur Donnithorne, Hetty Sorrel's craving for a life of fashion (which leads, tellingly, to her "transportation," a sentence lighter than the execution from which she is saved, but which as effectively removes her from the novel's frame), and Rosamond Vincy's seemingly easy mastery of the codes of provincial society to see that in Eliot's equation the polish of one's manners tends to stand in an inverse relation to the quality of one's character. We feel, too, that the kinds of mistakes that do organize Eliot's narratives, tragic, life-altering misapprehensions and errors whose philosophically necessary consequences are carefully orchestrated by a narrative mechanism barely discernible beneath the antique robes of Eliot's Nemesis, must exceed the minor embarrassments and lame failures that exert such force in James or Flaubert. We find in Eliot a narrator whose voice emerges from a certain tension between the social and the formal: on the one hand, that voice's moral authority keeps it clear of a merely social correctness; on the other, that voice *needs* merely social correctness in order negatively to produce its authority as timelessly and truly right.

Indeed, a measured carelessness about the local instance of bad form is a characteristic not only of what are taken as the best moments of Eliot's style but also of those often taken as her best people; opposed on the one hand to the disembodied violence of the conventional expressed in the gossipy communal chorus that is so regular an aspect of Eliot's novels and on the other to the damning egoism of Eliot's assorted slaves to fashion (those listed here are but a few) are the various nonconformist heroes and heroines who animate Eliot's novels, characters who express the strength of their ethical stuff most immediately through a surprisingly legible lack of style. Our first ideas about Dorothea Brooke, *Middlemarch*'s "later born Theresa," are formed on the basis of her outfit: "Miss Brooke had that kind of beauty which seems to be thrown into relief by poor dress."[2] Her own look, expressed in a disdain for ornament, in the simple cut of her clothes, and in a plain hairdo conspicuous given her time's preference for "frizzed curls," serves as a handy and immediately legible index of her ardent nature (16). Similarly, narration in *Felix Holt, the Radical* takes oddly obsessive notice of Felix's lack of a "waistcoat or cravat," an antisartorial detail that expresses with an almost conspicuous economy both his impatience with social convention and his deep idealism.[3] In both cases, char-

---

2. George Eliot, *Middlemarch*, ed. Bert G. Hornback (New York: Norton, 1977), 1; subsequent references to this work will appear in the text.

3. "There was rather a mischievous gleam in her face: the rap was not a small one; it came probably from a large personage with a vigorous arm. 'Good afternoon, Miss Lyon,' said Felix, taking off his cloth cap: he resolutely declined the expensive ugliness of a hat, and in a poked cap and without a cravat, made

acters are distinguished by a lack of style that expresses personal resignation as well as recognition of the structural and historical limits of convention: to follow convention is to be right only in a particular situation. Slavoj Žižek, building on Lacan's discussion of *Antigone* in *The Ethics of Psychoanalysis,* calls the ethical act that act which disregards the stated and unstated rules that structure social interaction so as to go "beyond" the reality principle; and as Antigone's demand for her bother's proper burial is never situated within the rules of her society and is thus "an intervention into social reality that changes the very coordinates of what is perceived to be possible," so is the stylelessness of Eliot's ardent heroes and heroines meant to denote a somewhat impossible ethical freedom from "not merely the explicit symbolic rules regulating social interaction but also the intricate cobweb of unwritten, implicit rules."[4] What Felix and Dorothea strive for and share (and we see it as well in Dinah Morris, Daniel Deronda, Maggie Tulliver, and Mary Garth) is just that: a radical ethical position that would transcend social and moral convention.

Predictably, this absence easily loses its shape. It is clear that for both Dorothea and Felix what is supposed to stand as freedom from convention, from

---

a figure at which his mother cried every Sunday, and thought of with a slow shake of the head at several passages in the minister's prayer" (chapter 10); "'What! that is young Holt leaning forward now without a cravat? I've never seen him before to notice him, but I've heard Tiliot talking about him. They say he's a dangerous character, and goes stirring up the working men at Sproxton'" (chapter 24); "It is true that to get into the fields they had to pass through the street; and when Esther saw some acquaintances, she reflected that her walking alone with Felix might be a subject of remark—all the more because of his cap, patched boots, no cravat, and thick stick. Esther was a little amazed herself at what she had come to" (chapter 27). George Eliot, *Felix Holt, the Radical,* ed. Fred C. Thompson (Oxford: Oxford University Press, 1988); subsequent references to this work will appear in the text.

4. It is worth pointing out that Dorothea's Quakerish beauty conjures for Ladislaw's German friend, Naumann, "a sort of Christian Antigone" (132). What's more, it is along lines similar to those articulated by Žižek that Eliot herself appreciates Antigone in her short essay "The *Antigone* and Its Moral": "The turning point of the tragedy is not, as it is stated to be in the argument prefixed to this edition [the volume for which Eliot's essay is a review], 'reverence for the dead and the importance of the sacred rites of burial,' but the *conflict* between these and obedience to the State. Here lies the dramatic collision: the impulse of sisterly piety which allies itself with reverence for the Gods, clashes with the duties of citizenship; two principles, both having their validity, are at war with each." We must recognize, however, that Eliot's feeling for the act is only one part of her social ethics; for while we can see in many of her characters reverberations from her own famously conspicuous breaks with convention (her youthful repudiation of religion and her later, even more dramatic decision to live with the already married G. H. Lewes as his wife), we can similarly see in almost every case a reassertion of the social, of the importance of community that seems sometimes to take the bite out of the initial act; she concludes her essay on Antigone: "Perhaps the best moral we can draw is that to which the Chorus points—that our protest for right should be seasoned with moderation and reverence." Slavoj Žižek, Melancholy and the Act," *Critical Inquiry* 26 (2000): 671–72, 657; George Eliot, "The *Antigone* and Its Moral," in *Selected Critical Writings,* ed. Rosemary Ashton (Oxford: Oxford University Press, 1992), 243–44, 246. For more on Antigone and "going beyond" the reality principle, see Jacques Lacan, *The Ethics of Psychoanalysis* (New York: Norton, 1992), 243–87; and Alenka Zupančič, *The Shortest Shadow Nietzsche's Philosophy of the Two* (Cambridge, MA: MIT Press, 2003), 78–80.

the small-minded appreciation of a material, merely temporal beauty, shifts easily into its opposite. Felix's politically eloquent undress works to draw the reader's attention repeatedly to his bare neck, a move that, along with a steady attention to his other physical qualities—he is "shaggy-headed, large-eyed, strong-limbed"—converts a gesture of social resignation into a sexy kind of excess. The fact that Felix is described over and over again as being without a tie is his *thing*, a mark that, like a verbal tic in Dickens, identifies him as having continuity of character; as a result, a contradiction that occurs at the thematic level around the relation between style and sexiness reappears at the formal level: although going without a tie is supposed to free Felix from being merely typical, it tends formally to reassert the importance of typology in *Felix Holt*.

So it is with Dorothea, whose sartorial austerity is meant to provide a point of functional contrast to the various fashion-hungry characters who populate *Middlemarch*. We are at the novel's earliest moments meant to feel the contrast between Dorothea and her sister Celia, whose moral immaturity is matched by her adolescent attention to her good looks. The narrator admits, though, that there is really little difference between the appearances of the Brooke sisters: "Celia wore scarcely more trimmings; and it was only to close observers that her dress differed from her sister's, and had a shade of coquetry in its arrangements; for Miss Brooke's plain dressing was due to mixed conditions, in most of which her sister shared" (1). And there is little doubt that Dorothea's plain style not only, as that first sentence tells us, throws her beauty into relief but also exploits quietly the forty-year difference between the novel's setting and its publication to assert paradoxically both style and its absence:

> She would perhaps be hardly characterised enough if it were omitted
> that she wore her brown hair flatly braided and coiled behind so as to
> expose the outline of her head in a daring manner at a time when pub-
> lic feeling required the meagerness of nature to be dissimulated by tall
> barricades of frizzed curls and bows, never surpassed by any great race
> except the Feejeean. (16)

The detail contributes in this instance to what we might call both a morality effect and a reality effect insofar as the flatness of Dorothea's hair points not only to her authenticity as a moral agent but also to the *roundness* of her character; the briefly derided frizzed hairdos seem, in other words, to stand recessed as a conventional backdrop to the detail-rich but fashion-poor "characterization" of Dorothea's hair.

If, however, Dorothea's hair seemed strange and austere to her contemporaries, Eliot's first readers would have had an altogether different reaction to the plainness of her style; by the time *Middlemarch* appeared, "brown hair flatly braided" was simply *in*. Joan Nunn tells us that as "skirts were drawn back in the mid to late 1860s, so the hair was also drawn up and back to reveal the ears, for so long covered, but kept flat on top, with curls or a small twist at the back of the head reflecting the back interest on the dress."[5] If, in other words, a style that "exposed the outline of the head" would have been something "daring" in 1829, it was, by the time of the novel's publication just another *thing to do*. In other words, the temporal lag so important to *Middlemarch*'s structure allows Dorothea to come off to the book's readers in 1871 as a fashion visionary instead of a fashion victim, as a trendsetter instead of merely trendy; rather than transcending time with all the authority of a style that is never stylish, Dorothea finds herself falling into history exactly because she is so—but only just so—fashion-forward.

Eliot is, in other words, exploiting a tension that exists within the very concept of style. Looking to the *OED*'s definition of the term, we see that "style" is experienced paradoxically as both the very particular and the perfectly general. On the one hand, style is "a particular manner of life or behaviour" or "a particular mode or fashion of costume," a means of differentiating one way of looking or doing from every other. On the other hand, style can also refer to context-unspecific "beauty or loftiness" or to the "absolute" qualities of "good or fine style." To have style in this sense is to look good, is to be good regardless of what everyone else is doing or wearing. The difference is important: style in the first sense is to be caught up in the fraught temporal experience that I referred to in chapter 1 as fashion's "ridiculous teleology"; to be *in style* is to subordinate oneself to the rules of the moment, to risk the necessary obsolescence of the merely stylish or a damning ethical interestedness in the hope of achieving identity with a set of historically situated rules and conventions. To *have style*, however, is instead to look good without needing ever to be *in style* in the first sense; it is to transcend the conventional, to get altogether out of fashion's game. Indeed, style in the second sense appears as a negation of the first. The presence of the one is the absence of the other. What's more, that style as absence needs a degraded style's presence, that ethical style needs the conventional forms of fashion to secure its own shape, suggests that any style that tries to escape history's drag is in for a fall.

But even if the idea of the absence of style (or of style as absence) crumbles when touched, we see that it continues nonetheless to appear throughout Eliot's work as a privileged mode of being, an ethical high ground in a moral

5. Joan Nunn, *Fashion in Costume: 1200–2000* (London: Herbert Press, 2000), 159. An 1867 issue of *Godey's Lady's Book and Magazine* tells us about "coiffure for a young lady": "The hair is slightly waved, and brushed to the back of the head, where it is caught up in short curls, bound in with a very heavy plait of hair."

universe in which agents cannot escape the philosophically necessary consequences of every action. So, even if style's absence always turns out finally to be just another style, it manages nonetheless to maintain its ethical form thanks to a rigorous policing of its more obvious moments of pure presence; that is, where fashion rears directly its time-bound and ethically ugly head, Eliot is often quick, following the lead of a previous century's sansculottes, to lop it off. Early in *Adam Bede,* Dinah Morris scares the hell out of the town flirt, Bessy Cranage:

> "Ah! Poor blind child!" Dinah went on, "think if it should happen to you as it once happened to a servant of God in the days of her vanity. *She* thought of her lace caps, and saved all her money to buy 'em; she thought of nothing about how she might get a clean heart and a right spirit, she only wanted to have better lace than other girls. And one day when she put her new cap on and looked in the glass, she saw a bleeding Face crowned with thorns. That face is looking at you now."[6]

Although Dinah's evangelical logic is less than clear (the sight of Christ's face, which is a figure for salvation, is presented at once as a threat to be avoided and as some kind of description of the encounter that Bessy and Dinah are at that moment sharing), it nonetheless does the trick. Bessy, gripped suddenly by the fear of God, tears "her earrings from her ears" and throws them to the ground, a violent reaction that, if we buy Dinah's pitch—that Jesus Christ really cares about style—is appropriate enough. Of course, Bessy's moment of revelation is introduced primarily to offer in miniature the system of rules according to which Hetty Sorrel, another flirt at the center of a much more important plot, is at last judged; for if in the legal logic of *Adam Bede* Hetty is transported for infanticide, her real crime within the novel's narrative economy is something less contingent: a "kittenish" style of beauty that Eliot marks as falsely innocent and "slily conscious."[7] Even worse, this overly aware beauty is accompanied by a love of ornament made ridiculous as Hetty, alone before an old mirror, paces "with pigeon-like stateliness backwards and forwards along her room, in her coloured stays and coloured skirt, and the old black lace scarf round her shoulders, and the great glass earrings in her ears."[8] This ridiculous beauty, both cause of and companion to what Eliot views as

---

6. George Eliot, *Adam Bede* (Oxford: Oxford University Press, 1996), 31.

7. Ibid., 83.

8. Ibid., 152. Mary Ann O'Farrell points to the way in which the material and commercial particularity of Hetty's style ("white stockings" and "Nottingham lace") allow Dinah's less narratable look to achieve the status of a value: "The novel is most clearly interested in Hetty's tastes insofar as they are set as vanities against the tastes of the preacher Dinah, whose 'absence of self-consciousness' goes along with 'no blush,

Hetty's misguided longing to escape the limits of her class by attaching herself to the feckless Arthur Donnithorne, is what results in her abjection; in these terms, the pregnancy and infanticide that lead to her public disgrace in the final scenes of the novel are less actions that result in punishment than punishments themselves. The novel's narrative structure responds, shapes itself to reflect an explicit moral logic that demands that Hetty's brand of beauty be shamed out of existence, physically removed, or both. The very narrative force of *Adam Bede*'s briskly paced narrative conclusion appears less as the logical result of the novel's crimes and punishments than as the working-through of a certain relation to style.[9]

D. A. Miller, writing about Jane Austen, has described the necessary role that style and its chastening have in the novel; in the Austenian marriage plot, the stylish heroine needs to pass through style, to have had and to have lost it, in order to achieve a fully social and, in the context of the marriage plot, fully *marriageable* personhood that has its structural analogue in that form's seemingly inevitable narrative closure: "But what brings this plot to fruition—what gets *her* [the Austen heroine's] desire to quicken, too—is a moment of mortification when, the better to acquire the selfhood she had never before wanted, the heroine *forsakes* style; or rather, what is much more demeaning, she flattens it into a merely decorative reminiscence of itself, like a flower pressed into a wedding album."[10] In other words, style is cast in the Austenian marriage plot as a developmental stage necessarily and shamefully passed through in order to produce the marriageable self. And, if Hetty's humiliation and punishment are conditions necessary both to her personhood and to the narrative resolution that is Adam's marriage to Dinah Morris (a sequence that offers an only slight twist to the marriage plot's most familiar patterns), the fate of style is even more clear in the case of Esther Lyon in *Felix Holt, the Radical*. Esther, who received her education at a "French school" and is suspected by some residents of Treby of having "contracted notions not only above her own rank, but of too worldly a kind to be safe in any rank," is distinguished by perfect French, a feeling for fashion, and adventurous tastes in reading (104).[11] All this

---

no tremulousness,' and 'no keenness in the eyes,' to delineate a negative femininity unsupported by finery and refined by pleasures disallowed." Mary Ann O'Farrell, "Provoking George Eliot," in *Compassion: The Culture and Politics of an Emotion*, ed. Lauren Berlant (New York: Routledge, 2004), 154.

9. And though there is this relation between style and narrative in *Adam Bede*, the narrator does not seem to have needed this process of working through to have arrived at an early and certain judgment about Hetty Sorrel: the disdain that the novel feels for her character is discernible in the earliest descriptions of her, descriptions that in the disproportionate relation between external and internal details sentence Hetty not only to badness of character but to emptiness—which, in the novel, might be the worse fate.

10. D. A. Miller, *Jane Austen, or the Secret of Style* (Princeton, NJ: Princeton University Press, 2003), 45.

11. The trouble with style in *Felix Holt* is figured bluntly in Felix's strange linguistic performance in chapter 10: picking up one of Esther's French novels (clear symbols to this point of her unfortunate feel

adds up to a style that attracts the stern attention of Felix and encourages him after his first meeting with her onto the following thoughts about Esther and on marriage in general:

> "I'll never marry, though I should have to live on raw turnips to subdue my flesh. I'll never look back and say, 'I had a fine purpose once—I meant to keep my hands clean, and my soul upright, and to look truth in the face; but pray excuse me, I have a wife and children—I must lie and simper a little, else they'll starve'; or, 'My wife is nice, she must have her bread well buttered, and her feelings will be hurt if she is not thought genteel.' That is the lot Miss Esther is preparing for some man or other. I could grind my teeth at such self-satisfied minxes, who think they can tell everybody what is the correct thing, and the utmost stretch of their ideas will not place them on a level with the intelligent fleas. I should like to see if she could be made ashamed of herself." (63)

The barely restrained violence of Felix's misogyny, reduced to its basic narrative function, is meant to expose his badly disavowed romantic interest in Esther Lyon, a fact underscored by the familiar bombast of the claim that he will never marry, a prediction that in the context of the traditional novel must set into motion narrative machinery as irresistible as anything in Sophocles. The negative tropological work of the statement (he says he will never marry, so that the novel reader knows perfectly well that he will) does not, however, make sense of the violence of his response or of his explicit desire to shame Esther; for, although the narrative content of the claim that he will never marry is undermined and finally contained by *Felix Holt*'s marriage plot, his own plot to shame Esther proceeds without deviation or self-consciousness. The very next report of a meeting between the two characters offers (partly in the free indirect style) the following insight into Esther's feelings about Felix:

> Felix ought properly to have been a little in love with her—never mentioning it of course, because that would have been disagreeable, and his being a regular lover was out of the question. But it was clear that, instead of feeling any disadvantage on his own side, he held himself to

---

for fashion), Felix demonstrates that he can *read* French as well, we are to take it, as she can. As she mocks him, however, for his poor pronunciation, we see an ethical system emerge that allows Holt to reap the benefits of what is cast in the novel as an essentially stylish language while distancing himself from its contaminating influence. This somewhat strained compromise suggests what is delicate about remaining *smart* without seeming *thin* in Eliot's ethical world; that the reader of *Felix Holt* needs also to read (but not to speak?) French to read this passage only further complicates matters.

be immeasurably her superior: and, what was worse, Esther had a secret consciousness that he was her superior. She was all the more vexed at the suspicion that he thought slightly of her; and wished in her vexation that she could have found more fault with him. (102–3)

And a little later:

She felt as if she should for evermore be haunted by self-criticism, and never do anything to satisfy those fancies on which she had simply piqued herself before without being dogged by inward questions. (106)

In a development that suggests an almost Wordsworthian faith in the power of thoughts over the world, Felix's privately considered wish to shame Esther seems immediately to produce that effect; what's more, where we might expect his wish to result in the same kinds of narrative complication as his predictions about marriage, there are no similar moments of complication or ambiguity: he wants to shame her, she is shamed, and thus she becomes someone Felix can marry. The shame is cast explicitly as newfound capacity for self-reflection, the emergence of a self-consciousness that the novel, adhering to a familiar Romantic ethical program, takes as a prerequisite for moral action and personal development.[12]

Style functions not only as a developmental necessity in Eliot's account of the progress of a character from the unsocial to the social but also—as was suggested at the outset—as a differential methodology for making clear the structural position of a character within a particular social and narrative system. For, if style and its absence are especially economical means of signifying something, we see that the force of that signification relies on the differential relation between characters.[13] We might in this instance consider Casaubon,

12. Though this pattern is especially to be found in the case of Eliot's women, we can see a less brutal version working with some of her male characters; Lydgate's famous "spots of commonness" are, it seems, identical to his effortless ability to wear the right clothes, his expensive taste in furniture, and his nice cambric handkerchiefs. These, and his style of thinking about them, are of course what put him in debt, force him into a closer relation to Bulstrode than he wants, and result finally in the ruin of his scientific aspirations. We can see something like this, too, in the case of Deronda, a beautiful man whose certain success in society is traded for a life of religious questing that removes him (with, it should be said, a nice new set of luggage from his uncle) from England altogether. The list could go on (Arthur Donnithorne, Harold Transome, Grandcourt, etc.); it should be stressed, though, that partly because of the sexist nature of the society that Eliot describes and partly because of the demands of her ethical system, women always seem to get the rougher time of it when it comes to style.

13. Alex Woloch has seen a similar logic at the base of the "asymmetrical" system that is *Pride and Prejudice*: "*Pride and Prejudice* is saturated with comparisons among the five Bennet sisters. The novel does not simply assume a static fixed hierarchy among the five sisters but constantly reasserts, and modulates,

someone whose often remarked upon lack of character would seem to absent him from the style system with which we have so far been concerned. We would expect Eliot's arid scholar to fall lamely between two obvious positions: on the one hand, the ethical absence of style and, on the other, style's guilty but still attractive presence. One of our earliest views of Casaubon, in fact, suggests that his, compared with Esther's too-rich style or Dorothea's stylish no-style, is simply a bad style: anxious that Dorothea is in danger of becoming too close to Casaubon and ignorant of the fact that she is already engaged to him, Celia offers the following criticisms in a famously funny exchange with Dorothea:

> "Is any one else coming to dine besides Mr. Casaubon?"
> "Not that I know of."
> "I hope there is some one else. Then I shall not hear him eat his soup so."
> "What is there remarkable about his soup-eating?"
> "Really, Dodo, can't you hear how he scrapes his spoon? And he always blinks before he speaks. I don't know whether Locke blinked, but I'm sure I am sorry for those who sat opposite to him if he did." (31)

What exactly are we to take from this exchange? We have no reason, because of their inherent triviality, to doubt either of the charges: Casaubon makes nasty noises when he eats, and he blinks unpleasantly. What is put in question rather is how we are meant to understand these aspects of Casaubon's character. The narrator does not give us at this point any idea of an objective context into which to insert these details but does offer an implicit description of the kind of reader who would interpret bad manners to the detriment of their owner's character. Celia, who has to this point been distinguished by a common sense and social pragmatism hid beneath a misleadingly innocent exterior, is given slightly rougher treatment here, as Eliot describes her "rather guttural voice" and Dorothea's anxiety about the damage her "pretty carnally-minded prose" could do (31). Bad manners, in other words, are not *forgiven* in the passage; we are left to feel still that it is best not to make noise while eating soup or to blink lots. Rather, Eliot turns Celia's notice of those manners into *another* instance of bad form, something guttural and carnal. In other words, the identification of bad manners and a bad character is not negated

---

the comparative judgments that privilege Elizabeth over the rest of the family. In other words, the asymmetrical organization that sustains the narrative is maintained only through a continual process of social judgment." Alex Woloch, *The One vs. the Many: Minor Characters and the Space of the Protagonist in the Novel* (Princeton, NJ: Princeton University Press, 2003), 69.

but simply deferred in this passage, which allows the quality of one's character to appear to exceed one's facility with social observances and which makes the relationship between Casaubon's manners and his other more important failures something less than perfectly necessary, but likely nonetheless.

At an earlier point, after Dorothea first meets and is first taken with Casaubon, the narrator intrudes: "Because Miss Brooke was hasty in her trust, it is not therefore clear that Mr. Casaubon was unworthy of it" (15). This figure of deferral—one way of thinking about things is obvious, but we should remain open to other readings and in all fairness wait and see—is repeated throughout Eliot's whole work. Casaubon has already been shown to be a little pretentious, curt when discussing subjects not his own, and unsociable. These qualities coupled with the rashness of Dorothea's ardent response to the arid scholar encourage in the practiced reader of novels a *conventional* response that the narrator seems to feel it important to discourage. To avoid the conventional sequence of events is, we see, not only to come closer to what both Eliot and G. H. Lewes had begun to theorize as a really successful realism but also to achieve what is itself a conventional kind of moral breadth (one should not judge a book by its cover). In this way, the comment defers the moment of judgment, suggesting meaningfully that the world does not work according to the same rules that structure novels. The line and the deferral it demands become, then, a particular species of reality effect: on the one hand, it stands in simply as the other of convention, a recognition that events, although they must follow a necessary logic of cause and effect, exceed familiar novelistic patterns; on the other, it suggests the possibility of a specifically moral realism, the existence of an ethical position that goes beyond the stupidities of social convention and the literary verisimilitude that is that convention's textual equivalent.[14]

But that deferral is not maintained for long; for, if it is only on the basis of minor differences that a watchful observer would be able to differentiate between two sisters who could not be any more different ("it was only to close observers that her dress differed from her sister's"), no such scrutiny is required to call the respective styles of Dorothea and her stiff husband-to-be. The exchange of letters that is Casaubon's proposal and Dorothea's "I accept" exposes most clearly the difference between the two characters. Casaubon's style is labored and affected; he resorts to lame figures pinched imprudently from bad models and stiffly prevaricates where, we see, frankness was required:

14. See Eliot's "Silly Novels by Lady Novelists," in *Selected Critical Writings*, ed. Rosemary Ashton (Oxford: Oxford University Press, 1992), 260–96; and G. H. Lewes's "Realism in Art: Recent German Fiction." *Westminster Review* 14 (October 1858): 488–518.

> To be accepted by you as your husband and the earthly guardian of
> your welfare, I should regard as the highest of providential gifts. In
> return I can at least offer you an affection hitherto unwasted, and the
> faithful consecration of a life which, however short in the sequel, has
> no backward pages whereon, if you choose to turn them, you will find
> records such as might justly cause you either bitterness or shame. (28)

The forced grammatical inversion in the first sentence, the whole passage's
lack of clarity, its pretentious diction, and the absurdity of its extended clos-
ing metaphor are all, we're to take it, absolutely just causes of bitterness and
shame. The letter is a kind of hodgepodge of styles and strategies, the result
of the insufficient digestion of a lifetime's reading.[15] If anything, the letter is
too bad. And while Dorothea's response—frank, simple, and direct—stands
perfectly opposed to Casaubon's as a rebuke to the scholar's dry style, we must
recognize that her plain style derives a good deal of its attraction from a stylistic comparison that Eliot leaves implicit.[16] What's more, Eliot leaves no room
for mistake; in case the reader missed, as Dorothea did, all that is wrong with
Casaubon's letter, the narrator adds: "How could it occur to her to examine
the letter, to look at it critically as a profession of love?" This narrative aside
not only flags the letter for the reader's careful consideration but also suggests
that if Dorothea had only looked more closely at the letter's style, she never
would have married; as it turns out, her lack of attention dooms her to one of
the nineteenth-century novel's best bad marriages. If, however, she had read
the relation between style and character that Eliot's ideal reader takes stupidly
for granted, she could have escaped.

---

15. Seth Lerer has seen another point at which a hard-earned intellectual stiffness seems to corrupt
Casaubon's more personal moments. When asked by Mr. Brooke if he has read Southey, Casaubon
responds with what Lerer hears as "an almost tongue-twistingly alliterative denial": "I have little leisure
for such literature just now." As in the case of his letter, the sentence is a bad one precisely because it calls
attention to itself *as* language, because its resistance to the tongue reminds us of a necessary difference
between form and content that good form would have us forget. Seth Lerer, *Error and the Academic Self:
The Scholarly Imagination, Medieval to Modern* (New York: Columbia University Press, 2002), 105.

16. The passage encourages, in fact, an anxiety that one feels at work in many of the classic arguments
for the plain style as the best style. "The term is right, and has its essential beauty, when it becomes, in
a manner, what it signifies, as with the names of simple sensations. To give the phrase, the sentence, the
structural member, the entire composition, song, or essay, a similar unity with its subject and with itself—
style is in the right way when it tends towards that." The perfect collapse of word into object which Pater
nonchalantly identifies as "tending toward" good style leads to the possibility that in good style expression,
or character—all in fact that we think of as style—would fall into superfluity. Or we could think of another
staple of the composition class, "Politics and the English Language," to notice that rules are articulated
and bad examples given, but with the strange exception of the King James Bible, *good* examples seem to
generate insufficient friction to allow for direct description. Walter Pater, *Appreciations, with an Essay on
Style* (Oxford: Blackwell, 1967), 22.

In the abandoned final paragraph of *Middlemarch*, Eliot asks why no one stopped Dorothea from making what we know was a bad marriage:

> Among the many remarks passed on her mistakes, it was never said in the neighbourhood of Middlemarch that such mistakes could not have happened if the society into which she was born had not smiled on propositions of marriage from a sickly man to a girl less than half his own age—on modes of education which make a woman's knowledge another name for motley ignorance—on rules of conduct which are in flat contradiction with its own loudly-asserted beliefs.[17]

Critics of the novel expressed confusion at this line, suggesting that, in fact, Dorothea's neighbors had objected to the marriage; one critic asked, "What more could Dorothea's friends have done unless they had put strychnine in Casaubon's tea?" Beyond the narrative problems that this line suggests, critics may also have been responding to the sense that if Dorothea and Casaubon were ill suited to one another, they were at least *perfectly* ill suited. In other words, the antithetical resonance of their relationship exhibits a kind of *bad complementarity*, a oppositional quality that seems to stand in as some weird other version of the perfect complementarity of the couple that the marriage plot takes as one of its ethical, formal assumptions. This is not to say simply that without Dorothea's mistake there would have been no plot (although this is a point worth making), but that, as the mutually definitive courting letters suggest, the "completion" that we expect from the inevitable narrative coupling of the marriage plot could come as well from a structurally productive hate. Perhaps it is for this reason that Casaubon's passing feels so clunky: on the one hand, death is the only deal-breaker potent enough to undo a marriage so perfectly bad; on the other, it is only appropriate that that death, which awkwardly jump-starts Dorothea's plot back into narratability, would be drawn with something like a ham-fist.

Style works in a couple of different ways for Eliot. On the one hand, style is presented as an aspect of a developmental theory of character that has an important role in the making of social subjects; insofar as style represents in Eliot a period of moral and social immaturity, a character—usually a woman—can no more do without having once had it than she can get on with it when she reaches, in narrative terms, a marrying age. On the other hand, style functions in Eliot as a structural means of differentiating between ideas within the

17. George Eliot, *Middlemarch: A Study of Provincial Life*, vol. 4 (Edinburgh: William Blackwood and Sons, 1872), 370.

novel. We know that Dorothea's style is good without Eliot telling us because Casaubon's is so bad; the minor differences between Celia and Dorothea are meaningful only because of the very fact of difference; Dinah looks right because poor Hetty ends up so wrong. In other words, style and the characters who have or want it not only fulfill an important role in the articulation of the moral system that Eliot's novels assume but also function as definite if demeaned points around which a theory of character develops.[18]

Who, in that case, better than Rosamond Vincy to suffer at the altar of style? *Middlemarch's* efforts to make absolutely certain the relation between Rosamond's stylish beauty and her badness have tended to attract the attention of readers: R. H. Hutton, reviewing the novel's sixth book in 1871, wonders why it is that Rosamond always seems to "catch it" from narration. More recently, Karen Chase has written, "If it is undoubtedly true that we should hesitate before blaming Rosamond, it is also true that the narrator scarcely hesitates at all."[19] Responses like these suggest that the affective intensity with which Rosamond is "blamed" by *Middlemarch* might undermine a distance between narration and character on which the novel as a coherent form counts. For starters, Rosamond does double duty in *Middlemarch*, standing as a kind of point of structural contrast not only to Dorothea but also to Mary Garth, whose attractive simplicity would have little shape without the structuring presence of Rosamond's badness. The opposition comes across clearly in the following passage:

> Rosamond and Mary . . . stood at the toilette-table near the window while Rosamond took off her hat, adjusted her veil, and applied little touches of her finger-tips to her hair—hair of infantine fairness, neither flaxen nor yellow. Mary Garth seemed all the plainer standing at an angle between the two nymphs—the one in the glass, and the one out of it, who looked at each other with eyes of heavenly blue, deep enough to hold the most exquisite meanings an ingenious beholder

18. In this way, Eliot is developing a strategy that Deidre Lynch has seen at work in novels from an earlier moment: "The character system that structured many of their novels was one of the chief mechanisms by which inner meaning became recognizable and desirable. The manner in which the novelists divided attention between reticent heroines and forward, overdressed beauties helped to reorganize romantic-period reading as an experience in exercising personal preferences—in choosing not only among texts, but also among characters and ways of regarding them." Eliot, as we have seen, is interested not only in the *choice* but also in the way in which the favored reticence of the one comes to look like an effect of the forwardness of the other. And Miller sees something similar at work in Austen: "The stylothete aims not simply at finding (her) Style *reflected* (as a concern in the fictional world, or in the 'real elegance' of a character) but at finding it reflected *in bad imitations*." Deidre Shauna Lynch, *The Economy of Character: Novels, Market Culture, and the Business of Inner Meaning* (Chicago: University of Chicago Press, 1998), 151; Miller, *Jane Austen*, 42.

19. Karen Chase, *George Eliot*, Middlemarch (Cambridge: Cambridge University Press, 1991), 62.

could put into them, and deep enough to hide the meanings of the owner if these should happen to be less exquisite. (76)

One does not need much in the way of genius to recognize the moral differences that the passage works to indicate. Mary's "brown" plainness is presented as singular, original, and morally superior to Rosamond's appearance, which, although it appears in and out of a mirror, is cast in neither case as a reflection: the "two nymphs" in the passage are perfectly equivalent in the description. In other words, in refusing to differentiate between original and copy, the passage offers an implicit criticism of Rosamond, suggesting that although she might be beautiful, she is as empty as a mirror is flat; what's more, her beauty, insofar as it is cast as perfect and thus something about which there is nothing really to say, seems to form a kind of closed narcissistic circuit and to encourage narration on to "a kind of semantic prattle," a superabundance of description that resembles the complicated but frivolous layers of her outfits.[20] Whatever narration has to say about Rosamond's beauty can only be *excessive* insofar as any description of a beauty like hers is, as Paul Valéry suggests, language "used for producing what strikes dumb, and expresses dumbness."[21] Rosamond, in other words, is exposed as bad because what is cast in the novel as narcissistic self-identity prevents her from meaning anything in particular to anyone else; we can see, in other words, that narration associates Rosamond with what Freud will call primary narcissism, a state that characterizes the earliest form of the ego, that is the result of "an original libidinal cathexis of the ego," and that is in turn characterized by an undifferentiated but false wholeness and a faith in the "omnipotence of thoughts." And, if the relation between Mary and Rosamond is meant to perform for the reader the difference between good and bad, Rosamond, in her relation to reflection—"reflection" taken in its other sense as the fact of ethical self-awareness—is shown as blind exactly to differences that Eliot's moral system takes as necessary for the cultivation of moral sense; if we think back to what Dinah said to Bessy Cranage, we can see that one particularly stern model for ethical reflection, one that appears throughout Eliot's work, is to look in the mirror and see something *different*, in that case "a bleeding Face crowned with thorns."[22]

20. Roland Barthes, *S/Z: An Essay*, trans. Richard Miller (New York: Hill and Wang, 1974), 79.

21. Paul Valéry, *Analects*, trans. Stuart Gilbert (Princeton, NJ: Princeton University Press, 1970), 562–63.

22. We might read this moment as the mirror stage without the "*méconnaissances* that constitute the ego"; in other words, the confidence with which Rosamond takes her reflection as perfect and perfectly representative precludes the psychoanalytically rich *identification* with the thing in the mirror as something other that Lacan suggests allows the subject to develop the ego and the relationship to the ego that, he says, will determine the range of social relationships later available to the subject. In other words, Rosamond

The passage is also one of the first in the novel to use an adjective that comes back with a strange persistence in relation almost only to Rosamond: Eliot calls her infantine. The term stands out for a number of reasons: first, it is an unusual adjective; second, it suggests from its first use a contradiction between Rosamond's infant looks and an almost crassly artificial style that will only gain in clarity and that contributes much, we're to see, to Lydgate's ruin; third, the word is almost always used in contexts in which Rosamond is compared to someone else—in this case Mary and, later, Dorothea. For instance, when Will Ladislaw happens to be present when Dorothea drops in on the Lydgates, he is given the opportunity—although he does not take it—to make explicit a comparison that has been working almost from the novel's beginning:

> The gentleman was too much occupied with the presence of the one woman to reflect on the contrast between the two—a contrast that would certainly have been striking to a calm observer. They were both tall, and their eyes were on a level; but imagine Rosamond's infantine blondness and wondrous crown of hair-plaits, with her pale-blue dress of a fit and fashion so perfect that no dressmaker could look at it without emotion, a large embroidered collar which it was to be hoped all beholders would know the price of, her small hands duly set off with rings, and that controlled self-consciousness of manner which is the expensive substitute for simplicity. (298)

The scene, as is clear, reactivates some of the work that Eliot has already done: the difference between hairstyles was one that allowed the reader in the first pages of *Middlemarch* to begin to see the moral difference between Dorothea and her historical background. What was, however, generalized as a style of the times ("tall barricades of frizzed curls and bows") is tied to the particular person of Rosamond; her clothes are proof of a general tendency toward conspicuous consumption, and even her self-consciousness is offered, oddly, as something "expensive." All this is, of course, set against the simplicity and thrift of Dorothea's style, a comparison that counts almost clumsily on the reader's dumb faith that "the best things in life are free." That the women are of the same height and can thus look one another in the eye encourages us to return to the image of the mirror offered in the passage; here again, Eliot

---

experiences what Bersani calls "the jubilation with which the infant . . . anticipates a unifying ego," but she experiences it without "the subject's paranoid suspicion that the other is deliberately withholding the subject's being." Jacques Lacan, *Écrits*, trans. Alan Sheridan (New York: Norton, 1977), 6; Leo Bersani, "Sociality and Sexuality," *Critical Inquiry* 26 (2000): 645.

places Rosamond in a situation in which her expensive and thus detachable beauty is reflected heuristically in the better looks, morals, and style of another.[23] Finally, although the passage begins as a comparison between two kinds of character, only Rosamond is really described; this points not only to a kind of contagious quality of this beauty, a kind of overdetermined material richness that comes to color the prose that describes it, but also to the functional difference between two kinds of beauty: Rosamond's can be described where, apparently, Dorothea's cannot.[24] Although narration tells us that Will can't take his eyes off Dorothea, it abandons a potentially passionate moment of the free indirect style to focus instead on Rosamond's looks. Thrift and simplicity have a value in the passage only insofar as they stand silently opposed to the prattle of expense and expensive embroidery. But why, again, is this aspect of Rosamond's beauty best captured by the word "infantine"?[25]

23. Sandra Gilbert and Susan Gubar go to some lengths to demonstrate that the differences between the two characters are less important than the similarities: "But we have already seen that Dorothea is involved in a 'form of feminine impassibility' that Rosamond more overtly typifies. Both, moreover, are called angels, each achieving her own perfect standard of a perfect lady, and both are considered beautiful. Both are victims of a miseducation causing them not to 'know Homer from slang,' and neither, therefore shows 'any becoming knowledge.' Experiencing the frustrating truth of Mrs. Cadwallader's remark, 'A woman's choice usually means taking the only man she can get,' Dorothea and Rosamond can only express their dissatisfaction with provincial life by choosing suitors who seem to be possible means of escaping confinement and ennui." Although this argument has considerable force, one feels nevertheless that it offers a reading of the novel at the expense of an important aspect of the novel's architecture. Sandra Gilbert and Susan Gubar, *The Madwoman in the Attic: The Woman Writer and the Nineteenth-Century Literary Imagination* (New Haven, CT: Yale University Press, 1979), 514–15.

24. Audrey Jaffe finds a similar effect connected with the almost oppressively beautiful Daniel Deronda: "Though the absence of resemblance between Deronda's features and those of Sir Hugo's family tells of his lack of blood relation to them, it also seems to tell of an absence of relation to any ordinary human family. But the description, giving readers the opportunity to fill in Deronda's blank features with their own designs (imagine for yourself 'the most memorable of boys'), is in fact more specific than it appears: the vacancy established by referring the business of description to 'you,' like the vacancy that characterizes Eliot's descriptions of Deronda, invites the constitution of a subjectivity in effect already constituted—a space to be filled with images whose specific referents, hanging on the walls of the National Gallery, are assumed to be the cultured reader's intellectual property." Although Eliot's privileged form of beauty is given a kind of referent here, the museum art which Mordecai scans for ideas about the kind of man with whom he could have sympathy, this is not a referent that lends stability to Daniel's beauty; instead of providing an anchor that might allow one to *describe* beauty, the relation merely lets one refer to something else that, assuming this is an aesthetic problem that extends beyond the confines of Eliot's novel, is similarly resistant to description. In other words, if Mordecai's gallery hopping is meant to solidify the relation between beauty and description, it fails because it only initiates an infinite regress: a tour guide gives us a set of rules with which to understand a picture; we then ask for a set of rules with which to understand those rules; and so on and so on. Audrey Jaffe, *Scenes of Sympathy: Identity and Representation in Victorian Fiction* (Ithaca, NY: Cornell University Press, 2000).

25. We come across it again on another occasion when Dorothea and Rosamond meet: "Looking like the lovely ghost of herself, her graceful slimness wrapped in her soft white shawl, the rounded infantine mouth and cheek inevitably suggesting mildness and innocence, Rosamond paused at three yards' distance from her visitor and bowed" (547). That she looks like a ghost of herself is yet another way for Eliot to

In one sense, the term manages nicely the relation between innocence and aggression that characterizes Rosamond and primary narcissism both. For, if Rosamond is a baby, we can see from the violence she does and the aggression she is able to express that she is more like the infant of Freudian and post-Freudian psychoanalysis than mother's little angel.[26] The infant in D. W. Winnicott's scheme hovers between the two poles of hallucination and awareness of external reality without needing necessarily to decide, through the work of reality testing, between the two. This allows the child to desire with what Winnicott calls a "primitive ruthlessness," a desire that stands without the care that comes from a recognition of the external world as real instead of as something produced out of the simple strength of that desire. If there are no other subjects "out there," as the felt strength of infantine omnipotence might suggest, there can be no reason to feel the guilt (the depressive position) that results from Kleinian acts of oral aggression against the good/bad object (at first the good or bad breast, a partial object, and later the whole good or bad mother):

It is characteristic of psychoanalysts that when they try to tackle a subject like this, they always think in terms of the *developing individual.* This means going back very early and looking to see if the point of

---

introduce the problem of reflection that seems to haunt Rosamond; for, as Diana Fuss points out, "Identification invokes phantoms. By incorporating the spectral remains of the dearly departed love-object, the subject vampiristically comes to life. To be open to an identification is to be open to a death encounter, open to the very possibility of communing with the dead." Although nobody is dead here, the strange appearance of Rosamond's ghost does suggest a narcissistic identification that has, again, short-circuited, allowing the *identification* to walk the earth in place of the subject doing the identifying, a reversal that tellingly *makes no difference* for Rosamond. Diana Fuss, *Identification Papers* (New York: Routledge, 1995), 1.

26. The relation of Eliot's thinking about infancy to this strain of psychoanalytic thinking is not simple anachronism; different strains of Victorian psychology, with which Eliot was of course familiar, were interested in the infant for a variety of reasons. Most obviously the infant embodied "the warmly-discussed question, whether conscience is an innate faculty—each man's possession anterior to and independently of all the external human influences, authority, discipline, moral education, which go to shape it; or whether, on the contrary, it is a mere outgrowth from the impressions received in the course of this training" (Sully, in Taylor and Shuttleworth, 344). This question is of course central not only to Eliot's social thinking but also to her narrative method. Perhaps more to the point, though, is the ambivalence about infancy that runs through Victorian psychology; for while the infant was often represented as a sentimentally passive point at which phylogeny and ontogeny collapse, a safe, domestic version of "savage life, with its simple ideas, crude sentiments, and naïve habits" (Sully, in Taylor and Shuttleworth, 342), infancy also encouraged the kind of suspicion that we are here discussing: "The child lives in the present; the emotion of the desire of the moment is large enough to blot out for him the whole world; he has no foresight, and is the easier given up to his instincts and passions; our passions, as Hobbes said, bring us near to children. Children are naturally egoists; they will commit all enormities, sometimes, to enlarge their egoistic satisfaction. They are cruel and inflict suffering on animals out of curiosity, enjoying the manifestations of pain" (Ellis, in Taylor and Shuttleworth, 351). Selections from *Embodied Selves: An Anthology of Psychological Texts, 1830–1890,* ed. Jenny Bourne Taylor and Sally Shuttleworth (Oxford: Clarendon Press, 1998).

origin can be determined. Certainly it would be possible to think of the earliest infancy as a state in which the individual has not a capacity for feeling guilty. Then one can say that at a later date we know that (in health) a sense of guilt can be felt, or experienced without perhaps being registered as such in consciousness. In between these two things is a period in which the capacity for a sense of guilt is in the process of becoming established.[27]

What Winnicott offers here is a short account of the emergence of guilt that is as true for style's development in the novel as it is for the child's development as imagined by psychoanalysis; it is a virtue of psychoanalysis that it addresses developmental logics, logics that, as we have seen, need not be limited to infant lives. In other words, in the same way the child begins to develop a sense of guilt based on its early efforts at reality testing, so in the case of style in Eliot do we see that some person or event challenged the omnipotence of a character's style in order to allow that character to enter as a fully social subject into the social world that is the subject of Eliot's work. Style in this reading begins its life as a kind of infantine omnipotence, a feeling of control close to that which is achieved within the context of a novel by narrative omniscience.

In all the cases discussed so far, Eliot presents the stylish character as one who expresses a control over the world through a combination of hallucination and artifice. Esther works early in *Felix Holt* to turn the interior of her dissenting minister father's house into the closest possible approximation of a stately home; Hetty looks into the mirror decked out in glass earrings and antique scarves, unable to differentiate fully between the character she creates and her own self; and Rosamond is throughout *Middlemarch* blind to the economic facts of her life with Lydgate and the social consequences of her actions. In all these cases, the moment of style is represented, as has been touched on already, as a necessary and immature stage in the development of the social subject, a stage that must be passed through to render the character socially recognizable. And insofar as reality testing is a process that enforces the individual's relation not to the Real but to the social, the dissolution of infantine omnipotence in the novel will be best represented in what the form traditionally has had, maddeningly, to offer as its perfect moment of social and formal resolution: the happy marriage.

And it is this stage that Rosamond, paradoxically, never seems to pass through.[28] Rosamond, unlike almost every other stylish character in Eliot's

---

27. Winnicott, *Home Is Where We Start From*, 81.

28. In this, Rosamond resembles the figure Winnicott calls the "creative artist," a figure "who, in a way he doesn't explain, is apparently exempt from the benign circle he has described, who in fact dispensed with

work, gets off the hook and remains in that state of "jubilation" that Eliot's system identifies with an especially aggressive kind of social immaturity. Rosamond, as we know from the novel's end, gets what she wants: her husband becomes a prosperous society doctor who works between London and the bathing resorts.[29] More important, what has been taken as the classic instance of Rosamond and style's pedagogical shaming is, on close inspection, something quite different. Readers of *Middlemarch* will point to the dramatic moment of reconciliation between Dorothea and Rosamond in chapter 81 as evidence that Rosamond goes through precisely the same sort of moral chastening that has seemed necessary to the development of character in the other cases described; what's more, that chastening is exposed here as not only a narrative or developmental necessity but also an opportunity for high moral melodrama, an event that can structure a novel's aesthetic and ethical relation to its readers. The initial description of Rosamond's reaction to Dorothea's deeply felt advances would suggest exactly the kind of chastening with which we have been concerned: Dorothea's unexpected kindness "made her soul totter all the more with a sense that she had been walking in an unknown world which had just broken in upon her" (549). If, however, the scene starts profoundly, it ends obscurely: Rosamond's development, which seems initially to lead toward the development of the sort of disinterested moral consciousness that *Middlemarch* privileges, falls back into a strategic egoism: "As she went on she had gathered the sense that she was repelling Will's reproaches, which were still like a knife-wound within her" (550–51). What looked like an ethi-

---

this circle altogether. For this person reparation, and the gratitude and sense of indebtedness it implies, is irrelevant, simply the creation of an obstacle. Characterized by his ruthlessness, the artist's particular kind of socialization 'obviates the need for guilt feeling and the associated reparative and restitutive activity that forms the basis of ordinary constructive work.'" Adam Phillips, *On Kissing, Tickling, and Being Bored: Psychoanalytic Essays on the Unexamined Life* (Cambridge, MA: Harvard University Press, 1993), 36–37.

29. The degree to which narration "hates" Rosamond has long been a source of discomfort for readers: R. H. Hutton, for instance, wrote in a contemporary review of *Middlemarch*'s early books that "it is quite clear that George Eliot decidedly dislikes the type of pretty, attractive, gentle, sensible, limited young ladies so common in modern life, and loses no opportunity of plunging the dissecting-knife into them. Celia Brooke and Rosamond Vincy are the two representatives of this species in the upper and middle spheres of Middlemarch society, and Celia Brooke and Rosamond Vincy are, to use an expressive, though rude, schoolboy phrase, 'always catching it' from their authoress, till we feel decidedly disposed to take their sides." It is this feeling, perhaps, that leads Gilbert and Gubar to such lengths to recuperate, in a kind of critical anamorphosis, Rosamond for the novel, pointing out, for instance, the ways in which she represents the most successful version of resistance that the novel offers. This is undoubtedly true, and there is a kind of heady pleasure associated with the strength of Rosamond's position and, in spite of narration's constant attacks, what amounts to her final victory. To project, however, this pleasure onto *Middlemarch* is not only to obscure an unmistakable misogyny that is at times at work in the novel but also fundamentally to misconstrue its formal structure. In other words, we must recognize that to save Rosamond is to risk sinking *Middlemarch*. *The Critical Response to George Eliot*, ed. Karen L. Pangallo (Westport, CT: Greenwood Press, 1994), 295.

cal approach toward a categorical imperative slides into just another instance of pathological jockeying for position, a reversal that suggests a failure of the narrative conversion away from style that is otherwise so central to Eliot's character system. Rosamond thus stands as a double exception to "the structure of double surrogation" that Neil Hertz has rightly seen at work throughout Eliot's oeuvre. That is, if characters are "paired emblematically to embody a series of telling binaries—as good or bad, idealistic or narcissistic," and so on, Rosamond's especially resilient narcissism does two things. First, it resists in a way that we have still to understand the descent into "growing anger and despair" that otherwise marks the temporal experience of narcissism in Eliot.[30] And, second, because it does not change, it does not make itself available to the dialectical movement that otherwise characterizes these relations; the bad half of the pair is usually sublated by the end of Eliot's fictions, murdered to make way for his or her better half or chastened into a dimmer, supporting version of the good. That Rosamond maintains the hard shell of her narcissism and lives to tell the tale threatens the usual developmental sequence of Eliot's plots. In other words, this swerve away from the usual developmental story points not only to the manner in which *Middlemarch* at once counts on and denies the conventions of the classic realist novel but also to Rosamond's special exemption from the trajectory of style and shame that we have seen as so usual within Eliot's novels. Such an exemption leads us to believe that, as she escapes from a developmental logic that is otherwise inexorable, she also plays a more than usual structural part within the system that is *Middlemarch*. What is that function? How, now, to account for it?

Toward the late middle of *Middlemarch*, George Eliot gives Rosamond Vincy some dirty work to do. The novel's most vital "love problem" threatens by chapter 59 to stall because a crucial bit of news has been withheld from Will Ladislaw. What he does not know is that the late Mr. Casaubon had amended his will to deny Dorothea his property were she ever to marry him. This is something that by chapter 59 everybody but Ladislaw seems to have heard. Will is the last to know for a few reasons. First of all, the novel suggests that while news travels fast among the members of a community who share a robust interest in other people's business, the difficulty in breaking bad news to those whom it actually concerns is something more complicated.[31] We

30. Neil Hertz, *George Eliot's Pulse* (Stanford, CA: Stanford University Press, 2003), 101.

31. For discussions of *Middlemarch* and gossip, see D. A. Miller, *Narrative and Its Discontents: Problems of Closure in the Traditional Novel* (Princeton, NJ: Princeton University Press, 1981); Patricia Meyer Spacks, *Gossip* (New York: Knopf, 1985); Alexander Welsh, *George Eliot and Blackmail* (Cambridge, MA: Harvard University Press, 1985); Rosemarie Bodenheimer, "George Eliot and the Power of Evil-Speaking," *Dickens Studies Annual* 20 (1991): 201–26.

see later in the novel that Mrs. Bulstrode and Rosamond are left in the dark about their respective husbands' humiliation until Mr. Vincy—brother to one and father to the other—takes what is in both cases represented as the difficult and moral step of telling what he knows about where they stand. Second, the novel's structure requires that Will remain for a time in ignorance about his complicated legal relation to Dorothea Casaubon. If, we see, Will had known immediately about the will, honor would have demanded that he leave town before he could become fully acquainted with Lydgate and Rosamond, a connection that sets the stage for Dorothea's all-important crisis in chapter 80 and that provides an important point of structural contact between the novel's two primary plots, Dorothea's and Lydgate's.

But by chapter 59 somebody has to tell him. Because the news is painful and because it is the sign of scandal, its transmission carries with it a burden. To tell is, as Eliot and Lydgate see, maybe to believe Casaubon's posthumous calumny. Thus it is that Eliot has Rosamond, whom we already distrust, do this dirty work. In an improbable and somewhat labored bit of plotting, Fred, who has had little contact with his sister and almost none with Ladislaw, tells her what he has heard:

> When she repeated Fred's news to Lydgate, he said, "Take care you don't drop the faintest hint to Ladislaw, Rosy. He is likely to fly out as if you insulted him. Of course it is a painful affair."
>
> Rosamond turned her neck and patted her hair, looking the image of placid indifference. But the next time Will came when Lydgate was away, she spoke archly about his not going to London as he had threatened.
>
> "I know all about it. I have a confidential little bird," said she, showing very pretty airs of her head over the bit of work held high between her active fingers. "There is a powerful magnet in this neighborhood."
>
> "To be sure there is. Nobody knows that better than you," said Will, with light gallantry, but inwardly prepared to be angry.
>
> "It is really the most charming romance: Mr. Casaubon jealous, and foreseeing that there was no one else whom Mrs. Casaubon would so much like to marry her as a certain gentleman; and then laying a plan to spoil all by making her forfeit her property if she did marry the gentleman—and then—and then—oh, I have no doubt the end will be thoroughly romantic." (414)

Thanks to Rosamond, the plot of the novel can now proceed in a way it had threatened not to. Ladislaw sees suddenly where he stands in Middlemarch and, more important, in relation to Dorothea. Lydgate, the character closest to Ladislaw, has been spared the demanding and, we're to take it, demeaning work of spreading or even showing that he has heard loose talk.

As if to demonstrate the propriety of Rosamond's taking on this vulgar but necessary narrative work, the preceding scene takes every opportunity to make her revelation as ugly as possible; it foregrounds the negative qualities that we have already been taught to associate with Rosamond: she is disingenuous to Lydgate, suggesting through her "placid indifference" that she will not tell. Her will-to-tell is accented with "little airs," empty displays of flair that suggest style without substance. She tells Ladislaw not out of concern but out of aggression; what she intuits as Dorothea's place in Will's thoughts produces jealousy, and the form her disclosure takes forces him to acknowledge his affection for Dorothea in a way that must embarrass. When Will "strikes out" as Lydgate predicted, Rosamond responds with the same aggression that we recognize from her fireside chats with poor Lydgate: "'Now you are angry with *me*,' said Rosamond. 'It is too bad to bear me malice. You ought to be obliged to *me* for telling you'" (415). In other words, Eliot salts this brief exchange with instances of almost all of Rosamond's bad qualities. On the one hand, it goes simply to solidify an impression of her character that the novel has worked steadily to encourage; on the other, connecting the dissemination of bad news with Rosamond, a character already sufficiently ruined in the novel, allows that important though dirty narrative work to occur without risk of contamination for any of the other characters in *Middlemarch* or for the voice that narrates it. Eliot's narrator is able, in other words, to disavow the moment while reaping its necessary narrative benefits not only by putting the news neatly into the mouth of a character whom we already distrust but also by making its appearance the single best reason for our distrust.[32]

There is something, however, about the way in which Rosamond tells Will that exceeds this otherwise balanced moral economy. That is, Rosamond's telling appears as one of the more abstractly *plotted* moments in *Middlemarch*. Rosamond, rather than simply telling, makes a story out of it, turning what she has heard from Fred into something "charming." Rosamond's schematic approach lays quite bare the narrative machinery that gives this news its interest; the story has everything: a romantic triangle, a jealous husband, narrative complications complicated enough to sustain the story, and an appropriately deferred moment of closure. That she speaks in almost technical terms about plotting and genre lends what seems like an unnecessary methodological precision to what she has to say. What's more, her brief sketch is not only nicely

---

32. In fact, in a review of book 6 of *Middlemarch*, a chastened R. H. Hutton, who, we remember, worried in reviews of earlier portions of the novel about Rosamond's "always catching it," points to this scene as one that provides evidence not only that Rosamond is really bad but also that she has been really bad all along.

composed in an aesthetic sense but also true.[33] Although Eliot disavows the necessary narrative work of telling tales by giving that task to Rosamond Vincy, she gives the act an aesthetic weight that suggests an identification of the novel's narrative system with Rosamond; for what does Rosamond do but render in a few compressed lines a plot that *Middlemarch* lingers over for 500 pages. Indeed, we might compare Rosamond's method here to that of various theorists of narrative who have worked to distill stories down into their most essential parts; like Propp or Bremond, Rosamond theorizes *Middlemarch* down to the very bone. What's more, the process carries with it something like the danger that always accompanies certain styles of narratology: if Rosamond's extreme narrative economy can in some sense account for *Middlemarch*, it also threatens to expose as boring what had seemed so very interesting.

The difference, we see, should come with Rosamond's very different sense of form. Where the content of Rosamond's narrative and *Middlemarch* are identical, they stand methodologically at odds. Rosamond's approach toward form is evident not only in her cultivated facility for meaningless "work" or her "pretty airs" but also in her narrative style: Rosamond tells, the narrator informs us, "in order that she might evoke effects" (415). This, we see, is a moral problem in Eliot: a narrative strategy that forgoes the aesthetic whole in order to produce discrete feelings through merely local effects is in every sense a bad strategy. In other words, Rosamond as a narrator lacks *Middlemarch*'s form at least insofar as she fails to distinguish between the isolated effect and what Eliot took to be really good form: "The highest Form . . . is the highest organism, that is to say, the most varied group of relations bound together in a wholeness which again has the most varied relations with all other phenomena."[34] Eliot offers this description of good form just a year before she begins work on *Middlemarch*, a text the subject of which is the search for exactly this highest form (Casaubon's "key to all mythologies," Lydgate's "primary tissue," Mr. Brooke's "documents," etc.). Rosamond's real lapse in *Middlemarch*—her inability to recognize the propriety of the whole—is offered not only as an

---

33. Rosemarie Bodenheimer, in an essay that points to the intensity of George Eliot's many narrative and social reactions to gossip, also notices that Rosamond is oddly right: "Like every other light-minded gossip Rosamond fails to comprehend the rage of peculiar feeling this news arouses in Will as he storms out saying, 'Never! You will never hear of the marriage!' Yet she is right, as all Middlemarch gossips are right in their ways; it is really the most charming romance." Bodenheimer stops short of differentiating between the truth that she addresses in her essay, a truth revealed by a gossip that "functions as a mirror of what the subject represses," and the truth to which Rosamond has weird access at this point in the novel. Rosamond does not, in other words, expose the repressed past but the *future*: she engages in a prescient form of plotting reserved usually for narration. Bodenheimer, "George Eliot and the Power of Evil Speaking," 219.

34. George Eliot, "Notes on Form in Art," in *Selected Critical Writings*, ed. Rosemary Ashton (Oxford: Oxford University Press, 1992), 356.

expedient means of achieving a necessary narrative end but also as an aesthetic error, a model of what *not* to do in a good novel.[35] Where the really good novel is the whole thing capable of dealing with the greatest number of discrete parts, Rosamond's style results in an effective but limited aesthetic fragment; it might be good at what it does, but, according to Eliot's moral-aesthetic scheme, it is bad art all the same.

Bad as it might be, Rosamond's style does work; if her goal is to "evoke effects," we see that her narrative has quite immediate somatic effects on its audience:

> "Great God! what do you mean?" said Will, flushing over face and ears, his features seeming to change as if he had had a violent shake. "Don't joke; tell me what you mean."
>
> "You really don't know?" said Rosamond, no longer playful, and desiring nothing better than to tell in order that she might evoke effects.
>
> "No!" her returned, impatiently.
>
> "Don't know that Mr Casaubon has left it in his will that if Mrs Casaubon marries you she is to forfeit all her property?"
>
> "How do you know that is true?" said Will, eagerly.
>
> "My brother Fred heard it from the Farebrothers."
>
> Will started up from his chair and reached his hat.
>
> "I dare say she likes you better than the property," said Rosamond, looking at him from a distance.
>
> "Pray don't say any more about it," said Will, in a hoarse undertone extremely unlike his usual light voice. "It is a foul insult to her and to me." Then he sat down absently, looking before him, but seeing nothing. (414–15)

Will reacts to Rosamond's narrative as if to an attack; his features change, and he flushes "over face and ears"; his voice loses its usual quality to become "hoarse"; his gestures and his look turn absent and automatic in a way that suggests a neurasthenic reaction. Will's coloring about the ears and neck is an index of embarrassment; his ravaged voice suggests exhaustion or depression; and his automatic response to Rosamond seems like the symptom of a surprise or disappointment powerful enough to call shock. More than simply registering emotional response, Eliot's description takes pains to ensure that the reader will see Will's response as especially somatic.

The object of this play of identification and disavowal is thus not loose talk but rather that of which loose talk is just an example: an aesthetic strategy

---

35. Gilbert and Gubar have noticed a less problematic identification between Eliot and Rosamond as narrator: "And she [Rosamond] is constantly plotting, devising futures for herself which she sometimes

that chooses the local somatic effect over a total moral appeal to the reader. At least as it is an expression of Rosamond's aggression, we see that the evocation of physical effect is a narrative style that, because of what is offered as its banality, brutality, and poverty, Eliot would work hard to disavow. Clearly opposed to Rosamond's appeal to the body is the cerebral approach that readers regularly take as *Middlemarch*'s *thing*. For what, we are again and again asked, is *Middlemarch* if not a novel with brains to spare?[36] If, however, *Middlemarch* is a novel that theoretically eschews the somatic cheap shot, it cannot seem to get enough of that shot's description: the novel is filled with blushes, flushes, and feelings of shock.[37] The novel recognizes that low as it might be to go simply for effect, to renounce entirely that narrative style would be to give up a means of encouraging an authentic affective response in its readers. In other words, this scene points generally to a problem in *Middlemarch*'s formal system; while readers have tended to buy the novel's claims to structural and moral breadth, the complicated intensity of its disavowal of Rosamond's narrative style suggests a conflict within the novel's economy, a conflict between serious and silly novels, between the cerebral and the somatic, and between what it offers at different points as good form and bad.

Disavowals of this kind are, of course, not foreign to the business of the classic realist novel; as we have seen elsewhere, narration derives some measure of its authority precisely from a contest with character that it always (at least in theory) wins. That is, where a character is limited both in terms of his or her ability to know as well as in his or her ability to make narrative, narration is hemmed in by neither of these limitations. But—and this is a subject treated in the previous chapter—this freedom is less a real attribute

---

manages to actualize. In short, like Eliot, she is a spinner of yarns, a weaver of fictions." While this is helpful, it does not take into consideration, because it treats all narratives as equally representative synechdoches for *Narrative*, the stylistic differences between *Middlemarch*'s narrator and Rosamond; this not only flattens out a potentially useful distinction but also simplifies the structure of narration in the novel. More particularly, insofar as Rosamond's is a purely conventional version of *Middlemarch*, it fails precisely as what Eliot and Lewes would have identified as a successful realist novel. Realism was, among other things, an originality, a distance from the simply conventional. In Lewes's essay "Realism in Art," for instance, he complains bitterly of the tendency of some German novelists to represent characters in only the most conventional of terms; Rosamond's abridged version of the narrative would fail because it reduces character to convention. The question remains, though, whether this shorthand version of the narrative is something against which we can identify what is valuable about *Middlemarch* or an indictment of the conventions that remain in play somewhere within *Middlemarch*. Gilbert and Gubar, *The Madwoman in the Attic*, 520.

36. In a letter to Grace Norton, Henry James writes: "To produce some little exemplary works of art is my narrow and lowly dream. They are to have less 'brain' than *Middlemarch*; but (I boldly proclaim it) they are to have more *form*."

37. For more on the mechanics of the blush in Eliot, see Mary Ann O'Farrell, *Telling Complexions: The Nineteenth-Century English Novel and the Blush* (Durham, NC: Duke University Press, 1997), 118–22, 124.

than a phantasmatic structural position: the narrator is only what the character, stuck in the hopelessly limited position of person, is *not*.[38] It is in that
case curious that the moment we have been discussing appears as one of the
narrator's most explicit efforts at the disavowal of character; Rosamond is
often singled out as the novel's least sympathetic character and is for that reason all too easy to repudiate. We are allowed, as Eliot herself seems to do, to
sympathize with the novel's other morally ambiguous characters—Casaubon
and Bulstrode, for instance—in a way that we are not, I think, with Rosamond. Rosamond's abjection would in that case seem to make her an ideal
and easy candidate to take the position of the thing against which narration
would secure its authority. Because, however, she is most a sitting duck while
she is narrating, the narrator's move against Rosamond is a move not against
narration's opposite—the epistemologically circumscribed character—but
against another kind of narration: it is precisely when Rosamond is engaged
in the act of narrating that she appears *most* abject.

If, in other words, Rosamond, morally weak and set up for a fall from her
first appearance, is that thing against which narration would define itself,
the fact that she is herself a kind of narrator creates a problem. For, if we expect narrative's play of oppositions to produce on either side of the net fairly
recognizable representatives of the mutually exclusive positions narrator and
character, what *Middlemarch* instead gives us is the difference between *styles*
of narration, a difference that in some sense jeopardizes the stability of both.
If narration is opposed to Rosamond's style in *Middlemarch*, what is produced
is not impersonality or the authority of omniscience but rather a cerebral
style, which, after all, might be that thing which is most recognizably Eliot's.
Against the physicality of the effects that Rosamond would evoke, the crudity
of her narrative style, and the baseness of what Eliot offers as her intention
would stand or, rather, would emerge the balanced, brainy, ethical position
that we recognize most readily as Eliot's style.

Rosamond's style, a style that, because it focuses so intently on affecting
the body, is not only fragmentary instead of whole but also *sensational* in
something like the literary sense in which the term was used in the 1860s.
Rosamond's version of Eliot's story is a banalization of *Middlemarch* insofar
as it ignores the complex moral and social problems that animate the novel in
favor of a generic treatment that foregrounds some of the hallmark features of
the sensation genre: an unhappy domestic scene; wills mysteriously altered at
the eleventh hour; a hint, if not of bigamy, of at least adultery; the hardened

---

38. Like Rosamond's *Middlemarch*, this is a pretty brisk version of one of Audrey Jaffe's principal
arguments in *Vanishing Points: Dickens, Narrative, and the Subject of Omniscience* (Berkeley: University of
California Press, 1991).

cruelty and deserved demise of an elder husband.[39] In converting the details
of her audience's own life into sensation fiction, Rosamond remains almost
excessively true to what a reviewer in the *Quarterly* called a "great element of
sensation"—proximity: "It is necessary to be near a mine to be blown up by
its explosion; and a tale which aims at electrifying the nerves of the reader is
never thoroughly effective unless the scene be laid in our own days and among
the people we are in the habit of meeting."[40] More important, Rosamond's
style appears to have exactly the kind of electrifying effect that is so central to
the sensation novel (she is more than once called a "torpedo"): "Instead of a
basic unit of sense perception, *sensation* now [in the 1860s] means some extraordinary shock or thrill to the reader's nervous system, with no specific or
necessary truth content involved in the transaction. Nevertheless, shocks or
thrills can have epistemological implications. In the discourse about sensation
fiction, the novel becomes, metaphorically, a weapon or missile, aimed at the
mind or, rather, the nerves of the reader."[41] In other words, Rosamond aligns
herself with the popular genre of the sensation novel in order to exploit its
tested and seemingly aggressive ability to evoke effect. What left the sensation
novel open to the criticism that it was a low genre was the very fact that it
worked; the genre was less immoral than it was amoral, bypassing altogether
the cognitive faculties that one would call on to differentiate between right
and wrong. So, the immediacy of physical response was both what invited
suspicion and what made the genre so exceedingly popular in the decade preceding *Middlemarch*'s publication. We can see, too, that this interest was not
limited to the production and consumption of the novels of Wilkie Collins
and Mary Elizabeth Braddon; rather, the relation between physiological reflex
and aesthetic affect was one that gained in interest as the nineteenth century

---

39. Although Patrick Brantlinger reasserts Eliot's implied disavowal of the sensation form in *The
Reading Lesson*, a number of other critics have noticed a return of that particular repressed in Eliot: Lyn
Pykett, in a few pages from her book on the sensation novel, points to a number of devices in Eliot's
work in general and in *Middlemarch* in particular that seem to come from the sensation genre: two love
triangles (Dorothea-Casaubon-Ladislaw, Rosamond-Lydgate-Ladislaw), Bulstrode's "secret skeleton from
his past," and Raffles, who "turns up as if from a sensation novel." Joseph Litvak notices that the story of
Madame Laure's "transgressiveness" in chapter 15 "bears a strange resemblance to the extremism and the
excess of the sensation novel." And Ann Cvetkovich suggests that "the ties between the sensation novel and
George Eliot's work are . . . stronger than she might have been willing to admit." Patrick Brantlinger, *The
Reading Lesson: The Threat of Mass Literacy in Nineteenth-Century British Fiction* (Bloomington: Indiana
University Press, 1998), 160, 164; Lyn Pykett, *The Sensation Novel from* The Woman in White *to* The Moon-
stone (Plymouth, U.K.: Northcote House, 1994), 70; Joseph Litvak, *Caught in the Act: Theatricality in the
Nineteenth-Century Novel* (Berkeley: University of California Press, 1992), 147; Ann Cvetkovich, *Mixed
Feelings: Feminism, Mass Culture, and Victorian Sensationalism* (New Brunswick, NJ: Rutgers University
Press, 1992), 129.

40. Quoted in Winifred Hughes, *The Maniac in the Cellar: Sensation Novels of the 1860s* (Princeton, NJ:
Princeton University Press, 1980).

41. Brantlinger, *The Reading Lesson*, 143.

progressed and that continued to produce an anxiety that blurred the differ-ence between low art and what seemed essentially low in the human nervous system: "Considering not only the visual but the corporeal shocks, recourse to physiology and psychiatry explains why the shocks, the jolts in the viewer oc-curred and how they are linked to the unconscious, instinct, hysteria or—in the shorthand of the period—the 'lower orders.'"[42]

Indeed, G. H. Lewes's work on the nervous system, work with which Eliot was of course familiar, not only suggests a similar division between high and low but also works to shift the accepted terms of nineteenth-century neuro-physiology to make that division implicitly *aesthetic*. Lewes's thinking about the nervous system runs self-consciously counter to the mainstream of neuro-logical thought, which, following Marshall Hall's influential work on the re-flex arc in the 1830s, offered a strict functional division between the brain and the rest of the nervous system based on what Lewes identifies as that camp's two primary hypotheses, "that Reflex Action did not involve Sensibility, and that the Brain was the sole Organ of the Mind."[43] Lewes instead argues for a holistic account of the nervous system that takes a fundamental identity in *function* as the logical conclusion of what had been recognized through mi-croscopic analysis as the *structural* identity of the brain and spinal tissues: if the brain and spine were made from the same stuff, they must, he reasoned, do something like the same work. This holism does not, however, do away entirely with the high-low distinction in the nervous system:

> It will be understood that by the word Mind we do not designate the
> intellectual operations only. If the term were so restricted, there would
> be little objection to our calling the Brain the organ of the Mind. But
> the word Mind has a broader and deeper signification; it includes all
> Sensation, all Volition, and all Thought: it means the whole psychi-
> cal Life; and this psychical Life has one special centre: it belongs to
> the whole, and animates the whole. The Brain is a part of the whole,
> a noble part, and its functions are noble; but it is only the organ of
> special mental functions; as the liver and lungs are organs of special
> bodily functions. It is a centre, a great centre, but not *the* centre. It is
> not the exclusive Sensorium. Its absence does not imply the absence of
> all consciousness, as I shall prove by experiment. It cannot therefore be
> considered as the organ, but only as *one* organ of the Mind.[44]

42. Rae Beth Gordon, "From Charcot to Charlot: Unconscious Imitation and Spectatorship in French Cabaret and Early Cinema," *Critical Inquiry* 27 (Spring 2001): 523.

43. G. H. Lewes, "Sensation in the Spinal Cord," *Nature* 9 (December 4, 1873): 83–84.

44. G. H. Lewes, *The Physiology of Common Life*, 2 vols. (Edinburgh: William Blackwood and Sons, 1860), 2:4–5.

Although this is a kind of throwback to earlier "spinal soul" theories of mind, it does not so extend the definition of thought as to unseat the brain from its cognitive throne.[45] In other words, what Lewes does is to preserve for the brain higher order cognitive functions while demonstrating that the nervous system was capable of processing *certain kinds* of sensation without the brain, an idea that people like Hall would have said was unacceptable.[46]

So where anxiety about a "lower order" aesthetic style, one that would evoke effects through sensation without encouraging thought, would be meaningless to Hall, exactly that kind of anxiety might be seen as the result of a vision of the nervous system that could allow a body literally without its brain to experience meaningful if cognitively poor sensations. *Sensation fiction* might come, then, to have a more complicated meaning for Lewes and Eliot: "sensation" could refer to a lower order evocation of effects that would not need to call on the ability to organize material into a coherent whole that Lewes would have continued to identify as one of the "intellectual operations" of the brain. Indeed, the novel's anxiety about this anticerebral style erupts weirdly into its content in the form of Farebrother's "lovely anencephalous monster," for which Lydgate trades "some sea-mice" and Robert Brown's *Microscopic Observations on the Pollen of Plants* (118–20). Anencephalic infants are regularly discussed in Lewes's work to strengthen arguments resulting from his experiments on brainless animals, and demonstrated to Lewes that humans without brains could, albeit for short periods of time, respond with something more than reflex to certain kinds of sensation. And although

45. For a lucid account of William Alison's ideas about the spinal soul—derived in part from his contact with Scottish philosophy—and of the debates between Alison and Hall that eventually resulted in the elevation of Hall's reflex theory to the status of common sense, see Ruth Leys, *From Sympathy to Reflex: Marshall Hall and His Opponents* (New York: Garland, 1990).

46. To prove his point, Lewes engaged in sometimes extreme experiments that involved removing a live animal's brain and then subjecting that animal to various kinds of painful sensation (poking, boiling, burning, etc.). As weird as these experiments were, they not only fall within a long tradition of neurophysiological study that contributed much to Anglo-American psychology and behaviorism but also stand as one source for a whole tradition concerned with the relation of biology and aesthetics: we might think of the James-Lange thesis, which held that what had been taken as somatic effects caused by emotion were in fact emotion's real content; or we might think of later researchers like Philip Bard, who continued into the twentieth century to annoy "decorticate" cats in order to determine to what extent animals without whole brains were capable of feeling not only physical pain but also, in a phrase with a suspiciously Jamesian ring to it, *sham rage*. We might think of I. A. Richards's attempts at isolating through experiment and statistical analysis the physical component in the experience of reading poetry; in a related context "tests were conducted by screening films and monitoring subjective response at dramatic or comic moments, measuring the exact intensity of sensations (which were then interpreted as emotions) in the spectator. According to late nineteenth-century physiology, successive stages of intensity in aesthetic emotion correspond to changes in the body." Philip Bard, "On Emotional Expression after Decortication with Some Remarks on Certain Theoretical Views," *Psychological Review* 41 (1934): 309–29; Gordon, "From Charcot to Charlot," 518.

Robert Greenberg suggests that Lydgate's love at first sight for the bottled monster suggests an identification between Rosamond and the brainless infant, it seems rather that the infant is a strange figure for the ideal reader of Rosamond's style; or, rather, insofar as Lydgate is susceptible to Rosamond's ability to evoke effects, he accepts a cognitive condition the description of which would be identical to the infant's.[47]

We can see, then, that the opposition between narration and Rosamond's style is not only a difference internal to *Middlemarch* but also a difference that counts on and mobilizes a range of cultural terms that would invest in that difference an ethical value that would exceed its structural use; as Rosamond is different from narration, so is the sensation novel different from *Middlemarch* and the body different from the brain.[48] If, however, we take it that the shock is the figure that would have best represented what was wrong both with the style of the sensation genre and with the lower aspects of the body, we find again that what would seem to secure the distinct and distinctly ethical identity of narration in *Middlemarch* is also what compromises that identity: *Middlemarch*, which is supposed to stand against the evocation of effects, is filled with merely physical effects. These begin with the strange correspondence between Lydgate's galvanic experiments in chapter 15 and his experience of shock at the sight of Laure's murder during her melodramatic performance in Paris: the coincidence of his electrical experiments on rabbits and frogs and his own physical shock upon witnessing the stabbing in chapter 15 (like a frog under the application of current, "Lydgate leaped and climbed, he hardly knew how") not only looks like a joke but also suggests the extreme figural mobility that shock comes to have in the novel.[49] After this first substitution, more follow: Dorothea is shocked at fragmentary Rome and the unhappiness of her marriage; she shows symptoms of shock again when she sees

---

47. Robert A. Greenberg, "Plexuses and Ganglia: Scientific Allusion in *Middlemarch*," *Nineteenth-Century Fiction* 30 (1975): 33–52.

48. In fact, in the reconciliation scene discussed earlier, Rosamond is once again explicitly aligned with lower order nervous response: "With her usual tendency to over-estimate the good in others, [Dorothea] felt a great outgoing of her heart towards Rosamond for the generous effort which had redeemed her from suffering, not counting that the effort was a reflex of her own energy" (551). Put in terms of Lewes's neurophysiology, Rosamond's greatest moral moment remains hollow because it is a nervous response, a reflex, that does not need the brain; it is not cognitive and is thus not moral. Rosamond's strange nonrelation to Lydgate's brain is underscored late in the novel: "He once called her his basil plant; and when she asked for an explanation, said that basil was a plant which had flourished wonderfully on a murdered man's brains" (575). If Rosamond is a torpedo, so, it appears, is she a zombie.

49. It is worth pointing out that Lydgate's experiment, taken simply, is a *bad one*; if he is looking to connect nervous motion with animal electricity, then the fact that his animals are, contrary to the popularly imagined galvanic experiment that tended conventionally to stick to frogs' legs and convicts' corpses, *alive* and apparently conscious (narration tells us that when he goes to the theater, he leaves them to wonder at the "trying and mysterious dispensation of unexplained shocks") would prevent him from

what looks like a scene of courtship between Will and Rosamond—and they are in turn shocked by the fact that they are seen. These scenes—and there are many more—share enough qualities to begin to suggest a coherent and nearly autonomous subgenre within *Middlemarch*. Each is self-consciously stagy (the Parisian melodrama and Rome both turn on a confusion between real life and the aesthetic, and the final scene is curiously still and seems *posed* in a manner that suggests a *tableau vivant*); each is among the novel's key moments of personal or narrative crisis; and each not only uses a vocabulary familiar to the shock but also represents the novel's characters as responding to the world in a manner very similar to Will's nearly automatic response to Rosamond's style. And if these shocks were not enough to suggest the tenacity of a style that *Middlemarch* has otherwise sought to repress, a final shock is offered in chapter 83: as an electrical storm begins to brew outside her window, Dorothea shares with Will what appears to be a final farewell:

> While he was speaking there came a vivid flash of lightning which lit each of them up for the other—and the light seemed to be the terror of a hopeless love. Dorothea darted instantaneously from the window; Will followed her, seizing her hand with a spasmodic movement; and so they stood, with their hands clasped, like two children, looking out on the storm, while the thunder gave a tremendous crack and roll above them, and the rain began to pour down. . . . Her lips trembled, and so did his. It was never known which lips were the first to move toward the other lips; but they kissed tremblingly, and then they moved apart.
>
> The rain was dashing against the window-panes as if an angry spirit were within it, and behind it was the great swoop of the wind; it was one of those moments in which both the busy and the idle pause with a certain awe. (559)

Again we recognize what have become, by this point, familiar aspects of a particular effect: spasmodic movement, the more than metaphorical role of electricity, and the curiously staged, conventional setup of the scene. What's more, even without the scene's euphemistic pan to a rain-swept windowpane,

---

distinguishing between purely reflexive motion resulting from contact with an electrical current and conscious motion resulting from the sensation of physical pain. One wonders if Eliot leaves the animals alive to avoid the censure of groups like the Royal Society for the Prevention of Cruelty to Animals and Society for the Protection of Animals Liable to Vivisection, both organizations with which Lewes was engaged in very public and possibly embarrassing disputes. For more on not only the historical but also the formal relations between Eliot and vivisection, see Richard Menke, "Fiction as Vivisection: G. H. Lewes and George Eliot," *ELH* 67:2 (2000): 617–53.

we would see that where the melodramatic is supposedly a thing to disavow, this scene, one that offers an inevitable resolution familiar to readers of the traditional novel, embraces exactly the conventions of melodrama. The storm is not only corny insofar at it exploits without subtlety the pathetic fallacy but also a little cheap as it replaces the authentic character motivation that Eliot's realism would seem to demand with a canned sublimity that takes over where plot gives up. And, as the scene is a culmination within the novel, so is it a kind of logical end point within the trajectory of the shock. The first sight of the shock comes with Lydgate's experiments, a situation barely described that seems only to provide background detail. Beginning, however, with the figurative substitution that is Lydgate's experience at the theater, the shock becomes increasingly comprehensive and increasingly potent: Lydgate shocks the frog; Laure shocks Lydgate; and, as the shocks becomes more central to the novel's plot, narration shocks its characters.[50] This final scene, however, takes this progression one step further; for while we might say that Eliot has to this point only described an effect within the world of her novel, the coincidence of the marriage plot's closure with the oldest trick in the book suggests that this last shock is meant especially for the reader of *Middlemarch*. Making the electrical charge purely atmospheric, placing it *outside* the novel's horizon, appears as a means both of figuring the final stage in a process of increasing comprehensiveness that has been at work from that first substitution and of suggesting that the sort of melodramatic shock that Madame Laure directed toward Lydgate in chapter 15 is in this final scene directed out toward the reader of *Middlemarch*. And, given our discussion so far, the only thing worse than the failure of this scene would be its success. If, in other words, there is nothing worse than giving up on the ethical demands of one's realism in order to "evoke effects," this scene is not only a problem given the choices that narration itself has made but also a final point of identification between narration and Rosamond Vincy. Where we have seen narration engaged in the disavowal of a bad style that would secure the identity of good one, we find at the moment of narrative closure, the moment that would validate not only a certain idea of the social but also the very idea of the traditional novel, a strange slip from good form to bad that offers vertigo where resolution was wanted.

---

50. Of course, Rosamond's relationship with Lydgate is another substitution for what comes more and more to look like a kind of primal scene in *Middlemarch*; on the one hand, narration's name for Rosamond, "torpedo," strengthens the figurative relation between Rosamond's style and shock that Madame Laure produces; on the other, certain conspicuous similarities in character such as an inability to become really ruffled under any circumstances and a tendency to act ("She was by nature an actress of parts that entered into her physique: she even acted her own character, and so well, that she did not know it to be precisely her own") offer insight into not only Lydgate's bad judgment but also the novel's own typological system.

The identification of Rosamond with narration in *Middlemarch* not only points to what Eliot recognizes as a necessary narrative strategy and the disavowal that that strategy necessitates but also suggests something about the shape of narration itself. Rosamond is given a chance to narrate precisely because of her relation to an aggression that *Middlemarch* identifies as infantine. What *Middlemarch*'s system suggests is that Rosamond's *right* to narrate comes, as it were, with the very quality that makes her abject: an infantine aggression that resembles the cognitive and ethical plenitude that we reserve within the novel for omniscient narration. The wholeness, the omnipotence, the aggression that we would negatively associate with primary narcissism and with Rosamond Vincy are, thought of from an only slightly different angle, the virtues of omniscient narration in *Middlemarch*. Eliot's narrator stands not only as some *other* to character in *Middlemarch* but also as a kind of ego ideal for the characters whose systems fail in the novel, an ego ideal that Freud, writing as if he had Rosamond in mind, recognized as "the heir to the original narcissism in which the childish ego enjoyed self-sufficiency."[51] Critics have often noted the connections between Casaubon and Lydgate's endeavors and Eliot's own; in all cases, they are in search of some means of resolving the incoherent parts of a particular discipline or field into a coherent whole. The characters fail not because of any essential stupidity in that desire but because they can only come up with bad totalities, "little systems" the sense of which is obliterated by the introduction of any new content that cannot be made to fit within them. And what is *Middlemarch* supposed to be if not a successful system? Eliot, we remember, called the "highest" form "the most varied group of relations bound together in a wholeness which again has the most varied relations with all other phenomena." Regardless of the actual success of Eliot's novel (and who would argue with its success?), we can see that within the novel's system, the novel itself stands as that perfect form against which the failures of the characters that inhabit it must be measured. In that case, narration comes to have a necessarily identificatory relationship with its characters insofar as narration is itself an ideal version of the thing that they work toward and desire.[52] In other words, the narrator stands as more than a supervisory or prohibitory voice, a disembodied conscience that

51. Sigmund Freud, *Group Psychology and the Analysis of the Ego*, trans. James Strachey (New York: Norton, 1959), 110.

52. Neil Hertz, talking about Casaubon, has pointed to "the play between the imaginer and the imagined, between author and character, and the possibility of a narcissistic confusion developing between the one and the other." For Hertz, this "confusion" amounts to a play between a misrecognition that obtains in any relation between subjects in language and a recognition that is, paradoxically, that misrecognition's repression. Neil Hertz, *The End of the Line: Essays on Psychoanalysis and the Sublime* (New York: Columbia University Press, 1985), 82.

would limit and define the good and the bad for the inhabitants of *Middle-march*. Narration in the novel is often embodied in asides that, whether they attract admiration or distaste, constitute something like a character. Because that character works successfully at exactly the kind of project that inevitably fails within the novel's frame, it also works as an ideal object that thus initiates a chain of identifications between character and narrator, novel and reader. These identifications, because they are mobile, potent, unruly, make indissolubly knotty the ethical and formal relation between narration and what it narrates in *Middlemarch*.

What we see, in that case, is not that narration is bad but that narration is both especially incommensurate with and irresistibly drawn to what it narrates for reasons that go beyond the demands of narrative structure. In the next chapter we will see that in Henry James's *The Sacred Fount*, the transformation of his usually supersubtle third-person narrative voice into its first-person equivalent produces a person who is not only socially but also essentially *crazy*; in *Middlemarch* the always correct, always balanced voice that is narration, were it to appear among the citizen-characters of *Middlemarch*, might look more like Rosamond Vincy than Dorothea Brooke. If Rosamond's ability to evoke effects is inseparable from her greatest fault, her feeling that "no woman could behave more irreproachably than she was behaving," we might imagine as painful the descent of a narration that *always knows* into a community bitterly suspicious of those who would "put on airs," a community, in other words, like *Middlemarch*.

CHAPTER 4

Hanging Together in Henry James

You haven't a vulgar intonation, you haven't a common gesture, you never make a mistake, you do and say everything exactly in the right way.
—Henry James, The Princess Casamassima[1]

When we first see the grown Hyacinth Robinson enter Amanda Pynsent's shabby parlor, the narrator tells us that, although he carries traces of a day's labor on his clothes, one can see that there is "an idea in his dress" (104). That is, the parts of his outfit fall into place around some governing intention, some principle that turns the discrete sartorial detail into something that works toward an end, that contributes to the sense of the whole. Hyacinth's body is in this way like the classic realist text, a thing made of its details but guaranteed by its intention, a denotative anchor on which we, readers of a readerly text, are asked to count. If, however, there is an intention at work here, the precise nature of that intention is withheld. The narrator tells us that there is an idea, but not what that idea is. We are left, then, with a possible contradiction in the looks of Hyacinth Robinson: if there is in

1. Henry James, *The Princess Casamassima*, ed. Derek Brewer and Patricia Crick (London: Penguin, 1987), 337; subsequent references to this work are included in the text.

fact an "idea in his dress," Hyacinth's style is secure; if not, he is merely stylish and maybe vulgar. Because an idea is indicated but unnamed, both possibilities seem to coexist within Hyacinth.

If it is Hyacinth's problem that his style might stand without an intention, that it might be unmotivated, we can see that, at least as critics have taken *The Princess Casamassima*, this was James's problem too. Readers at the time of its publication did not like *The Princess Casamassima* because of the uncertain relation between its body, its intention, and its style: "That want of virility with which Mr. James has been taxed certainly becomes a distinguishing trait in *The Princess Casamassima*. In order to be nice and elegant whenever he can he sprays his subject as with a perfumed atomizer."[2] The body of James's text is in that case maybe too much like Hyacinth's. Its plot is, the critic suggests, too thin to withstand the too vigorous spray of the Jamesian style. To be "nice and elegant," the critic implies, is to accentuate the style of a work at the expense of its body. What's more, James's perfume isn't simply overpowering; it's bad:

> To do this well calls on the best abilities of a capital perfumer. All sweet-smelling roots must be carefully ground, triturated, mixed, and no scent must be too much in prominence. *The Princess Casamassima* is not precisely of this kind. Rather a pomander, or belike a vinai-grette. The case, a perfection of neatness, shows sharp chiselings, is worked up *ad unguam*, but from the inside comes whiffs redolent with the acrid sharpness of thieves' vinegar.[3]

We see then that James's fault is not only that he sprays his novel too liber-ally with a stylish odor but also that the scent is cheap: one part sticks out and smells. Where the expensive scent complements the body to which it is applied, the cheap overpowers and distorts. On the one hand, comparing James's prose to bad perfume figures the easy slide between style and vulgarity that has often been taken to characterize James's writing.[4] On the other hand, it says something specific about the structure of *The Princess Casamassima*: like oil and vinegar, it just won't hang together.

The uncertain intention behind Hyacinth's look not only threatens the style of James's novel but also becomes an important aspect of that novel's

---

2. "A 'Slumming' Romance," *New York Times*, November 21, 1886, in *Henry James: The Contemporary Reviews*, ed. Kevin J. Hayes (Cambridge: Cambridge University Press, 1996), 179.

3. Ibid., 181.

4. Joseph Litvak suggests that certain of James's characters' "desire for and identification with this vulgarity . . . opens a space for *James's* enactment of his own similar relationship to what he would *bafouer*." Joseph Litvak, *Caught in the Act: Theatricality in the Nineteenth-Century Novel* (Berkeley: University of California Press, 1992), 237.

plot. It is exactly this ambiguity of intent, an ambiguity reflected in the mysterious circumstances of his birth, the unstable class position he occupies, and the unclear orientation of his sexual desire, that allows "little Hyacinth Robinson" to join the ranks of the revolutionaries at the Sun and Moon (the pub where Paul Muniment and his fellow would be revolutionaries meet) and to be taken up by the arch-anarchist Hoffendahl as a paradoxically effective terrorist (the paradox: his conspicuous perfection renders him perfectly inconspicuous). We find in Hyacinth Robinson not only an uncertainty of intention that structures his character and that character's relationship to its context but also a disposition that causes an ability perfectly *to see* (an ability associated both with *The Princess Casamassima* in particular and with James in general) to fall somewhat apart. His body, always "little," and his style, which, we know, is better than it should be, both stand out in the novel and achieve a kind of social opacity that allows him not to defy authority but to avoid it altogether.

What is at stake here is the very possibility of coherence for character and narration in *The Princess Casamassima*. Where does the absence of intention I have begun to describe leave James's text? Although we might see that this is an especially knotty problem in *The Princess Casamassima*, we might ask this question of every system, textual or otherwise. In *The Intentional Stance*, Daniel Dennett describes the practical necessity of projecting into systems too complicated to understand an intention to account for their various behaviors: "The intentional strategy consists of treating the object whose behavior you want to predict as a rational agent with beliefs and desires and other mental stages exhibiting what Brentano and others call *intentionality*."[5] If a thermostat has too many parts to comprehend all at once, we say that the thermostat *wants* to warm the room when it is cold, although we understand perfectly that a thermostat cannot meaningfully *want* anything. Intention, thought of in these terms, is not something that we *possess*; it is rather something that we *project* on to other things in order to give them meaning and to make them useful. If we leave aside for the moment the possibility that every intention, human or otherwise, is only an enabling fiction, we can see that intention in the language of literary criticism has tended to do something like the work Dennett describes.[6] For once we recognize that novels—even at their least loose and

5. Daniel Dennett, *The Intentional Stance* (Cambridge, MA: MIT Press, 1989), 15.

6. I take Dennett not only as a useful supplement to familiar literary critical debates around the nature of intention (Wimsatt and Beardsley, Knapp and Michaels, Frye, de Man, etc.) but also as working along similar lines to, if at a distance from, some of de Man's similarly derived arguments in favor of a "not necessarily subjective" version of intention: "Intention is inseparable from the concept of meaning; any meaning is to some extent intentional. Any language oriented to meaning is at least intentional, precisely by virtue of the fact that it intends meaning. Intention is, therefore, not subjective." Paul de Man, *The Resistance to Theory* (Minneapolis: University of Minnesota Press, 1986), 94.

baggy—escape perfect Aristotelian comprehension (they are too complex and too long to hold all in one's head), we find ourselves treating them as systems that *want* to do this or that thing. To complicate matters further, coherence is, in the context of the literary, not merely pragmatic; rather, an almost always out-of-reach coherence is taken as one of the principal qualities that make the traditional novel valuable. So where the thermostat just "lets" intention happen to it, the novel has had to court coherence, to seek out its intelligibility as a textual effect in order to secure its aesthetic value. Coherence, like good form, is a structuring ideal rather than an achievable state of being.

Because, however, intention is thrown repeatedly into question in James's novel, the question of coherence in *The Princess Casamassima* becomes its principal thematic interest as well as its principal structural problem. Not only does the novel turn, as I have begun to describe, on an uncertainty of intention within both the character of Hyacinth Robinson and its own larger structure, but what has come over the course of this book to look like one of the surest ways to secure the reader's sense of coherence—the mistake—is also compromised. Counting on a familiar bit of folk wisdom that suggests that it is human to make mistakes, the novel form "hopes" (in the same way the thermostat "wants") that the presence of mistakes in character can make that very slippery system seem more human; put in different terms, mistakes in character produce the effect of coherence. If the visible mistake is, as we have seen in previous chapters, one way to produce the effect of coherence in character and in the traditional novel, we are left with a problem: Hyacinth, we are told at key moments in the novel, never makes a mistake. What follows will work to describe the relationship between coherence, the mistake, and what can and cannot be seen in *The Princess Casamassima*.

We might take it as James's own fault that very different ideas (seeing spying narrating) have become so inextricably tangled up in the critical response to his work.[7] The elevation of "showing" over "telling" in the prefaces to the New York Edition (or at least in the post-Jamesian theoretical consolidation of those prefaces) and a style of plotting that turns on sudden and "scenic" disclosures encouraged early theorists of the novel inspired by James (most notably Percy Lubbock) not only to understand James's novels primarily in terms of their ability to engage vision but also to take this effect as an element necessary to the success of the novel form in general.[8] It would seem

---

7. See, for example, Mark Seltzer, *Henry James and the Art of Power* (Ithaca, NY: Cornell University Press, 1984).

8. See Wayne C. Booth, *The Rhetoric of Fiction* (Chicago: University of Chicago Press, 1983), for an early and sustained response to what Booth perceives as a tyranny of this opposition in writing about the novel and its generic value.

inevitable, in that case, that as criticism grew increasingly suspicious of the complicity of vision and power, it would grow equally suspicious of Henry James.[9] This tendency finds early and vitriolic expression in the criticism of the self-proclaimed "anti-Jacobite" Maxwell Geismar:

> James has been praised over and over again (by the James cult, I mean) for having removed the "auctorial presence" of the nineteenth-century novelists from the novel form. But the "points of view," or the "centers of illumination," which he substituted were all completely *James's* point of view. Behind them he lurked, he plotted and planned and schemed, more despotic and dictatorial than any old-fashioned novelist lecturing his readers about the sins and frailties of human character.[10]

In a manner that anticipates more recent work on James, Geismar suggests that where "the James cult" would see James's method as approaching a narrative style objective enough to lend the novel form the purest kind of cultural authority, that objectivity is in fact merely a screen for tyrannical interestedness. In other words, where James's supporters would suggest that his novels had achieved a kind of disinterested ethical purity by virtue of the formal development of a neutral narratorial position, Geismar says that the form of James's novels instead enforces through a dictatorship underwritten by surveillance a very specific and very judgmental sort of vision.[11]

Related to this vision is the idea that narration in James not only enforces social rules within the novel but also looks to become fully identical to those rules (it is important to note that Geismar is not opposing narrative omniscience to limited narration, but a really good, impersonal omniscience to the bad, ersatz omniscience he sees in James). In this, the bad narrator might remind us of *The Portrait of a Lady*'s Gilbert Osmond:[12]

9. I am thinking primarily, but not exclusively, of Michel Foucault's influential equation of vision and power: "The prosecutor is not just the agent of law who acts when the law is violated; the prosecutor is, above all, a gaze, an eye constantly trained on the population. The eye of the prosecutor must transmit information to the eye of the attorney general, who in turn transmits it to the great eye of surveillance, which at the time was the minister of police. The latter transmits information to the eye of the one who is at the highest point of society, the emperor—who, as it happens, then [in the early years of the nineteenth century] used the symbol of the eye." Michel Foucault, "Truth and Juridical Forms," in *Power: Essential Works of Foucault, 1954–1984*, vol. 3, ed. James D. Faubion, trans. Robert Hurley (New York: New Press, 2000), 73.

10. Maxwell Geismar, *Henry James and the Jacobites* (Boston: Houghton Mifflin, 1963), 6–7.

11. This criticism rhymes with a recent and influential strain of James criticism best represented by Seltzer, *Henry James and the Art of Power*. His work on *The Princess* appears on pages 25–59.

12. Jonathan Freedman points out that recent criticism has, in ways that again remind us of Geismar, seen James as something like his own worst character, as "a second Gilbert Osmond." Jonathan Freedman, *Professions of Taste: Henry James, British Aestheticism, and Commodity Culture* (Stanford, CA: Stanford University Press, 1990), xiv.

"You say you don't know me, but when you do you'll discover what a worship I have for propriety."

"You're not conventional?" Isabel gravely asked.

"I like the way you utter that word! No, I'm not conventional: I'm convention itself."[13]

Osmond's fantasy is that he might be able to identify, incorporate, and thus perfectly reproduce the whole set of rules that structure the social world, a dream that would result, if it were possible, in the sovereign identity of Osmond and that ordered world, a condition that I have called "good form."[14] This would mean not only that Osmond's manners would be perfect but also that his being wrong within the context of the social would be impossible. Simply to act would be to exert the kind of disciplinary control over the social that Geismar takes as James's dirty trick on the reader: what Osmond wants to be in relation to his world, he implies, narration is in relation to its own.

If, however, Geismar implicitly aligns James with Osmond, that move runs against the grain of James's novel, one that systematically values the flawed and the abyssal both in character and in narrative structure. In the first case, we might remember the moment at which, in order to image the cause of his discontent with his wife, Osmond compares Isabel Archer to an antique teacup in which he has spotted a flaw, a mistake: "It already has a wee bit of a tiny crack" (436). Although Osmond invokes the crack to counter Madame Merle's implicit recognition of Isabel's innate preciousness, it is precisely the crack, we see, that gives Isabel a value that exceeds the merely collectible, just as it is Osmond's failure to recognize that value that exposes him once and for all as fatally tacky.[15] What Osmond takes as Isabel's flaw is in fact what has made her so interesting; that she is not perfectly resolved into an undifferentiated, hollow vessel is what has allowed all those who see her to ask, "What

13. Henry James, *The Portrait of A Lady*, ed. Robert D. Bamberg (New York: Norton, 1995), 265; subsequent references to this work will appear in the text.

14. See chapter 1 for more on good form.

15. James provides ample evidence for Osmond's literal tackiness. Freedman points out that Osmond's taste suffers diminishment over the course of the novel: "Lord Warburton, as we have already seen, identifies Osmond's taste as a product of the more ephemeral sort of fashion; Ned Rosier is even more unsparing. 'It's papa's taste; he has so much,' Pansy tells him; 'he had a good deal, Rosier thought; but some of it was bad.' As indeed it is: when Rosier walks his way through Osmond's collection, he notes for us, through the delicate modulations of the *style indirect libre*, the aesthetic gaucherie represented by the 'big cold Empire clock' in Gilbert's living room, the diminished imagination registered by his collection of miniatures. As the novel progresses, Osmond's taste becomes progressively, even incrementally, diminished." We might connect the failure of Osmond's taste to the problem of Hyacinth's dress as sketched out in this chapter's opening: the sketchiness of Osmond's style might point finally to that all but fatal lack of an idea or organizing intention; instead, and this is Freedman's point, Osmond, a caricature, can only perform taste and cannot have it. Freedman, *Professions of Taste*, 150–51.

will she do?" To go without that crack would be not only less interesting but also really monstrous: "Far from containing emotions (or, for that matter, judgments) or possessing a consciousness capable of directing feelings, a 'truly in-dividual, un-divided' being would lack the self-differentiality that makes experience possible at all."[16] The way in which the crack lends Isabel Archer a value that Osmond cannot appreciate leads us to a second case: in James's preface to the novel he points to one scene as his finest:

> She sits up, by her dying fire, far into the night, under the spell of recognitions on which she finds the last sharpness suddenly waits. It is a representation simply of her motionlessly *seeing*, and an attempt to make the mere still lucidity of her act as "interesting" as the surprise of a caravan or the identification of a pirate. It represents, for that matter, one of the identifications dear to the novelist, and even indispensable to him; but it all goes on without her being approached by another person and without her leaving her chair. It is obviously the best thing in the book, but it is only a supreme illustration of the general plan. (14–15)

The scene that James describes is the novel's most sustained look at Isabel Archer, a look cast in the form of a kind of reported interior dialogue, questions and answers that perform the presence of the internal. The possibility of holding a discussion with oneself (we might call this consciousness) is a kind of crack like the crack in the cup, the slight gap or difference in the self that at once makes impossible full knowledge about what it is that one means and helps, when represented, to produce the effect of interiority in the traditional novel. What's more, this enabling difference reappears as a narrative effect in the scene: James represents the whole of the scene in the free indirect style, an approach that in this context serves not to erase the distance between narration and Isabel Archer but to give that distance the status of legible form. The scene, which can of course only point toward the internal, performs the impossibility of knowing really what goes on inside another person or, for that matter, inside oneself. We might take it that this is the sense in which the scene is an exemplary expression of the "great plan" of James's novel; the room at its center, an interior that is the interior of James's Isabel Archer, is, at last, nowhere to be found. Where the scene seems initially to put the Jamesian eye right up to the keyhole (as opposed to one of the house of fiction's many windows), its pleasure is not that of the Peeping Tom; what, after all, do we call

---

16. Rei Terada, *Feeling in Theory: Emotion after the "Death of the Subject"* (Cambridge, MA: Harvard University Press, 2001), 81.

the perversion associated with *not* seeing? That narration is at its best when it *identifies* with Isabel's objectless vision suggests not the force of its own powers of surveillance but the curious value the novel places on what is not seen.

The difference between the internal and external is precisely that which makes possible the narratable process of epistemological osmosis on display throughout the novel. An Osmondian identity between the external and internal worlds (an Osmondian osmosis!) would not be narratable; *that* comes, in *The Portrait of a Lady*, from the wee and tiny but nonetheless interesting crack that separates the world from an interior we can only guess at. The free indirect style of the passage, the compromised position of narrator and reader in relation to Isabel's thoughts, might in that case be taken not as the overbearing style of the know-it-all, a disciplinary consciousness in touch with all others within its system, but as yet another figure for that crack. As much, in other words, as we recognize the free indirect style as a novelistic innovation that gives narration a power that it so regularly displays in the nineteenth-century novel, the clustering of intentions and perspectives that allows for the irony that frequently accompanies that style's appearance not only exposes blind spots in character but also tends to compromise any clear sense of a novel's intention.[17] Where critics of the too powerful glare of Jamesian vision say that he sees too much, the novel instead offers the play of seeing and not seeing, of knowing and not knowing as its great source of interest and as a model for what narration does when it does good.

The relation between knowing and not knowing, so central to *The Portrait of a Lady*, returns with a vengeance in *The Sacred Fount*. In that novel, a first-person narrator alive to the faintest of shifts in his social world goes for a weekend party to Newmarch, a country estate some distance from London. Newmarch, whose hosts we never meet, appears in the novel as the ideal form of a party, a pure instance of the sociable that encourages its guests on to social perfection and that seems to exist only to facilitate the coming together of clusters of brilliant people talking brilliantly. As, however, it begins to analyze those people, the novel offers up a set of odd logical problems: because Mrs. Brissenden looks ten years younger while her husband, "poor Briss," looks that much older, the strange increase in Gilbert Long's social intelligence must point to an equivalent enfeeblement of his secret lover (whoever that is!). The world, as it is here and as it appears to the novel's narrator, seems as if it is governed by social forms as autonomous as any natural law: "'One of

---

17. "The pleasure of the text is that moment when my body pursues its own ideas—for my body does not have the same ideas I do." The same goes, we should say, for the body of the text. Roland Barthes, *The Pleasure of the Text* (New York: Farrar, Straus and Giroux, Inc., 1975), 17.

them always gets more out of it than the other. One of them—you know the saying—gives the lips, the other the cheek.' 'It's the deepest of all truths.'"[18]

The very limited sense we have of what may or may not exist outside the party world of Newmarch underscores its sociable character; the problems and mysteries of the weekend will, it appears, break up when the party does.[19] The bounded nature of the party is in this sense like an ideal version the novel form: it is a closed system; its rules are, we take it, internally coherent and refer only to content within the system for which they are rules; its temporal influence ends with the end of the novel. The closed nature of the party is what turns it into a text available to the narrator's too, too subtle hermeneutic. What happens, however, in *The Sacred Fount* troubles the closed nature of both the sociable situation and the novel form.

As in the case of James's other first-person pieces, *The Sacred Fount*'s narrator is not reliable, a fact brought into poignant relief in the novel's final scene. After digging into the relations of his fellow guests for 200 pages, the narrator is at last confronted by the astute Mrs. Brissenden: "My poor dear," she tells him, "you *are* crazy, and I bid you good-night!" (187). The narrator, on whom we have counted for our impressions and who has seemed really drunk on his own—"It comes back to me that the sense thus established of my superior vision may perfectly have gone a little to my head" (105)—is done in with a word:

> When once I had started to my room indeed—and to preparation for a livelier start as soon as the house should stir again—I almost breathlessly hurried. Such a last word—the word that put me altogether nowhere—was too unacceptable not to prescribe afresh that prompt test of escape to other air for which I had earlier in the evening seen so much reason. I *should* certainly never again, on the spot, quite hang together, even though it wasn't really that I hadn't three times her method. What I too fatally lacked was her tone. (187)

We have felt the craziness of the narrator throughout the novel, and it is a craziness that would seem to be the inevitable result of the introduction of

---

18. Henry James, *The Sacred Fount* (London: Penguin, 1994), 49; subsequent references to this work will be included in the text.

19. As has been the case, I use "sociable" here in Simmel's sense. Again, for him, sociability exists as the formalization of social behavior into an end in itself. Where in everyday life making money is a matter of life and death, in sociability it takes what he sees as the harmless form of gambling. What's more, the sociable event is internally coherent insofar as every participant must have a sense of where everyone else fits because the perception of superiority, he says, has no place in and in fact ruins the sociable situation. Georg Simmel, "Sociability," in *On Individuality and Social Forms*, ed. Donald N. Levine (Chicago: University of Chicago Press, 1971), 129.

the Jamesian narrative voice into the mix of the story he tells.[20] Peter Brooks
has seen that while the narrator must at least entertain the notion that he is
crazy, the structure of the novel nevertheless preserves his great idea: "But it
(the narrator's madness) is no more provable than it is provable that a game
of chess is crazy. The point is what can be done within the perfect closure
and the rules of the game."[21] The problem here is that Brooks does not learn
the novel's lesson, that the narrator's discovery that "one of them always gets
more out of it than the other," challenges, insofar as it exposes, the dynamics
of power concealed behind sociability's screen, the very idea of perfect social
or aesthetic autonomy. The form of sociability is not strictly autonomous in
relation to its social content, just as the perfect form of the narrator's game
cannot be perfectly closed. Power, labor, difference: all these stand just to the
side of sociability as *mostly* silent rebuke. What the "last word" of Mrs. Briss
does is to obliterate the integrity of a narrative perspective that we as readers
have counted on and that finds, in the case of *The Sacred Fount*, literal embodiment in our potentially crazy narrator. What we have, in other words, is
a specific but nonetheless exemplary failure of the sociable system that is *The
Sacred Fount*.

The narrator does not fail in spite of his method: he fails because of it. The
difference between method and tone ("What I too fatally lacked was her tone")
is that while the former is an a priori category, a thing necessarily external to
the particular system it would address, to have tone is rather to breathe in the
very substance of that system, the air and atmosphere of that closed world.[22]
We can see that the necessary distance between the narrator and what the narrator narrates creates a hole or a rupture within the sociable system of James's
novel. The unnamed narrator of *The Sacred Fount* is nowhere just prior to the
end of the novel not only because his function has exhausted itself with the
completion of the work (indeed, it seems to end suddenly, even prematurely)
but also because his structurally necessary inability to meet the tone of the
Newmarch system has rendered him so obviously unfit to participate within

20. In this way, *The Sacred Fount* enacts at the level of its plot an observation of Dorrit Cohn's: "Our
discussion up to this point suggests a relation of inverse proportion between authorial and figural minds:
the more conspicuous and idiosyncratic the narrator, the less apt he is to reveal the depth of his characters'
psyches or, for that matter, to create psyches that have depth to reveal. It almost seems as though the
authorial narrator jealously guards his prerogative as the sole thinking agent within his novel, sensing
that his equipoise would be endangered by approaching another mind too closely and staying with it too
long . . . " This loss of "equipoise" might be taken as equivalent to what James thinks of as "not hanging
together." Dorrit Cohn, *Transparent Minds: Narrative Modes for Presenting Consciousness in Fiction* (Princeton: Princeton University Press, 1978), 25.

21. Peter Brooks, *The Melodramatic Imagination: Balzac, Henry James, Melodrama, and the Mode of
Excess* (New Haven, CT: Yale University Press, 1976), 176.

22. For more on "tone and method," see chapter 1 for my discussion of Gadamer, sociability, and *sensus
communis*.

the social world of that novel; insofar as narration insists on a privileged point of perspective both outside and in the closed system of sociability, to narrate is to be crazy. To see enough to narrate is to claim a position other than one in the game, which is in turn to fail ever to "hang together."

What *The Sacred Fount* shows us, then, is something different from the simple collapse of seeing and authority. Where Geismar wants us to feel that the Jamesian narrator is nothing if not a disciplinarian, we feel poignantly that it is the bright-eyed narrator of *The Sacred Fount* whose wrist gets slapped hardest by that novel's end. Sociability, Simmel tells us, turns the tragic to play:

> For "good form" is mutual self-definition, interaction of the elements, through which a unity is made; and since in sociability the concrete motives bound up with life-goals fade away, so must the pure form, the free-playing, interacting interdependence of individuals stand out so much the more strongly and operate with so much the greater effect.[23]

What happens, though, when the narrator tries to bring a perspective to the oppressive couple system that seems to express Newmarch at its most sociable is exile: "The narrator's perception of relation in *The Sacred Fount* endangers the homeostatic and motivating fantasy of the couple; doing so, it proclaims itself a perception afforded the outsider, the uncoupled, the excluded, the exiled, the sensitive single gentleman: social pressures compel the narrator's departure from Newmarch before the party's end."[24] The heteronormative form of the couple is a perfect expression of Simmel's best hopes for sociability: difference in the couple is regulated, ironed out by an ideology of static complementarity. The narrator's neatly Hegelian discovery of that "deepest of truths" (one gives where the other takes—the couple system, never equivalent, is marked exactly by the fact of that difference) points to the lie in that particular form of the sociable. As a result, however, of exposing, of naming the ideology behind the sociable, the narrator/character is chased right out of the novel, bringing *The Sacred Fount* to an end.

It is, in that case, significant that James saw the potentially unruly collapse of narration and what it narrates as a productive as opposed to catastrophic problem for *The Princess Casamassima*. The novel is, James suggests in his

---

23. Simmel, "Sociability," 129.

24. Mary Ann O'Farrell, *Telling Complexions: The Nineteenth-Century English Novel and the Blush* (Durham, NC: Duke University Press, 1997), 133.

preface, both an early and an ideal example of a method that would come to define his work, a method that consists of "placing advantageously, placing right in the middle of the light, the most polished of possible mirrors of the subject" (42). The danger here is that the mirror, the responsive consciousness of some central character, might shine too brightly, might come off as "too *interpretative* of the muddle of fate, or in other words too divinely, too prig-gishly clever" (37). This danger, familiar to us from *The Sacred Fount*, might be seen as pouring too freely into the vessel of character the interpretive force of narration, a danger that James tries to prevent with his assertion of an important difference:

> To find his [Hyacinth's] possible adventure interesting I had only to conceive his watching the same public show, the same innumerable appearances, I had watched myself, and of his watching very much as I had watched; save indeed for one little difference. This difference would be that so far as all the swarming facts should speak of freedom and ease, knowledge and power, money, opportunity, and satiety, he should be able to revolve around them but at the most respectful of distances and with every door of approach shut in his face. (34)

The difference here is only in part the very obvious difference in the social positions of an American novelist in London and that novelist's diminished surrogate: a little cockney bookbinder. For while it is true that James would have had access to homes whose doors remain closed to his proletarian hero, the spectral ability everywhere on display in *The Princess Casamassima* to pass through those doors, to watch anywhere and anytime, to command "all the swarming facts," is associated more with James as omniscient narrator than James as a man-about-town. That difference, which we have seen in previous chapters as a structurally precarious one, does in this case count on class for its stability. Where in *The Sacred Fount* the obliteration of that difference produced a character that other characters see as *crazy*, the relation between narration and character in *The Princess Casamassima* relies on a set of social distinctions less slippery if also less obviously formal. Where, as we have seen in previous chapters, narration's structuring difference from character tends by itself to waver, social differences might be pointed enough to give narration its much needed definition; narration, as James describes it in his preface, draws some of its form from a social difference that the novel takes as one of its principal themes.

It is significant, in that case, that it is exactly that social difference that collapses so spectacularly in the person of Hyacinth Robinson. With Hyacinth torn between the low conditions in which he was raised, his fuzzy aristocratic origins, and the bad example of his murdering French mother, his problem is that he seems not to fit anywhere within the social order, a fact that not only

seems to give him that ability to see which threatens to render him "too prig-
gishly clever" but also allows him to elude the hard looks of others.[25] It is, after
all, because of his indistinct origins that he is so quickly "picked up" by the anarchist movement: Hyacinth, because of his peculiar sense of style, would be
able smoothly to infiltrate with pistol or bomb the enclaves of the aristocracy.
It appears, in other words, that there is something about the cultivated character of Hyacinth Robinson, something perfect that seems to exceed the otherwise perfect vision of the law. For if it is the failure of most anarchists that
they look too much like anarchists, Hyacinth, in ways that go quite beyond
the novel's often strained naturalist logic, arrives dressed for success. After
delivering a rousing speech at the Sun and Moon that surprises even himself,
Hyacinth is invited by Paul Muniment to meet and plot with the great revolutionary, Hoffendahl. It is not, however, on the strength of his oration that
Hyacinth ascends to a higher degree within the anarchist movement:

> "Are you going now—to see Hoffendahl?" Hyacinth cried.
>   "Don't shout it all over the place. He wants a genteel little customer
> like you," Muniment went on.
>   "Is it true? Are we going?" Hyacinth demanded eagerly.
>   "Yes, these two are in it; they are not very artful, but they are safe,"
> said Muniment, looking at Poupin and Schinkel.
>   "Are you the genuine article, Muniment?" asked Hyacinth, catching
> this look.
>   Muniment dropped his eyes on him; then he said, "Yes, you're the
> boy he wants." (296)

What secures Hyacinth's position in the group is first a look and second his
looks. The moment is in the first case an orchestrated exchange of glances the
meaning of which depends not on the firm convictions of a revolutionary
party or even simple clear-sightedness but on a flirty play of unspoken if suspected intentions conveyed but never guaranteed by significant but opaque
acts of seeing. There is also the question of Hyacinth's *looks*. We are reminded
throughout *The Princess Casamassima* of Hyacinth's difference from the others of his class, a difference easily registered by the other disgruntled almost-
anarchists at the Sun and Moon. "A genteel little customer," Hyacinth holds
on to his place at the pub not through a shared and stable class identity or

---

25. Sara Blair notices that a naturalist logic which should serve typologically to "place" Hyacinth within
a social field falls weirdly short in *The Princess Casamassima*: "Although apparently 'foredoomed' to a double life framed by the warring instincts of the 'bastard' and the 'gentleman,' Hyacinth never convincingly
embodies the 'mixed, divided nature'—the fatal self-division—dictated by his blood." Sara Blair, *Henry
James and the Writing of Race and Nation* (Cambridge: Cambridge University Press, 1996), 94.

through any particular proof of political commitment but through an explicitly sentimentalized narrative of his origins, a narrative related, Hyacinth guesses, with appropriate national pride by Hyacinth's French friend and co-worker, Eustache Poupin:

> He had an intimate conviction—the proof of it was in the air, in the sensible facility of his footing at the "Sun and Moon"—that Eustache Poupin had taken upon himself to disseminate that anecdote of his origin, of his mother's disaster; in consequence of which, as a victim of social infamy, of heinous laws, it was conceded to him that he had a larger account to settle even than most. He was *ab ovo* a revolutionist, and that balanced against his smart neckties, a certain suspicious security that was perceived in him as to the *h* (he had had from his earliest years a natural command of it), and the fact that he possessed the sort of hand on which there was always a premium—an accident somehow to be guarded against in a thorough-going system of equality. (282)

Of course, the qualities that make Hyacinth barely suited to be a member of the class for which he wants to do battle are exactly those that suit him for the job of terrorist. His "smart neckties," his bearing, his hold on his aitches: all these will allow Hyacinth a proximity to the upper classes for which the chemist Muniment—with his visibly work-stained hands—could never hope. Hyacinth, because of his weird sophistication, will pass unnoticed, invisible by the guardians of the rich. The preceding passage suggests another uncanny point of identification between Hyacinth and the voice that would describe him. Narration follows its mention of Hyacinth's lucky knack for the standard aitch—a knack that facilitates the pronunciation of Millicent Henning and Hyacinth's own name—with the phrase, "he had had," a conspicuous and slightly nervous demonstration of narration's own natural command of that particular class indicator. We might take this as another point at which the disciplinary stability of the narrative position seems somewhat compromised, a moment where Hyacinth picks up some of narration's authority and where narration, nervous at the novel's superabundance of class passing, slumming, and social mobility, asserts its status in a way that stands as a familiar symptom of creaturely social anxiety.

Hoffendahl himself is clear about what he sees or, rather, *doesn't see* in Hyacinth Robinson:

> To be sure, Hoffendahl had known nothing about him in advance; he had only been suggested by those who were looking out, from one day to the other. The fact remained however that when Hyacinth stood

before him he recognized him as the sort of little chap that he had in his eye (one who could pass through a small orifice). (334)

The whole phrasing here is, needless to say, peculiar. What would it mean to have an object of interest "in one's eye"? The difference between having one's eye *on something* and having something *in one's eye* is quite the difference between the disciplinary gaze and a special kind of blindness, a blindness that would result from an obstruction in or on the eye itself. A blindness like this is the scotomization referred to by Freud in his essay on the fetish: "Scotomization . . . suggests that the perception is entirely wiped out, so that the result is the same as when a visual impression falls on the blind spot in the retina."[26] Scotomization differs from both neurotic repression and psychotic disavowal insofar as where the latter two processes involve a working over of material (affects in the first case and ideas in the second), "scotomization" suggests the obliteration of the material in question, a psychic vicissitude that runs quite counter to the parsimonious spirit of Freud's economic system. The thing repressed had once been seen, the thing scotomized, never. Hyacinth, in this case, is importantly neither repressed nor disavowed by Hoffendahl's vision (seen but ignored or figured into some other less distressing thing), but is in fact the index of his own cancellation. Hoffendahl doesn't just not see Hyacinth: he doesn't see *exactly* Hyacinth. Hyacinth is the perfect obstruction to the view of himself, a Hyacinth-shaped flaw on Hoffendahl's eye. It is thus strange that Hyacinth is the "sort of chap" who could pass *through* "a small orifice," since, at least in the case of Hoffendahl, it was exactly *in* a small orifice (his eye) that Hyacinth seems to have gotten stuck.[27]

Hyacinth's character, caught between different positions in the system in which the anarchists want him to operate, is at once hard to ignore and easy to miss. There is, in other words, something in Hyacinth's development that has produced a character that gets somehow to get past the close looks of the law while remaining entirely interesting to us. We might take as further evidence an exchange between the Princess and Hyacinth in which she tries

---

26. Sigmund Freud, "Fetishism," in *The Standard Edition of the Complete Psychological Works of Sigmund Freud*, 24 vols., trans. James Strachey (London: Hogarth Press, 1961), 21:153–54.

27. We must see, too, that Hoffendahl (or narration) is engaging in another of what Hugh Stevens has seen as "repeated suggestive *double entendres*, in which the secret holes of anarchist activity suggest both the furtiveness of homoerotic encounters and the more hidden apertures of the human body, [which] appear to [the reader as] knowing asides . . . which are embarrassing to the perpetually compromised Hyacinth." The preceding example is indeed another of these, a case that at least doubles the possible intentions that may or may not guarantee Hoffendahl's revolutionary agenda. And though Stevens leaves it as just a hint, we must wonder at what it would mean for Hyacinth to feel embarrassed about what his reader might be thinking. Hugh Stevens, *Henry James and Sexuality* (Cambridge: Cambridge University Press, 1998), 107.

to understand what it is that makes him tick. Hyacinth's initial introduction to the Princess is secured simply through the chance of his being an available poor person at the opera house where the Princess, Captain Sholto, and Madame Grandoni sit and watch *The Pearl of Paraguay* (the Princess has become interested in the "social problem" and wants to meet someone poor and angry). But it is not his class position that really hooks the Princess Casamassima. Later in the novel:

> The Princess admitted, frankly, that he would, to her sense, take a
> great deal of accounting for; she observed that he was, no doubt,
> pretty well used to himself, but he must give other people time. "I
> have watched you, constantly, since you have been here, in every detail
> of your behaviour, and I am more and more *intriguée*. You haven't a
> vulgar intonation, you haven't a common gesture, you never make a
> mistake, you do and say everything exactly in the right way. You come
> out of the hole you have described to me, and yet you might have
> stayed in country houses all your life." (337)

In the same way that being a "genteel little customer" becomes the paradoxical guarantee of Hyacinth's revolutionary credibility, so does Hyacinth (at least temporarily) attract the interest of the Princess with his strange and surprising perfection. It catches the Princess off guard to find that Hyacinth is so right in the same way that it surprised her to discover he "knew Schopenhauer" (329). But Hyacinth is not merely right here: he is, to the Princess's discriminating eye, never wrong. Hyacinth never makes a mistake.

What would it mean never to make a mistake? On the one hand, we see that this is another indicator of what is strange about Hyacinth's character: the mixed-up result of a generically canned affair between a debauched English aristocrat and a mad French seamstress followed by a petit bourgeois upbringing in an obscure corner of London, Hyacinth is most odd and most familiar (familiar, that is, to novel readers who know their genealogy plots) because of the way he manifests his complicated origins in good manners that give the game immediately away. On the other hand, even the most polished of gentlemen cannot be counted on *never* to make a mistake; in any case, Hyacinth's manners, as good as they are, don't begin to get him over that all-important definitional hump: "'Do you mean I am a gentleman?' asked Hyacinth, in a peculiar tone, looking out into the wet garden. She hesitated, and then she said, 'It's I who make the mistakes!'" (337). The Princess is embarrassed by the question; Hyacinth is embarrassed by her implicit answer; and we, we who know with James that Hyacinth is doomed, are embarrassed for them. It is, after all, Hyacinth's problem that he cannot fit in anywhere; he is not a gentleman, but he is also not *not* a gentleman.

Considered in its ordinary-language sense, the Princess's phrase seems to mean something different from what the genealogy plot could by itself suggest, something more like: everyone, even a gentleman, makes mistakes, so why don't you? In other words, Hyacinth's odd perfection not only doesn't allow him to blend in perfectly with high society but also denies him one of the qualities that we take as proof of the merely—or the really—human: people make mistakes. We have already seen that one of the ways in which the bourgeois novel produces its character effects is to suggest that a given character can make mistakes, an ability that we take as an index of interiority. More than this textual strategy, however, making mistakes is important not only in terms of the world of convention on which the novel often draws for its effects of verisimilitude but also in the sense suggested by Freud's account of the mechanism of the parapraxis in *The Psychopathology of Everyday Life*. If the mistake in general suggests the presence of an inside, in Freud it is an index of repression, the psychic process that not only manages what content we cannot allow into consciousness but also *produces* the psychic apparatus insofar as that apparatus is the relation between consciousness and an unconscious that is itself the structural result of repressions that eventually surface in the form of dreams, jokes, neuroses, and mistakes. Freud, as Strachey suggests in his introduction, counted on his work in *The Psychopathology* to make general ideas that might have seemed only to apply to extreme cases: "The special affection with which Freud regarded parapraxes was no doubt due to the fact that they, along with dreams, were what enabled him to extend to normal life the discoveries he had first made in connection with neuroses."[28] What Freud took as the normal process of making mistakes was tied directly to the process of repression so crucial to the workings and origin of the Freudian psyche. Repressed content, ideas, and information return in the form of what everybody knows as "slips." Mistakes are always explicable in terms of some reference to socially proscripted desire, which the mistake—a distorted compromise expression of that desire—allows us to leave safely beneath the surface of consciousness.[29] The mistake insofar as it is an index of repression in general is both a repetition and proof of the primary repression on the basis of which the psychic apparatus is as a whole structured; the mistake figures repression, which founds the unconscious, which, in turn, makes us human.

Hyacinth, in that case, poses a problem for the Princess not only because of the nonsense he seems to make of class distinction but also because he lacks

28. Sigmund Freud, *The Psychopathology of Everyday Life*, trans. James Strachey (New York: Norton, 1965), xiii.

29. For a critique of Freud's insistence on the relation between the mistake and repression, see Sebastiano Timpanaro, *The Freudian Slip: Psychoanalysis and Textual Criticism*, trans. Kate Soper (London: Verso, 1985).

for her, as he did for Hoffendahl, the socializing mark of repression; not to make a mistake is not to have repressed, is not, finally, to possess the hole in one's psychic life (the crack in one's cup) that Freud calls the unconscious. To go without that hole, without that proof of interiority while still making some kind of sense, is to run against the grain of a novel system as particularly invested in character as is James's. In other words, if it is by now routine to notice that literary characters do not quite hang together, that what subjectivity they seem to possess is merely a subjectivity effect and not the result of a real denotational anchor that might resolve discrete aspects of a character into a coherent whole (there is "an idea in his dress"), it is something different altogether to read a novel in which other characters nervously make that literary critical observation about one of their own.

The Princess's surprise at the fact that he never makes a mistake is indeed connected explicitly to Hyacinth's repeated claim that he comes from a hole: "You come out of the hole you have described to me, and yet . . . you never make a mistake." As we have begun to see, however, her surprise refers less to how it is that one could come from a hole and yet still never make a mistake and more to how it is that Hyacinth, *because* he never makes a mistake, hasn't a hole at all. So, when the Princess says that she is surprised that Hyacinth comes from a hole and yet makes no mistakes, we can take it that she refers not only to the material circumstances of his upbringing but also to the hole that every one is supposed to carry around, the lack or crack in the cup of the self that allows for the process of substitution that produces not only significant mistakes but also character as such. She begins, in other words, to wonder what kind of thing Hyacinth Robinson might be. Insofar as Hyacinth's problem is exactly the damning obscurity of his origins, we might read the Princess's take on his situation as a vulgar if elaborate pun: Hyacinth, a bastard, is a "mistake" who never makes mistake, which, we begin to see, is its own especially damaging kind of mistake.

The material hole that James provides for Hyacinth indeed makes us wonder. Although James seems engaged with the realist details of Lomax Place, the neighborhood in which Hyacinth grew up under the guidance of Amanda Pynsent and the fiddler Anastatious Vetch, it is hardly a hole if we take "hole" to mean some kind of a slum.[30] In fact, the "beastliness" of Lomax Place is something more like the dirtiness of the child Millicent Henning: Hyacinth, we are told, "hated people who were not fresh, who had smutches and streaks. Millicent Henning generally had two or three, which she borrowed from her

---

30. Hyacinth almost unfailingly refers to Lomax Place as a "hole": "'So it is; it's a beastly hole,' said the young man" (103); "'Very likely. That's the kind of rot they talk in that precious hole,' the young man said, without blenching" (110).

doll, into whom she was always rubbing her nose and whose dinginess was contagious" (62). If, however "contagious," Millicent Henning's doll is as bad as it gets in Lomax Place, Hyacinth's home seems neither very dirty nor very much like a hole. Where James might have taken Hyacinth's childhood home as an opportunity to flex realist muscle with a really foul depiction of a really foul place, he chooses instead to drop Hyacinth into a kind of "clean mess," a worn but respectable home whose "smutches and streaks" more *signify* poverty than gross us out. James's realism, or rather his naturalism, is not conveyed in the case of Hyacinth's home by some special detail, a usefully useless item that would like Flaubert's barometer signify the real instead of really representing anything.[31] Instead, it is for James the single stain, the single dirty spot that guarantees the quality of the scene. The overall and conspicuously clean realism of Hyacinth's neighborhood is naturalized by the presence of a smutch; like letters on a page, the degraded stain is not added to the waiting canvas of the real but rather works retroactively to naturalize the scene of James's labored literary realism.

It is, in that case, not surprising that the quality of James's realism would at this point have more to do with the conspicuous digestion of literary convention's light fare than with any "ripe round fruit of" documentary "perambulation" (33).[32] We can see, for instance, a marked similarity between certain aspects of poverty in James and the description of Ma Vauquer's boardinghouse in *Père Goriot*. Piles of stuff that seem as much to have grown up out of the furniture as to have fallen away from any dress in progress (Pinnie is a dressmaker), the details of shabby economy ("a small bottle which had formerly contained eau-de-cologne and which now exhibited half a pint of a rich gold-colored liquid"), and an assortment of by-the-way neighbors whose circumstances suggest some obscure "fall" (Mr Vetch: "he had . . . the glamour of reduced gentility and fallen fortunes . . . though he lived in a single backroom, in a house where she had never seen a window washed") all signify

---

31. Roland Barthes takes an incidental barometer from Madame Aubain's home in Flaubert's "A Simple Heart" as an exemplary instance of the reality effect, "an object which is neither incongruous nor significant, and which, therefore, at first sight, seems not to belong to the domain of the *notable*." Instead, suggests Barthes, of signifying anything in particular, such objects say through the very fact of their insignificance that "*we are the real.*" Roland Barthes, "The Reality Effect," in *French Literature Today*, ed. Tzvetan Todorov (Cambridge: Cambridge University Press, 1982), 11, 16.

32. In this oft-quoted 1884 note to Thomas Sergeant Perry, James seems to acknowledge, tongue firmly in cheek, the tepidness of his real commitment to literary naturalism: "I have been all the morning at Millbank prison (horrible place) collecting notes for a fiction scene. You see I am quite the Naturalist." Henry James, *Henry James: Letters*, 3 vols. ed. Leon Edel (Cambridge, MA: Belknap Press of Harvard University Press, 1974–84), 3:61.

rather than represent a mostly textual poverty taken generally from a realist and naturalist canon and from Balzac in particular.[33]

Hyacinth's hole, then, begins to emerge as a less and less surprising origin for his character. Hyacinth is a careful reader (with a taste for "advanced" French literature) and has been so since his childhood:

> He used to stand there for half an hour at a time, spelling out the first page of the romances in the Family Herald and the London Journal, and admiring the obligatory illustration in which the noble characters (they were always of the highest birth) were presented to the carnal eye. When he had a penny he spent only a fraction of it on stale sugar-candy; with the remaining halfpenny he always bought a ballad, with a vivid woodcut at the top. (54)

His tastes run toward the same kinds of materials that produced him. Or, to put it differently, Hyacinth's conspicuous sophistication comes at least in part from his mastery of and, in fact, his embeddedness in a system of literary reference.[34] Indeed, his coming to terms with his past is conducted mostly at

---

33. It is worth pointing out that, in his *other* naturalist novel, James uses the same technique in his lingering description of Basil Ransom's "shabby rooms in a somewhat decayed mansion which stood next to the corner of the Second Avenue." In a description that takes, in fact, much more from Balzac, James allows a somewhat more involved narrative eye to roam slowly over the details of the house, recalling as much in style as in the choice of particular details, the effect produced in the opening sequence of *Père Goriot*. What's more, James ends his description with an excuse for his lingering: "I mention it not on account of any particular influence it might have had on the life or the thoughts of Basil Ransom, but for old acquaintance sake and that of local color." In a novel that, with *The Princess Casamassima*, formed James's closest engagement with the naturalism of Zola, the brash lack of interest in the effects of environment on character is striking. And, while the appeal to acquaintance has been taken to refer to James's onetime residence in that area of New York City, we might take the line rather as a sly note of gratitude to another old acquaintance: Honoré de Balzac. Henry James, *The Bostonians*, ed. Charles R. Anderson (London: Penguin, 1984), 195.

34. *The Princess Casamassima* is an especially allusive book. On the one hand, Hyacinth as the sensitive cockney, who quotes "Ode to a Nightingale" to himself in order to acclimate himself to the strangely pastoral grounds of Medley cannot but remind us of Keats, one of James's favorite poets and a figure for whom class embarrassment was a well-known and determining issue. Or, on the other hand, the specter of Hyacinth's grandfather, the clock maker, reminds us of Rousseau's father in *The Confessions*, a connection that serves—as so many like details in the novel do—the French revolutionary foundation upon which James constructs his later anarchist's tale. One can also find in the novel persistent references to Delacroix, a figure who would have represented for James the same sort of temporal bind that structures the historical position of his novel: it cannot, in some sense, decide whether it describes the political situation in the 1880s or in the heat of the French Revolution; this same dilemma was productive for Delacroix's greatest works, though they were caught, as T. J. Clark suggests, more properly between the revolutionary promise of 1848 and the disappointing fact of 1851. Christopher Ricks, *Keats and Embarrassment* (Oxford: Clarendon Press, 1984), especially 115–42; T. J. Clark, *The Absolute Bourgeois: Artists and Politics in France 1848–1851* (Berkeley: University of California Press, 1999), 124–78.

the British Library as he looks over various newspaper reports on the circumstances surrounding his mother's murder of his alleged father.[35] This textual savvy, as we have seen, does a few things for Hyacinth. For one, it gives (or at least this is the hope of the great Hoffendahl) him a kind of social invisibility. Paradoxically, it is also what everyone notices about Hyacinth Robinson.

Hyacinth's style, if it is wrong, is wrong because it goes too far. The details of his clothes—his nice ties, his "soft circular hat"—these suggest, as I mentioned at the beginning, that there is "an idea in his dress," a style that his compromised class position should not allow. Or rather, although style suggests in Hyacinth's case the presence of an "idea" or an intention in his dress, a denotative center that would guarantee the coherence of his details and the wholeness of their effect, that idea is—as was suggested at the beginning of this chapter—finally withheld.[36] Hyacinth's childhood playmate, Millicent Henning, having grown into a "handsome young woman," sees Hyacinth right off as in costume: "What she liked was his face, and something jaunty and entertaining, almost theatrical in his whole little person. Miss Henning was not acquainted with any member of the dramatic profession, but she supposed, vaguely that that was the way an actor would look in private life" (104). When, later, she says as much to him, Hyacinth initially rebels but then holds back: "He was on the point of replying that he didn't care for fancy costumes, he wished to go through life in his own character; but he checked himself, with the reflection that this was exactly what, apparently, he was destined not to do" (109). Hyacinth's "own character" is overwhelmed by the details of his dress; his "costume" does too much for his body. The handsome Millicent Henning is cast, although she cares quite as much for her clothes as anyone, as an opposite sort of person:

> She was very handsome, with a shining, bold, good-natured eye, a
> fine, free, facial oval, an abundance of brown hair, and a smile which
> showed the whiteness of her teeth. Her head was set upon a fair,

35. Sara Blair, for instance, points out that James's generic commitment to naturalism is unstable in exactly these terms: Hyacinth, while marked throughout with the traces of his finally indeterminate racial origins, nevertheless emerges as an instance of Jamesian self-fashioning. "This idiom of inherited 'racial' type enables the redirection of James's signature interest in the self-fashioning of the finely aware intelligence profiting by cultural 'accumulations.'" Blair, *Henry James and the Writing of Race and Nation*, 95–96.

36. In a chapter with the charming title "Hats and *The Princess Casamassima*," Clair Hughes points out that Hyacinth's hat is an especially potent if finally ambiguous *vesteme*: "Confused by a tradesman in the wrong part of the house, by Hyacinth's style of dress—and by the fact that, seemingly *au fait* with the requirements of etiquette, he has removed his hat in the drawing-room and is waiting to greet his hostess before relinquishing it—the Prince, a straightforward if simple limited man, understandably wonders whether this bookbinder has designs on his status, his silver, or his wife." Clair Hughes, *Henry James and the Art of Dress* (London: Palgrave, 2001), 90.

strong neck, and her tall young figure was rich in feminine curves. Her gloves, covering her wrists insufficiently, showed the redness of those parts, in the interstices of the numerous silver bracelets that encircled them, and Miss Pynsent made the observation that her hands were not more delicate than her feet. (92)

Where Hyacinth comes off as an occasion for a tie, for a Frenchman's smock (he feels this even though "he had never before seen one"), or, really, for his unusually good French, Millicent is all body; she bursts with health through her fashionable clothes and holds on to—indeed, she cannot hide it—her bodily "character" regardless of what she wears.

How different for Hyacinth. Just as his is a textual body that emerges from a textual "hole" (the very literary Lomax Place), so is it composed out of details, discrete sartorial elements that hide or quite overpower whatever it is that we are to think he is. So, just as the hole of Lomax Place is a hole not because it is "really" filthy but because it instead is only textual, a description without a referent, so is Hyacinth's body textual, a clean mess of details that cluster precariously around Hyacinth's lack of a lack.[37] The relation of Hyacinth's outfits to his body seems like a material performance of the relation between the discrete semes that constitute what we can ever know about a character and the Proper Name around which they are clustered and which only appears to resolve them into a whole greater than the sum of their parts.[38] What makes Hyacinth different from other characters is that this is true not only in terms of our relationship to the character within the readerly text but also in terms of what other characters within the novel seem to feel about Hyacinth; where, we might say, other characters were put off in *The Sacred Fount* by the feeling that the narrator was always narrating, Hyacinth's troubled success in *The Princess Casamassima* is not only a matter of the overdetermination of his mysterious birth (a generic donée meant to convey meaning only through its rote familiarity) but also the result of the fact that other characters sense that Hyacinth is a literary character walking among them, a recognition we feel at work when Millicent sees that Hyacinth is an actor in need of "going about in character" or when Paul Muniment notices that he looks just "like a young man in an illustrated story-book" (210).

37. Indeed, when we first see the grown-up Hyacinth, we are told that a painter would like to make a sketch of him. That it would be a sketch instead of a painting is telling; where we take it that the painting is the effort to capture the whole of a subject, the sketch is rather a form that foregrounds an important detail in order to convey a broader, usually social significance. We might think of the police sketch: the artist re-creates the whole from only parts, only details.

38. Roland Barthes, *S/Z: An Essay*, trans. Richard Miller (New York: Hill and Wang, 1974), 94.

It is not, in that case, surprising that a creature as odd as Hyacinth would be well suited to participate in the attenuated political life that *The Princess Casamassima* looks to represent. His inability to "hang together," if we believe some of what has been written about the novel, might just resemble James's own vague relation to the political situation he describes. It has been a persistent criticism of *The Princess Casamassima* that the book exposes James's ignorance about the revolutionary scene he chose to depict; James's *not knowing* about his subject has been taken as a distortion, as that which would make what was to be an exercise in literary naturalism into something disturbing, into what Rebecca West called "a mad dream." A comparison of the first edition, published in 1886, and the New York Edition of the novel shows that James himself recognized that he had made a mistake or two about what real revolutionaries were really like. Among the many changes he made to the text of *The Princess* for the 1908 edition, one that stands out is a shift in political vocabulary. In the first version, Vetch, pumping Hyacinth for information, asks him about his relation to "the International," a term that, as Christine DeVine points out, would have functioned easily in the moral panic surrounding terrorism in the 1880s as a vague keyword for almost any kind of revolutionary activity: in the *Times,* for instance, the March 1881 assassination of Czar Alexander is vaguely attributed to "an international society, having for its watchword the murder of Monarchs and the overthrow of governments."[39] The idea of an "International" gave narrative focus and meaning to a disparate set of terrorist acts that contributed to James's famous "imagination of disaster" at the end of the nineteenth century: the assassinations of Czar Alexander and President Garfield, the Phoenix Park murders, the dynamiting of the underground in 1882, the explosion in the House of Commons in 1885, and so on. In January 1885, James wrote to Grace Norton: "There is very little 'going on'—the country is gloomy, anxious, and London reflects its gloom. Westminster Hall and the Tower were blown up two days ago by Irish Dynamiters." James is, in this regard, a man very much of his time, a man of that "half-century during which the bourgeois imaginary was haunted by the infamous figure of the bomb-throwing nihilist or anarchist."[40] One could imagine dealing with an

---

39. Quoted in Christine DeVine, "Revolution and Democracy in the London *Times* and *The Princess Casamassima,*" *Henry James Review* 23 (2002): 53–71. I am indebted to DeVine's piece in the passages that follow.

40. Mike Davis, in Jon Weiner, "Mike Davis Talks about the 'Heroes of Hell,'" *Radical History Review* 85 (2003), 227. Davis locates the beginning of that "half-century" in 1878. To associate that fear with the bourgeois imaginary is not, however, to say that there was no reason to be afraid. The first half of the 1880s was marked by a steady and often successful stream of assassinations and bombings in London and beyond; between 1883 and 1885, successful and unsuccessful attacks were made on the Local Government Board Offices in London, the offices of the *Times,* two underground railways, Victoria Station, Scotland Yard, St. James's Square, Nelson's Column, London Bridge, the House of Commons, Westminster Hall,

irrational but nevertheless singularly intentional "international"; how much harder to imagine regulating social and economic conditions that might produce local and spontaneous and unrelated expressions of dissatisfaction in the absence of any particular organization. If, however, the "International" had an appeal for James when *The Princess Casamassima* was first published, we can assume that it was the term's increasingly solid relation to the First International Working Men's Association, created in St. Martin's Hall in London on September 28, 1864, and the Second International, formed in 1889, that made the term all too particular for James by 1908. What's more, the very effect that James sought, the "sketchiness and vagueness and dimness" of pure violence, could easily be ruined by too material an association with any one thing. James's was not, after all, a history book.

As a result, James changes references to that organization in the later edition to "the Subterranean." The following is from a conversation between Vetch and Hyacinth in the first version of the novel:

> "Well, now the other matter—the International—are you very deep in that?" the fiddler went on, as if he had not heard him. (172)

In the New York Edition:

> "Well, now the other thing—what do they call it? The Subterranean?—are you very deep in that?" the fiddler went on as if he had not heard him.[41]

Where the first name threatened to reduce the effect of floating anxiety that James wished to capture to a particular historical problem, the Subterranean catches better the tone of violence's dispersed threat in the world of *The Princess Camassima*: politics is something essentially obscure, a thing that one falls deep into (the threat of "falling deeply" in the first version seems almost to have produced James's later and less referential name), something that doesn't necessarily hang together. And like the mostly textual hole from which Hyacinth emerges, the Subterranean is explicitly not some secret cave, not some

---

and the Tower of London (most of these attacks were connected to Irish nationalists). These local attacks were vaguely associated with attacks and assassinations occurring at the same time in Russia, France, Italy, Germany, and Spain. See DeVine, Trilling, and Derek Brewer's introduction to *The Princess Casamassima* for more on James's familiarity with terrorism in the 1880s. See also Paul Avrich, *Anarchist Portraits* (Princeton, NJ: Princeton University Press, 1988).

41. Henry James, *The Princess Casamassima*, New York Edition, vol. 5 (New York: Scribner's, 1908), 181.

real place; it is a place that isn't a place at all. It is one more hole that is no hole.[42]

In these terms, terrorism for James was not a historically knowable object but a kind of static in society, a dissonance within the political imaginary that during the period in which he wrote *The Princess* seemed to James to structure the political experience of social life. Lionel Trilling puts the case in this way:

> Henry James in the eighties understood what we have painfully learned from our grim glossary of wars and concentration camps, after having seen the state and human nature laid open to our horrified inspection. "But I have the imagination of disaster—and see life as ferocious and sinister": James wrote this to A. C. Benson in 1896, and what so bland a young man as Benson made of the statement, what anyone then was likely to make of it, is hard to guess. But nowadays we know that such an imagination is one of the keys to truth.[43]

Trilling is right to see that James managed early on to get at an anxiety that characterizes modernity and our own terrifying slice of it; still, what is there to *know* about such an imagination? What can one ever *know* about anxiety? We may feel with James and Hyacinth that there is something, anything bubbling beneath "the vast smug surface" of society without knowing finally what it is that we are so worried about. What Trilling suggests about James is important and runs against the grain of his famous defense of *The Princess Casamassima* as a historical document of particular accuracy: "For the truth is that there is not a political event of *The Princess Casamassima*, not a detail of oath or mystery or danger, which is not confirmed by multitudinous records."[44] In other words, politics in the novel is represented not by the International (a nameable, historical organization against which we can test the mimetic effect of James's writing) but—as James himself saw in 1908—by something *subterranean*, a figural hole that is not a hole around which the social sentiments of

---

42. We might compare James's Subterranean with the secret organization in G. K. Chesterton's *The Man Who Was Thursday*; if *The Princess Casamassima* finds some of its humor in the disparity between Hyacinth's high hopes and the bungling reality of Hoffendahl and his officers, in Chesterton, the joke is that anarchists *really do* live underground. After rocketing down a secret elevator that had moments before been a pub's table, Gabriel Syme, secret agent, gets his first look at the terrorist's "subterranean" headquarters: "In the door there was a sort of hatchway or grating, and on this Gregory struck five times. A heavy voice with a foreign accent asked him who he was. To this he gave the more or less unexpected reply, 'Mr. Joseph Chamberlain.' The heavy hinges began to move; it was obviously some kind of password." G. K. Chesterton, *The Man Who Was Thursday* (London: Penguin, 1986), 22.

43. Lionel Trilling, *The Liberal Imagination: Essays on Literature and Society* (Garden City, NY: Doubleday Anchor, 1953), 57.

44. Ibid., 64.

his characters are organized and which structures the novel itself. As we again and again learn, political life is inevitably, disastrously built exactly on the basis of what we do not know.

It is in these terms that James makes his famous defense of ignorance within the preface to the novel; James admits to his own not knowing not as a failing but as an indispensable element of composition in the whole of *The Princess Casamassima*:

> Let me at the same time not deny that, in answer to probable ironic
> reflexions on the full license for sketchiness and vagueness and dimness
> taken indeed by my picture, I had to bethink myself in advance of a
> defense of my "artistic position." Shouldn't I find it in the happy conten-
> tion that the value I wished most to render and the effect I wished most
> to produce were precisely those of our not knowing, of society's not
> knowing, but only guessing and suspecting and trying to ignore, what
> "goes on" irreconcilably, subversively, beneath the vast smug surface? (48)

There is in the structure of society a motivating blankness that, paradoxically, becomes a quantity well worth representing. James establishes a structural consonance between the shape of his own creative consciousness (a conscious-ness that does not, as he obliquely admits, know very much about politics), the limited experience of his protagonist, and it is implied, the epistemologi-cal structure of his novel. Throughout that novel, whenever Hyacinth works to express himself in political terms, he seems self-consciously to fade away as if he does not really believe or understand what he is saying. We might, on the one hand, take this as an expression of the ambivalence Hyacinth feels with regard to the revolution; he is in "too deep" in too many different ways to distance himself from the rhetoric of revolution. On the other hand, it seems clear that there is a real ignorance here, an ignorance that is not the failure of politics but one of its preconditions:

> "The manner in which [it] is organized is what astonished me; I knew
> that, or thought I knew it, in a general way, but the reality was a reve-
> lation. And on top of it all, society lives! People go and come, and buy
> and sell, and drink and dance, and make money and make love, and
> seem to know nothing and suspect nothing and think of nothing; and
> iniquities flourish, and the misery of half the world is prated about as
> a 'necessary evil,' and day follows day, and everything is for the best in
> the best of possible worlds. All that is one-half of it; the other half is
> that everything is doomed! In silence, in darkness, but under the feet
> of each one of us, the revolution lives and works. It is a wonderful, im-
> measurable trap, on the lid of which society performs its antics." (330)

What is he talking about? What exactly *has* he seen in his one, brief encounter with Hoffendahl? And what, in a meeting that included the somewhat absurd revolutionary trio of Schinkel, Poupin, and Paul Muniment, gave him the impression of a perfectly organized party of world revolution? The question doesn't finally matter. It is rather the fact of invisibility, of secrecy, of impenetrability that gives this threat its strength.

The maddening vagueness of the passage is reminiscent of the many points at which, in *The Bostonians*, Verena Tarrant makes her political speeches under the spell of mesmerism. On the occasions when we do hear them, we are inclined to agree with Basil Ransom that they make little sense. For the most part, however, James chooses not to focus on the speeches and rather describes almost anything else: "The historian who has gathered these documents together does not deem it necessary to give a larger specimen of Verena's eloquence, especially as Basil Ransom, through whose ears we are listening to it, arrived, at this point, at a definite conclusion."[45] This technique does two things. First, it releases James from the difficult task of writing political speeches. Second, and more important, it points to James's chief insight about the political in both *The Bostonians* and *The Princess Casamassima*: not knowing is a fact of composition not only in his novel about politics but also in politics as such.[46] Confusion, bad faith, hucksterism: these are not facts that James can simply discount. Rather, their positive role in the organization of political consciousness is central to the complicated theoretical project of *The Princess Casamassima*.

What, in other words, motivates the revolutionaries at the Sun and Moon as well as Hyacinth and the Princess is precisely the absence of direct knowledge of politics or anarchism. Or, as Peter Brooks puts it:

> The motor of their acts and their imaginings lies in the depths; they are driven by something occult, mostly hidden even to themselves. When the content of the abyss surfaces, it is in the form of the letter from Hoffendahl to Hyacinth, taken from its first envelope and delivered, unopened, by Schinkel, who has himself received it from an unnamed intermediary. The letter is a blank; we can never know its contents directly but must piece it together from Paul Muniment's

---

45. James, *The Bostonians*, 268–69.

46. Wendy Graham suggests that *The Princess Casamassima* tends to substitute criminal slang for the language of revolution: "The closest James comes to political speech is an occasional reference to social Darwinism; yet the novelist seems fully versed in the vocabulary of criminals." For Graham, the blurring of political dissidence and criminality points to anarchism's function as a "screen for the [novel's] underlying theme of sexual subversion." Wendy Graham, *Henry James's Thwarted Love* (Stanford, CA: Stanford University Press, 1999), 187, 179.

and Schinkel's deductions and from its deflected result, Hyacinth's suicide.[47]

Not knowing does not, James sees, prevent one from making choices, from contributing actively to history. In this way, *The Princess Casamassima*, often criticized or praised on the basis of its success or failure as a work of history, begins to look like a much needed theory of history: in this theory, it is what one doesn't know that makes one vote, speak, and act. How, then, does one represent a politics based productively—if dangerously—on what one doesn't know?

We should consider the most properly political moment in James's novel, a moment that is in fact never narrated directly. The culmination of Hyacinth's political career is the moment at which he makes his pact with Hoffendahl and the others to put himself at the service of the party of action; as he tells the Princess at Medley, "I took a vow—a tremendous, terrible vow—in the presence of four witnesses" (327). Hyacinth tells the Princess of his involvement with the revolutionaries and his agreement to sacrifice his life as soon as he is tapped by the great Hoffendahl. He narrates all this some time after it has occurred in a barely disguised effort to impress the Princess.[48] While, however, these details are given to us after the fact, the actual moment of political commitment is left quite out. The lines leading up to the moment are also the last of the novel's second book:

> They all walked away from the "Sun and Moon," and it was not for some five minutes that they encountered the four-wheeled cab which deepened so the solemnity of their expedition. After they were seated in it, Hyacinth learned that Hoffendahl was in London but for three days, was liable to hurry away on the morrow, and was accustomed to receive visits at all kinds of queer hours. It was getting to be midnight; the drive seemed interminable, to Hyacinth's impatience and curiosity. He sat next to Paul Muniment, who passed his arm around him, as if by way of a tacit expression of indebtedness. They all ended by sitting

---

47. Brooks, *The Melodramatic Imagination*, 173.

48. One element of the plot that critics have tended not to mention is its comedy. Hyacinth begins his dreadful story with the solemn statement "I'll give you no names." Of course, he proceeds to mention Paul Muniment and Eustache Poupin and to allude directly to Diedrich Hoffendahl within ten sentences. This is a recurring phenomenon in *The Princess Casamassima*: no one can keep a secret. Pinnie tells everyone she knows about Hyacinth's birth; Hyacinth, for whom those facts are his own deep and defining secret, tells anyone who will listen; Poupin betrays him to the others at the Sun and Moon. Secrets, of course, must be revealed in a novel to become narratable; this fact becomes for James a source of social amusement and a barely stated way of satirizing the questionable secrecy of secret agents.

silent, as the cab jogged along murky miles, and by the time it stopped
Hyacinth had wholly lost, in the drizzling gloom, a sense of their
whereabouts. (296)

The final dissolve in the passage is only the culmination of an ambiguity
that defines the whole of the scene. The errand on which the four men have
entered should be among the most motivated of the novel; no one, however,
seems to have much an idea what it's all about. The tone of the thing—the
hour, the weather, their mode of transportation—takes over, putting the atmospheric cart before the narrative horse and detracting somehow from what
could be intentional about the scene. What's more, the terms on which the
men (Paul and Hyacinth particularly) express the importance of the journey
seem somewhat out of place here. The arm that Paul passes around Hyacinth
appears only moments after the passage quoted earlier in which Hyacinth's
credibility as a possible terrorist is strengthened on the basis of a surprisingly inscrutable exchange of looks. James's sense of the embeddedness of the
political in a web of more personal, more erotic relations serves to bring the
reader to quite the same conclusion as Hyacinth: we lose, in other words, all
sense of our whereabouts.
     At the beginning of the next book, our confusion is only exacerbated:

Hyacinth got up early—an operation attended with very little effort,
as he had scarcely closed his eyes all night. What he saw from his window made him dress as rapidly as a young man could do who desired
more than ever that his appearance should not give strange ideas about
him: an old garden, with parterres in curious figures, and little inter-
vals of lawn which appeared to our hero's cockney vision fantastically
green. (299)

It is not for another full page or so that we realize that *three months* have
passed since the previous scene and that Hyacinth now finds himself waking
up in a spare room at Medley, a country house rented by the Princess. Until
that is clear—and the text seems to delight in withholding that information—we can have no idea really where Hyacinth is waking up. Our feeling
of being lost is made material as well by the fact that in the New York Edition
this break falls between the two volumes that constitute *The Princess Casamassima*; the three lost months that separate the evening with Paul and the morning with the Princess are left to hang in the air, dislocated and lost.[49]

---

49. John Carlos Rowe has seen this ellipsis as a means of exposing social contradiction in James's
novel: "The formal structure of the novel is the representation of such contradiction; the melodramatic
and suspenseful discontinuity in the narrative, which we have sketched above, is merely a synecdoche for

This confusion is exacerbated by James's excessive phrase about Hyacinth's dressing. What would make one want to look so normal? How exactly does one dress to convey that impression? And, most important, what is it that has happened to Hyacinth that he would want to prevent "strange ideas"? The answer becomes clear over the course of a few pages: Hyacinth is nervous about his stay with the Princess and wants obviously to make as nice an impression as possible. However, given the ambiguity in the passage, a number of ideas are suggested: for one, left still with the impression made by the errand that Hyacinth was engaged in the page before, perhaps he wants to look as little like an anarchist as he can. Or, if he is waking up in the home of another anarchist, perhaps he wants to look as little like someone who doesn't look like an anarchist as he can (we know that this has been his fear at other moments). Also, given the number of ambiguously amorous relationships that he cultivates over the course of the novel (Millicent, Paul, and the Princess all emerge as possible love interests), waking up in a strange bed might result in an anxiety that has little if anything to do with an anarchism either international or subterraneous.

And, if we learn finally why it is that Hyacinth would want to look so normal (and what poor boy wouldn't want to look normal in a place like Medley?), these other possibilities stick to Hyacinth not only because they are all suggested by the novel but also because we are dealing with a character who either has no insides or whose insides are especially unavailable to us. So, without the denotational guarantee that a hole in Hyacinth would provide, we are left with a cluster of competing connotations. We find then that Hyacinth's body, one described earlier as the sum of its details, has something else in common with the text of *The Princess Casamassima*. If Hyacinth's is a connotative body, if it is a body somehow without the denotational center that repression provides, we can see at the center of the novel a similar kind of slippage, a gap made almost vulgarly literal in the distance between the two volumes of a novel. The scene that was lost, a meeting that occurs between the end of book 2 and the beginning of book 3, is the dead center of *The Princess Casamassima*: it is the culmination of Hyacinth's flirtation with anarchism and the event that allows for the novel's denouement; the scene falls at the rough center, pagewise, of the novel; the scene would have been the only sighting of Hoffendahl, the master anarchist who, we are told, organizes the discrete details of not only his organization but also the world like the conductor of an orchestra or, indeed, the author of a novel.[50] Hyacinth's vow, the truth about

---

a pervasive feature of James's structural organization." John Carlos Rowe, *The Theoretical Dimensions of Henry James* (Madison: University of Wisconsin Press, 1984), 186.

50. "He had exactly the same mastery of them that a great musician—that the Princess herself—had of the keyboard of a piano; he treated all things, persons, institutions, ideas, as so many notes in his great

anarchists, and the presence of Hoffendahl: all these are facts that might have provided the anchor around which Hyacinth's character and the whole system of *The Princess Casamassima* might have been organized. Instead, exactly these things are perversely absented from the directly narrated fabric of the novel. We are with Hyacinth left hanging.

Hyacinth's odd condition, the key symptom of which is his lack of a social-izing repression (he never makes a mistake), is at once the source of his sophistication and that which makes him useful to Hoffendahl and the other anarchists. A character among characters who would be real people, Hyacinth, looking increasingly like the narrator of *The Sacred Fount*, begins to seem more and more inexplicable, less and less possible. The narrative result of this discontinuity, almost inevitably, is the suicide with which the novel ends; Hyacinth, not made for this world and not willing, finally, to shoot a duke, takes his life in the last pages of *The Princess Casamassima*. He shoots himself in the heart. As grisly as the scene might have been, its mess is curiously managed; the Princess sees the suicided Hyacinth stretched out on his bed:

> Her eyes had attached themselves to the small bed. There was some-thing on it—something black, something ambiguous, something outstretched. Schinkel held her back, but only for an instant; she saw everything, and with the very act she flung herself beside the bed, upon her knees. Hyacinth lay there as if he were asleep, but there was a horrible thing, a mess of blood, on the bed, in his side, in his heart. (590)

Although horrifying, the scene is remarkably if by now predictably neat: it is a mess that is not a mess.[51] Hyacinth's darkly clad little body shows up as a clearly defined if "ambiguous" *something* against the visual field of his bed,

---

symphonic revolt. The day would come when Hyacinth, far down in the treble, would feel himself touched by the little finger of the composer, would become audible (with a small, sharp crack) for a second" (334). The fantasy here is, of course, of the perfectly significant work: not a note, even the shortest, could be lost. In these terms, Hyacinth, whom we have seen has a problem with his details, dreams of be-coming significant under the little finger of the great social artist. There is here, in other words, yet another structural consonance between the novel and Hyacinth. That is, Hyacinth—the mistake who never makes a mistake—is willing here to become a detail to retain some control over his own details.

51. What makes it even neater is that it stands as kind of repetition of a scene from the novel in which we first met Christina Light, the Princess Casamassima: *Roderick Hudson*. Roderick, feeling that his genius has run dry and that his passion for Christina is a failed one, wanders off into the Swiss countryside and falls or jumps into a ravine: "He had fallen from a great height, but he was singularly little disfigured. The rain had spent its torrents upon him, and his clothes and hair were as wet as if the billows of the ocean had flung him upon the strand. An attempt to move him would show some hideous fracture, some horrible

just as his wound shows up as a single concentrated blot against the coherent visual form of his "sleeping" body. The description gets neater as it goes, tightening the focus from bed to body to side to heart. The tidiness of the wound is matched by a tidy formal symmetry: the look of Hyacinth's body against the bed reproduces the look of his body's wound against his body; like the "smutches and streaks" on Millicent Henning's doll and on the whole of Lomax Place, the traces of Hyacinth's suicide are presented as if they were nicely rendered marks on a page, signifiers pointing as much to the fact of signification as to any particular thing. We might compare Hyacinth's neat little corpse to what is left behind at the end of Zola's *Nana*: "What lay on the pillow was a charnel-house, a heap of pus and blood, a shovelful of putrid flesh."[52] Zola works to remove Nana's body from the realm of the representable, distorting it so completely, so messily, as to make it difficult to talk about her using words we at all associate with bodies. Hyacinth, however, remains perfectly composed, a textual body that does not much bleed because as we have seen—as everybody has seen all along—Hyacinth, doomed to live however briefly as character's effect, *would* have little blood to give.

---

physical dishonour, but what Roland saw on first looking at him was only a strangely serene expression of life. The eyes were those of a dead man, but in a short time, when Rowland had closed them, the whole face seemed to awake. The rain had washed away all blood; it was as if Violence, having done her work, had stolen away in shame." Both suicides are unusually, uncannily tidy; what makes Hyacinth's all the more so is that it is, a near and knowing quotation of another suicide from another, earlier book. Henry James, *Roderick Hudson* (New York: Penguin, 1986), 386.

52. Émile Zola, *Nana*, trans. George Holden (London: Penguin, 1972), 470.

Afterword: "J'ai envie d'foutre le camp"

*The war in Indochina is an accident, the cars have ac-
cidents, you don't get along with your wife it's an accident,
accident; that's the conclusion of the picture.*
     —*Jean Renoir on* The Rules of the Game[1]

W hat would it mean for bad form to end? When in either life
or literature would we stop making the mistakes that make
us color, stutter, and cringe? It is hard to imagine a life without
mistakes, and, indeed, it seems as if plenty of bad examples have
managed to outlive the good old days of the classic realist novel.
Isn't Prufrock's pathos simply the bathos of a bad form leavened
with difficulty and verse? "I grow old…I grow old… / I shall wear
the bottoms of my trousers rolled."[2] Can we say that much has
changed when, in Mary McCarthy's *The Group*, "Kay repeated
to Dottie what Harald had said of the etiquette of contraception,
which, as he explained it, was like any other etiquette—the code
of manners rising out of social realities"?[3] And is Patrick Bateman's

1. *Jean Renoir*, dir. David Thompson, 1993, included with *The Rules of the Game*, DVD
(New York: Criterion Collection, 2004).
2. T. S. Eliot, *The Waste Land and Other Poems*, ed. Frank Kermode (London: Penguin,
2003), 7.
3. Mary McCarthy, *The Group* (New York: Penguin, 1963), 51.

response to Paul Allen's beautiful business card in the film version of *American Psycho*—he trembles, sweats, and finally kills—anything other than a strong version of the panicky, aggressive response to good form that we have seen at work all along? "Look at that subtle off-white coloring. The tasteful thickness of it. Oh, my God. It even has a watermark."

While we can easily find these and other examples, they are different from the cases—in Flaubert, Eliot, James, and others—that I have discussed so far. They are different because they are *late theorizations* of bad form, self-consciously belated efforts to account for social conditions that had for a time produced the bourgeois experience of social life as *novelistic*: roughly homogeneous, necessarily meaningful, and productively embarrassing. The social mistake, as I have argued, takes on a particular significance in relation to a nineteenth-century culture invested in its open-ended commitment to reform: once reform (represented in the everyday by its light surrogates, fashion and etiquette) becomes a ruling concept, the mistake, which had stood previously as a legible index of one's distance from a fixed point of perfection, becomes not only a necessary fact of life but also an inevitable and reinforcing aspect of the social order as a whole. In the absence of stable values and verities, mistakes negatively make and remake the felt experience of social coherence. The mistake and the rules it made visible were thus necessary to the production of the *neutralized spaces* ("areas where people may meet without fear under the protection of clear, unchallenged rules") that Franco Moretti takes as characteristic of the European nineteenth century: "When a world enjoys a Hundred Years' Peace (as Polanyi defined European history between 1815 and 1914) neutralized spaces tend inevitably to increase in number, and to occupy a growing portion of social existence."[4] The end of that peace and its neutralized spaces comes with the end of faith in reform as a process that was progressive, interminable, and productive of the cultural conditions that made bad form necessary to the experience of coherence in literary form and social life. So while moments of bad form continue to appear after the period I have so far discussed, these later incidents must be taken as related to what Adorno identifies as *late style*. In the wake of their own diminished value, social mistakes come to "find expression as the naked representation of themselves."[5]

It is for this reason that one self-consciously late example will be my last. Maybe the best film about bad form, Jean Renoir's *The Rules of the Game* can, because it understands itself as the last gasp of a particular form of sociabil-

---

4. Franco Moretti, *The Way of the World: The Bildungsroman in European Culture* (London: Verso, 2000), 239.

5. Theodor W. Adorno, "Late Style in Beethoven," in *Essays on Music*, ed. Richard Leppert, trans Susan H. Gillespie (Berkeley: University of California Press, 2002), 565, 566.

ity, take seriously the social mistake, stand as a critical commentary on the tradition we have considered so far, and wonder aloud about what's next, indeed, what's left for the formal strategies and social anxieties that defined the nineteenth-century novel of manners. Not only does the film's big loser, the overearnest pilot André Jurieu, die as the result of what we are to see as poor play, but the film, one Renoir later called a war film without any "reference to the war," also suggests implicitly that a certain relation is marked for death: the relation between content and form, between social life and a curiously abstracted idea about social life that makes both Renoir's film and bourgeois sociability possible. World events, the film recognizes, were soon to shatter the lifestyle of a residual *haute bourgeoisie* whose play-drunk paralysis paved the way, Renoir thought, for exactly that shattering; as Stephen Tifft puts it: "Renoir conceived the film from the first as a means of expressing, however indirectly, his fury with the Munich appeasement agreement and his anxiety over the state of Europe on the brink of World War II."[6] Renoir, who thought of himself as a "man of the nineteenth century,"[7] also shares with Adorno a sense of the relation between fading forms of social life and equally tenuous forms of traditional narration: "The identity of experience in the form of a life that is articulated and possesses internal continuity—and that life was the only thing that made the narrator's stance possible—has disintegrated."[8] *The Rules of the Game* is an example of bad form's late style and as a result betrays an anxiety about the possibility of form in the face of that disintegration; a film *about* a novelistic experience of coherence on the verge of passing away, *The Rules of the Game* will give us our last look back at bad form.[9]

Games: "Vous comprenez, Corneille, c'est la vis de ma fauvette"

The Rules of the Game is stuffed with games: billiards, Ping-Pong, pinochle, bridge, *belote*. Even André Jurieu's transatlantic flight (completed in twenty-three hours!) is only the biggest of the film's games, a supremely pointless bit of heroism closer to the adventurer's ascent up Mount Everest (approached "because it was there") than to any motivated social act. These games (and

6. Stephen Tifft, "*Drôle de Guerre*: Renoir, Farce, and the Fall of France," *Representations* 38 (Spring 1992): 131.

7. Jean Renoir, *My Life and My Films*, trans. Norman Denny (New York: Atheneum, 1974), 171.

8. Theodor W. Adorno, "The Position of the Narrator in the Contemporary Novel," in *Notes to Literature*, vol. 1, ed. Rolf Tiedemann, trans. Shierry Weber Nicholsen (New York: Columbia University Press, 1991), 31.

9. Quotations from the film have been checked against Jean Renoir, *La Règle du jeu: Nouveau découpage intégral*, ed. Olivier Curchod (Paris: Librairie Générale Française, 1998).

there are many more in the film) are rarely distinguished from a general sense of everyday life as fundamentally attenuated; there is nothing left to this life other than light conversation, extended social visits, and the comic because meaningless exchange of lovers. Renoir described his world in this way: "Characters pass by and say something inane. 'Shall we finish our bridge game?' 'I hate bridge.' 'I love sea salt.' 'I hate sea salt.'"[10] Love or hate, sea salt or not: who cares? This state of affairs stands as a version of sociability so abstract that it erases the difference between winning at cards, winning at love, and flying one's plane across an ocean. It all and always amounts, as Robert's practiced ennui everywhere announces, to the same damn thing.

It is in that case odd that the thing that most gets Robert going is what best represents the purposeless purposiveness of the film's social play: his toys. Ingenious, useless, irritating, and delightful, Robert's many automatons, mechanical birds, and music boxes stand in on the one hand for the complexity of a social world driven by the smooth, meaningless interaction of who knows how many parts and on the other for that world's belatedness: relics from another time, Robert's love for his decaying Enlightenment toys (Octave: "Looks like the moths got to it!") points to the fact that the game of the film's title is one played without effect by a vestigial *haute bourgeoisie*, a "residual class" out of sync with what Lukács calls the "pure classes in bourgeois society."[11] And if Robert's rooms are filled with objects that are good because they are good-for-nothing, so does that quality seem at moments to seep directly into Renoir's style, a visual style that occasionally allows its forms to play without the guarantee of motivating consequence. For example: early in the film, Robert visits his mistress Genvieve with the intention of breaking up. The scene begins with a deep-focus shot of her in the foreground and him standing behind. As Robert moves to the left and she to the right, a shot-reverse-shot sequence is initiated and shows both Robert and Genvieve standing next to different figures of Buddha, details from Genvieve's *décor chinois*. What's odd about the scene is that the statues look uncannily like the characters: Genvieve's robe and attitude, and Robert's roundish, pale visage are weirdly doubled by their respective Buddhas. The effect is at once striking and strikingly meaningless: what could we learn from so purely formal a resemblance? Instead of meaning anything in particular, the scene, because of its lack of motivation, all but obliterates the difference between a life represented, the film that represents it, and so many bibelots.

10. *Jean Renoir, le patron: La Règle et l'exception*, dir. Jacques Rivette, 1966. Included with *The Rules of the Game*, DVD (New York: Criterion Collection, 2004).

11. Georg Lukács, *History and Class Consciousness: Studies in Marxist Dialectics*, trans. Rodney Livingstone (Cambridge, MA: MIT Press, 1971), 59.

Doubles: Genvieve and her statue. © Les Grands Films
Classiques–Paris

None of this accounts, however, for the uncharacteristically earnest dive
that Robert takes after dropping the screw that allows one of his mechanical
warblers to sing "every twenty minutes." Surrounded by a half dozen visibly
bored servants, Robert, moving as jerkily as one of his mechanical dolls, shifts
and crawls beneath the furniture to retrieve it. The scene is marked by an im-

Doubles: Robert and his statue. © Les Grands Films Classiques–Paris

mediacy of affect that Robert and the film rarely achieve (not when his wife leaves, not when his guest dies, not when he is himself nearly shot). The screw, it seems, means more to Robert than life itself. The fragility of toys and the hysterical, exaggerated activity required to protect them suggest an often and necessarily disavowed aspect of sociability: the labor that goes into making a space safe for play. This becomes all the more apparent during Schumacher's rampage. Late in the film, Schumacher, la Colinière's gamekeeper, charges through the house trying to kill Marceau, the poacher whom he has caught fooling around with his wife, Lisette. As Schumacher fires pistol shots into clusters of party guests, the film encourages us to worry less about *someone* than about *something* catching a bullet: the elaborate musical device that Robert displayed moments before as "l'aboutissement" of his career as a collector. A quick, disingenuous cut to the machine as Schumacher shoots in some other direction encourages us to think that it might be spectacularly struck (indeed, Robert's chief servant, Corneille, will later announce—in a tone that suggests the natural equivalence between his terms—that although no one was hurt, "the stuffed birds suffered a bit"). And, although the machine is not in fact shot, it nevertheless goes sympathetically haywire, producing a repetitive grinding sound as Schumacher is at last restrained and disarmed. The machine's malfunctioning exposes the inelegant mechanism necessarily pounding away behind society's seemingly easy play even as it allows us to imagine the machine's spectacular, probably inevitable, and somehow pleasing self-destruction. If we don't destroy it, it will destroy itself.

At the fête: Robert's greatest achievement as a collector. © Les Grands Films Classiques–Paris

This shot of Robert's machine threatened with violence follows an earlier appearance when Robert shows it off to his friends, a moment he imagined as the climax of the fête. This moment is similarly a break away from the film's narrative, a pause that suspends both action and its attendant anxiety. In this way, the machine stands in for our best hopes for sociability, a play form of the social that would assuage suffering through its distance from the sometimes troubling contents of life's myriad plots. The shot, a close-up on an uncharacteristically enthusiastic Robert and his musical toy, breaks from Renoir's usually neutral depth-of-field style, placing the viewer in an intimate and direct relation to the contents of a scene bookended by sharp cinematic cuts, a fact that further marks the moment as a suspended as opposed to situated narrative act, a flattened moment of pure spectacle opposed to the thoughtful, analytical attention of Renoir's usual deep-focus camera work. Where, however, that scene stands as a strange pause in the action, a moment that diverts interest from the film's content to an empty rotation of gears (a figure for both the abstraction of the rules of the game and the necessarily disavowed cinematic mechanism that allows for the capture of these images), the toy's later appearance, as Schumacher threatens it with his pistol, points to the threat of violence that the fragility of these mechanisms conjures into being. A war film without reference to the war, *The Rules of the Game* encourages us, on the one hand, to imagine and to desire destruction and, on the other, to wonder why sociability and a violence that is its other are in every text we have considered all but inseparable. What is the film's famous hunt sequence, if not proof that the two are sometimes even identical? Put differently, the film enacts what every spoilsport knows: even at its Schillerian best, social play can never fully ease the pain of bad form.[12]

Rules: "Et c'monde-là, ça a ses règles! Des règles tres rigoureuses!"

There is a curious absence in *The Rules of the Game*: although the film does represent different games and their respective rules, there are few clear rules to the all-important game of its title. We see that there is discipline and punishment, social success and social failure in Renoir's world. If, however, we

---

12. J. Huizinga notes that the spoilsport, the one "who trespasses against the rules or ignores them," "must be cast out, for he threatens the existence of the play community." As we have seen repeatedly, and will see again, a tendency toward identification that sometimes obscures the difference between narration and what it narrates can appear as a failure of play that results in a fate similar to that of the spoilsport, a fact that points to the *limits* of play in the traditional novel. J. Huizinga, *Homo Ludens: A Study of the Play-Element in Culture* (Boston: Beacon Press, 1955), 11.

were asked to explain the rules of the game to some new player, we would be hard-pressed to say much other than "don't get shot." We learn that a friend should tell a husband before running away with his wife, that it is "not done" to declare one's love for a married woman while doing an interview on the radio, and that the only way to make a potato salad is to pour wine over the potatoes while they're really hot. If, however, these rules are not to be broken, they are neither portable enough to stand as *the* rules of *the* game nor "deep" enough to account for the anxiety they produce. The film's moment of best form is Christine's strategic announcement about the nature of her past relations with Jurieu; she neutralizes the potential for gossip by owning with pride what might have seemed a disgrace. Although Christine's move works beautifully, it does not do so because it demonstrates an understanding of any special set of rules; it is, rather, an improvisation for which no corresponding rule had previously existed. There is, in other words, a kind of paradox at work in the film: although Octave explains to the doomed Jurieu that society "has some pretty stiff rules," these rules are rarely articulated, and, what's more, they neither prevent nor even condemn the many kinds of chaos that threaten to make nonsense out of social life in the film.[13]

Jon Elster writes that there "is no single end—genetic, individual or collective—that all norms serve and that explains why there are norms. Nor, for any given norm, is there always an end that it serves and that explains why it exists."[14] If what we sometimes look for in a text is the way in which it figures a particular social content or a distinct historical or ethical end, Elster's take on society's rules must be disturbing. For if rules cannot be definitively accounted for by looking into the rational bases for their existence, then the representation of social rules in something like *The Rules of the Game* begins to look simply like a representation of representation, an empty figural play the analysis of which can only lead us on indefinitely. We might think of this in terms of a Wittgensteinian "skeptical paradox": if someone asks me how I understand a thing, I say that I understand it be-

---

13. Richard J. Watts offers a nice sketch of two ways of thinking about the causal relation between rule and act in the sphere of what he calls (im)politeness: while "we tend to think that the appropriate forms of behaviour to display at, say, the ticket office of a coach station in some way 'exist' outside ourselves, perhaps in the form of social 'rules' of some kind," it might be better to think of those "rules" as the result of a kind of productive and performative repetition: "So by standing in the queue and doing what others (including ourselves) expect us to do, we actually help to reproduce that social activity. We are reproducing what the ethnomethodologist Harvey Sacks might have called 'doing being in a queue.' The reproduction of the social activity relies on the tacit agreement of those participating to 'do it all over again.'" Richard J. Watts, *Politeness* (Cambridge: Cambridge University Press, 2003), 117–18.

14. Jon Elster, *The Cement of Society: A Study of Social Order* (Cambridge: Cambridge University Press 1989), 125.

cause I know the rules that govern the thing and its use; if I am then asked how I understand those rules, I say that I understand them because I know some more rules that govern the rules that govern the thing and its use; and so on.[15] It is thus appropriate that the narrative of *The Rules of the Game* is structured more around a figural mobility that allows players to switch games, trade partners, and change positions without serious consequence than around a clear understanding of any particular rules. Even Jurieu's death is offered not as an event that might end or establish limits to the game but as something simply to redescribe: when Robert calls his death "a terrible accident," Saint-Aubin notes with a wry smile that that's "a new definition of 'accident.'"

It is for this reason, perhaps, that bad form is so important; while social norms seem always to elude articulation, to fail to take a form that would allow for their simple codification, the social mistake appears as an especially portable, adaptable, and productive social fact. After Jurieu's gaffe—he complains in a radio interview immediately after his transatlantic flight that Christine, Robert's wife and the woman for the love of whom he made his journey, does not appear to greet him—a series of shots beginning with one that pans up from within the electronic guts of a radio in Christine's bedroom show how André's goof finds its way across the airwaves into the homes of the film's principal characters. His mistake not only produces a narrative disquiet that will sustain the film until his death and its conclusion but also generates discourse in the form of the proliferating chatter that follows. The mistake brings the different places of the film together into a continuous and synchronized social space that will find its most material form in the dramatic unity offered by la Colinière and will be captured by Renoir's deep-focus shooting style. The "pretty stiff" rules that we imagined as a backdrop against which the mistake appears legible are instead the *result* of his mistake; they come into being only after a gaffe has occurred. If, in other words, it is hard to see what form prior to their breaking the rules of the game might take, what *is* eminently visible in *The Rules of the Game* is the form that the mistake gives to rules and aesthetic representation of them.

15. "This was our paradox: no course of action could be determined by a rule, because every course of action can be made out to accord with a rule. The answer was: if everything can be made out to accord with the rule, then it can also be made to conflict with it. And so there would be neither accord nor conflict here." Ludwig Wittgenstein, *Philosophical Investigations*, trans. G. E. M. Anscombe (New York: Macmillan, 1953), 81. See also Saul A. Kripke, *Wittgenstein on Rules and Private Language: An Elementary Exposition* (Cambridge, MA: Harvard University Press, 1982), 21.

Quits: "J'ai envie d'foutre le camp.... J'ai envie de...de disparaître, dans un trou!"

Why is Octave so depressed? Although he often plays the fool, he is also prey to bouts of extreme and seemingly inexplicable melancholy. In an otherwise antic scene in which he tries and finally manages to convince Robert to invite Jurieu to la Colinière, Octave—played by Renoir—suddenly loses his rhythm and falls into a surprising sadness: "Dis donc, vieux: j'ai envie d'foutre le camp....J'ai envie de...de disparaître, dans un trou!" Where, we wonder, will he go and what good will going there do him? On the one hand, Octave is simply playing the same card he did with Christine moments before when he threatened her with an especially dejected "adieu!" instead of an "au revoir." Octave, the amiable parasite, is not above manipulating one friend (Robert) in order to assist another (Jurieu). On the other hand, the intensity of his wish to disappear into a hole seems out of line, seems to go overboard in a context otherwise lightened by Robert's ubiquitous toys and conventional comic exchanges between Octave, Robert, Christine, and Lisette.

The shot is a deep one, but unlike the film's other signature depth-of-field shots, the room in this case is barely filled. Between the camera and the two characters—Robert and Octave—there is an ocean of evacuated space, a distance made all the more palpable by the scene's brittle acoustics. This distance, which makes it difficult to see clearly what either character is feeling, produces within the context of a long shot unpunctuated by close-up or

"J'ai envie d'foutre le camp": Robert and Octave. © Les Grands Films Classiques–Paris

montage a resistance to any effort to make sense of Octave's depression. His melancholy is left in the scene as a kind of narrative and affective excess. Later Octave makes good on his threat: after Jurieu's death—he is murdered by Schumacher, who mistakes him for one of his wife's several admirers—Octave simply leaves the film, walking out minutes before its resolution. This is strange not only within the world of the film but also in terms of its form: Octave has been a central character from the beginning, one whom we would have expected not only to be present at its last moments but also to have had some more vital role to play in the tying together of whatever loose strands might have remained. His work to that point had been to "orchestrate" social events (an activity he seems to have adopted as a compromised alternative to his stalled musical career), to bring characters together in a way that, as others have noted, underscores the relation between Octave the character and Renoir the director.[16] Renoir described Octave's role in this way: "My character is in fact a complement to the others. He's like a cork that can fit in the necks of different bottles or like a wedge you use to steady the furniture."[17]

How, in that case, is it conceivable that he could just up and leave the film before it is properly over? Where does the director go? Stanley Cavell takes Octave's premature departure as paradoxical evidence for the fact that a director is never really present in his or her film in the first place: "In *Rules of the Game*, the movie director's absolute absence from his work (accented if, *per accidens*, he appears in it) is fictionalized as Octave's departure from its scene of accident."[18] And Stephen Tifft, following Cavell, notes that in removing himself from the film, Renoir "enacts the familiar Derridean logic of the *pharmakos*, by which a strategy of scapegoating marginal elements to purify a system inevitably fails from an internal fatality that binds the scapegoat to the system. Renoir's peculiar twist on that logic is his attempt to scapegoat himself: rarely does the purveyor of a system condemn himself as its parasitic impurity."[19] We have seen again and again, however, that a troubling identification between character and narration in the novel, an identification that appears as the by-product of omniscient narration's structuring disavowals,

---

16. Late in the film and in an effort to cheer up Christine, Octave acts out a moment from the good old days: a moment when Christine's father (also Octave's mentor) strode out onto an English stage to conduct a performance before the king. Octave smiles, walks out onto an empty balcony, and mimes its first few seconds. When his performance of a performance is met, as it must be, with silence (we hear only the croaking of the frogs), Octave's clowning slides once again into the blackest of moods. The scene begs the question: is a sadness associated with conducting Octave's or Renoir's?

17. *Jean Renoir, le patron: La Regle at l'exception*, dir. Jacques Rivette, 1966, included with *The Rules of the Game*, DVD (New York: Criterion Collection, 2004).

18. Stanley Cavell, *The World Viewed*, enlarged edition (Cambridge, MA: Harvard University Press, 1979), 230.

19. Tifft, "*Drôle de Guerre*," 157.

tends to lead exactly to the threat of narration's expulsion. We remember, for instance, that *The Sacred Fount*'s narrator, a party guest who made himself increasingly unwelcome with mounting claims to omniscience, was told at last that he was "crazy." Like Octave, whose identification with Renoir and whose active and embedded role in orchestrating the events of the film blurs the difference between narration and what it narrates, that narrator had no choice but to leave. To narrate, which is in turn to lay claim to a difference that cannot be sustained, begins at last to look like the worst sort of bad form. In *The Rules of the Game*, Octave's otherwise unintelligible depression is, we now see, the melancholy of narration. Trying to maintain its form in the face of a series of seemingly inevitable identifications, narration, always looking most like what it narrates when it wants it least, can only agree, sadly, to get out.

The Party's Over

In a film otherwise full of people and things, the final shot of *The Rules of the Game* is oddly empty. André Jurieu is dead, Octave has flown the coop, and Robert, after apologizing urbanely for the night's events, has said goodnight. With little to do but go to bed and begin again in the morning, the party guests climb the stairs and head back into the great house. Instead, however, of following bodies as they make their way up the stone steps, we watch this last march in the form of a row of long shadows flowing over a wall and a few shrubs. The camera lingers; it watches as the shadows pass; it remains—for a

Goodnight: the party's over. © Les Grands Films Classiques–Paris

beat, for two beats—focused on the wall, the shrubs, and little else. Indeed, it lingers just long enough for these shapes to pass into a state of abstraction, into pure form instead of bad form.

Bad form has been my name for a social relation necessary to the structure of the classic realist novel; in the absence of other securities, bad form becomes an inevitable and yet tenuous structuring element in the novel and in social life. If, however, a certain form of sociability depends on the presence of the social mistake, so is bad form unthinkable without other people. One doesn't feel embarrassment, worry about the done thing, feel the force of the social mistake when one is really alone. It is in this way that Renoir's film at last goes beyond bad form: trading the densely packed, deep-focus interiors of la Colinière for this flattened, desolate space, *The Rules of the Game* imagines a world without people and the games they play. It imagines, in all this emptiness, a world without bad form.

Works Cited

Adorno, Theodor W. "Late Style in Beethoven." In *Essays on Music*. Edited by Richard Leppert. Translated by Susan H. Gillespie. Berkeley: University of California Press, 2002.

———. *Notes to Literature*. Edited by Rolf Tiedemann. Translated by Shierry Weber Nicholson. 2 vols. New York: Columbia University Press, 1991–92.

Agamben, Giorgio. *Homo Sacer: Sovereign Power and Bare Life*. Stanford, CA: Stanford University Press, 1998.

Althusser, Louis. *Lenin and Philosophy and Other Essays*. New York: Monthly Review Press, 1971.

Anderson, Amanda. "Victorian Studies and the Two Modernities." *Victorian Studies* 47 no.2 (Winter 2005): 195–203.

Armstrong, Lucie Heaton. *Good Form. A Book of Every Day Etiquette*. London: F. V. White, 1889.

Armstrong, Nancy. *Desire and Domestic Fiction: A Political History of the Novel*. New York: Oxford University Press, 1987.

Austen-Leigh, James Edward. *A Memoir of Jane Austen: And Other Family Recollections*. New York: Oxford University Press, 2002.

Avrich, Paul. *Anarchist Portraits*. Princeton, NJ: Princeton University Press, 1988.

Balzac, Honoré de. *Lost Illusions*. Translated by Herbert J. Hunt. London: Penguin, 1971.

———. *Père Goriot*. Paris: Flammarion, 1995.

———. *Père Goriot*. Translated by Burton Raffel. Edited by Peter Brooks. New York: Norton, 1994.

Banfield, Ann. *Unspeakable Sentences: Narration and Representation in the Language of Fiction.* Boston: Routledge and Kegan Paul, 1982.

Bard, Philip. "On Emotional Expression after Decortication with Some Remarks on Certain Theoretical Views." *Psychological Review* 41 (1934): 309–29.

Barrie, J. M. *Peter Pan.* London: Bloomsbury Books, 1994.

Barthes, Roland. *The Pleasure of the Text.* New York: Farrar, Straus and Giroux, Inc., 1975.

———. "The Reality Effect." In *French Literature Today.* Edited by Tzvetan Todorov. Cambridge: Cambridge University Press, 1982.

———. *S/Z: An Essay.* Translated by Richard Miller. New York: Hill and Wang, 1974.

Bell, Quentin. *On Human Finery.* New York: Schocken Books, 1978.

Bellos, David. *Balzac Criticism in France 1850–1900: The Making of a Reputation.* Oxford: Clarendon Press, 1976.

Bersani, Leo. *Balzac to Beckett: Center and Circumference in French Fiction.* New York: Oxford University Press, 1970.

———. *A Future for Astyanax: Character and Desire in Literature.* Boston: Little, Brown, 1976.

———. "Sociality and Sexuality." *Critical Inquiry* 26 (2000): 657–82.

Blair, Sara. *Henry James and the Writing of Race and Nation.* Cambridge: Cambridge University Press, 1996.

Bodenheimer, Rosemarie. "George Eliot and the Power of Evil-Speaking." *Dickens Studies Annual* 20 (1991): 199–227.

Booth, Wayne C. *The Rhetoric of Fiction.* Chicago: University of Chicago Press, 1983.

Bourdieu, Pierre. *Distinction: A Social Critique of the Judgment of Taste.* Translated by Richard Nice. Cambridge, MA: Harvard University Press, 1984.

———. *In Other Words: Essays towards a Reflexive Sociology.* Translated by Matthew Adamson. Stanford, CA: Stanford University Press, 1990.

———. *The Rules of Art: Genesis and Structure of the Literary Field.* Translated by Susan Emanuel. Stanford, CA: Stanford University Press, 1996.

Brantlinger, Patrick. *The Reading Lesson: The Threat of Mass Literacy in Nineteenth-Century British Fiction.* Bloomington: Indiana University Press, 1998.

Brombert, Victor. *The Novels of Flaubert: A Study of Themes and Techniques.* Princeton, NJ: Princeton University Press, 1966.

Brontë, Emily. *Wuthering Heights.* London: Penguin, 1995.

Brooks, Peter. *The Melodramatic Imagination: Balzac, Henry James, Melodrama, and the Mode of Excess.* New Haven, CT: Yale University Press, 1995.

———. *Reading for the Plot: Design and Intention in Narrative.* Cambridge, MA: Harvard University Press, 1992.

Butler, Judith. *The Psychic Life of Power: Theories in Subjection.* Stanford, CA: Stanford University Press, 1997.

Carlyle, Thomas. *Characteristics.* Boston: James R. Osgood, 1877.

Cavell, Stanley. *The World Viewed.* Enlarged edition. Cambridge, MA: Harvard University Press, 1979.

Chase, Karen. *George Eliot,* Middlemarch. Cambridge: Cambridge University Press, 1991.

Chasseguet-Smirgel, Janine. *The Ego Ideal: A Psychoanalytic Essay on the Malady of the Ideal.* Translated by Paul Barrows. New York: Norton, 1985.

Cheadle, Eliza. *Manners of Modern Society: Being a Book of Etiquette.* London: Cassell, Petter, and Galpin, 1872.

Chesterton, G. K. *The Man Who Was Thursday.* London: Penguin, 1986.

Clark, T. J. *The Absolute Bourgeois: Artists and Politics in France 1848–1851*. Berkeley: University of California Press, 1999.

———. *Image of the People: Gustave Courbet and the 1848 Revolution*. Princeton, NJ: Princeton University Press, 1982.

Cohn, Dorrit. *Transparent Minds: Narrative Modes for Presenting Consciousness in Fiction*. Princeton: Princeton University Press, 1978.

The Critical Response to George Eliot. Edited by Karen Pangallo. Westport, CT: Greenwood Press, 1994.

Culler, Jonathan. *Flaubert: The Uses of Uncertainty*. Ithaca, NY: Cornell University Press, 1974.

———. "Omniscience." *Narrative* 12, no. 1 (2004): 22–34.

———. *Structuralist Poetics: Structuralism, Linguistics, and the Study of Literature*. Ithaca, NY: Cornell University Press, 1975.

Curtin, Michael. "A Question of Manners: Status and Gender in Etiquette and Courtesy." *Journal of Modern History* 57 (September 1985): 395–423.

Cvetkovich, Ann. *Mixed Feelings: Feminism, Mass Culture, and Victorian Sensationalism*. New Brunswick, NJ: Rutgers University Press, 1992.

d'Alq, Louise. *Le nouveau savoir-vivre universel*. Paris: Bureau des Causeries Familieres, 1881.

Davidoff, Leonore. *The Best Circles*. London: Cresset Library, 1986.

Davidoff, Leonore, and Catherine Hall. *Family Fortunes: Men and Women of the English Middle Class*. London: Hutchinson, 1987.

de Bradi, Mme la Comtesse. *Du savoir-vivre en France au dix-neuvieme siècle, ou Instruction d'un père à ses enfants*. Paris: V. Berger-Levrault et Fils, 1858.

de Man, Paul. *The Resistance to Theory*. Minneapolis: University of Minnesota Press, 1986.

Dennett, Daniel. *The Intentional Stance*. Cambridge, MA: MIT Press, 1989.

DeVine, Christine. "Revolution and Democracy in the London *Times* and *The Princess Casamassima*." *Henry James Review* 23 (2002): 53–71.

Dickens, Charles. *Great Expectations*. London: Penguin, 1996.

du Puy de Clinchamps, Phillipe. *Le Snobisme*. Paris: Presses Universitaires de France, 1948.

Durkheim, Émile. *The Rules of the Sociological Method*. New York: Free Press, 1982.

Elias, Nobert. *The Civilizing Process: Sociogenetic and Psychogenetic Investigations*. Edited by Eric Dunning, Johan Goudsblom, and Stephen Mennel. Translated by Edmund Jephcott. Oxford: Blackwell, 1994.

Eliot, George. *Adam Bede*. Edited by Valentine Cunningham. Oxford: Oxford University Press, 1996.

———. "The *Antigone* and Its Moral." In *Selected Critical Writings*. Edited by Rosemary Ashton. Oxford: Oxford University Press, 1992.

———. *Felix Holt, the Radical*. Edited by Fred C. Thompson. Oxford: Oxford University Press, 1988.

———. *Middlemarch*. Edited by Bert G. Hornback. New York: Norton, 1977.

———. *Middlemarch: A Study of Provincial Life*. Vol. 4. Edinburgh: William Blackwood and Sons, 1872.

———. "Notes on Form in Art." In *Selected Critical Writings*. Edited by Rosemary Ashton. Oxford: Oxford University Press, 1992.

———. "Silly Novels by Lady Novelists." In *Selected Critical Writings*. Edited by Rosemary Ashton. Oxford: Oxford University Press, 1992.

Eliot, T. S. *The Waste Land and Other Poems*. Edited by Frank Kermode. London: Penguin, 2003.

Elster, Jon. *The Cement of Society: A Study of Social Order*. Cambridge: Cambridge University Press, 1989.

Embodied Selves: An Anthology of Psychological Texts, 1830–1890. Edited by Jenny Bourne Taylor and Sally Shuttleworth. Oxford: Clarendon Press, 1998.

Etiquette for the Ladies: Eighty Maxims on Dress, Manners, and Accomplishments. London: David Bogue, 1846.

Flaubert, Gustave. *Bouvard and Pécuchet with the Dictionary of Received Ideas*. Translated by A. J. Krailsheimer. London: Penguin, 1976.

Madame Bovary. Paris: Librairie Générale Française, 1999.

———. *Madame Bovary*. Edited by Paul de Man. New York: Norton, 1965.

———. *Madame Bovary*. Translated by Geoffrey Wall. London: Penguin, 1992.

———. *Selected Letters*. Translated by Geoffrey Wall. London: Penguin, 1997.

———. *The Temptation of Saint Anthony*. Translated by Kitty Mrosovsky. Ithaca, NY: Cornell University Press, 1981.

Foucault, Michel. "Truth and Juridical Forms." In *Power: Essential Works of Foucault, 1954–1984*. Vol. 3. Edited by James D. Faubion, 1-90. Translated by Robert Hurley. New York: New Press, 2000).

Freedman, Jonathan. *Professions of Taste: Henry James, British Aestheticism, and Commodity Culture*. Stanford, CA: Stanford University Press, 1990.

Freud, Sigmund. *Beyond the Pleasure Principle*. In *The Standard Edition of the Complete Psychological Works of Sigmund Freud*, volume 18.

———. *The Ego and the Id*. In *The Standard Edition of the Complete Psychological Works of Sigmund Freud, volume 19*.

———. "Fetishism." In *The Standard Edition of the Complete Psychological Works of Sigmund Freud, volume 21*.

———. *Group Psychology and the Analysis of the Ego*. Translated by James Strachey. New York: Norton, 1959.

———. "Negation." In *The Standard Edition of the Complete Psychological Works of Sigmund Freud*, volume 19.

———. "On Narcissism." In *The Standard Edition of the Complete Psychological Works of Sigmund Freud*, volume 14.

———. *The Psychopathology of Everyday Life*. Translated by James Strachey. New York: Norton, 1965.

———. *The Standard Edition of the Complete Works of Sigmund Freud*, 24 volumes. Edited by James Strachey et al. London: The Hogart Press and the Institute of Psychoanalysis, 1960.

Furst, Lillian R. "The Power of the Powerless: A Trio of Nineteenth-Century French Disorderly Eaters." In *Disorderly Eaters: Texts in Self-Empowerment*. Edited by Lillian R. Furst and Peter W. Graham. University Park: Pennsylvania State University Press, 1992.

Fuss, Diana. *Identification Papers*. New York: Routledge, 1995.

Gadamer, Hans-Georg. *Truth and Method*. Translated by Joel Weinsheimer and Donald G. Marshall. New York: Continuum, 2000.

Gaskell, Elizabeth. *Cranford*. Oxford: Oxford University Press, 1998.

Gay, Peter. *Pleasure Wars: The Bourgeois Experience: Victoria to Freud*. New York: Norton, 1998.

Geismar, Maxwell. *Henry James and the Jacobites*. Boston: Houghton Mifflin, 1963.

Genette, Gérard. *Narrative Discourse: An Essay in Method*. Ithaca, NY: Cornell University Press, 1980.

Gilbert, Sandra, and Susan Gubar. *The Madwoman in the Attic: The Woman Writer and the Nineteenth-Century Literary Imagination*. New Haven, CT: Yale University Press, 1979.

Girard, René. *Desire, Deceit, and the Novel: Self and Other in Literary Structure,* trans. Yvonne Freccero. Baltimore, MD: Johns Hopkins University Press, 1976.

Goffman, Erving. *Interaction Ritual: Essays in Face-to-Face Behavior.* Chicago: Aldine, 1967.

Gordon, Rae Beth. "From Charcot to Charlot: Unconscious Imitation and Spectatorship in French Cabaret and Early Cinema." *Critical Inquiry* 27 (2001): 515–59.

Graham, Wendy. *Henry James's Thwarted Love.* Stanford, CA: Stanford University Press, 1999.

Greenberg, Robert A. "Plexuses and Ganglia: Scientific Allusion in *Middlemarch.*" *Nineteenth-Century Fiction* 30 (1975): 33–52.

Gregg, Stephen H. "'A Truly Christian Hero': Religion, Effeminacy, and Nation in the Writings of the Societies for Reformation of Manners." *Eighteenth-Century Life* 25 (Winter 2001): 17–28.

Hartman, Geoffrey H. "Romanticism and Anti-Self-Consciousness." In *Beyond Formalism: Literary Essays 1958–1970.* New Haven, CT: Yale University Press, 1970.

Hayward, Abraham. "Codes of Manners and Etiquette." *Quarterly Review* 59 (1837): 395–439.

Hertz, Neil. *George Eliot's Pulse.* Stanford, CA: Stanford University Press, 2003.

———. *The End of the Line: Essays on Psychoanalysis and the Sublime.* New York: Columbia University Press, 1985.

Hughes, Clair. *Henry James and the Art of Dress.* London: Palgrave, 2001.

Hughes, Winifred. *The Maniac in the Cellar: Sensation Novels of the 1860s.* Princeton, NJ: Princeton University Press, 1980.

Huizinga, J. *Homo Ludens: A Study of the Play-Element in Culture.* Boston: Beacon Press, 1955.

Ingram, Rick E., Wiveka Ramel, Denise Chavira, and Christine Scher. "Social Anxiety and Depression." In *International Handbook of Social Anxiety: Concepts, Research and Interventions Relating to the Self and Shyness.* Edited by W. Ray Crozier and Lynn E. Alden. New York: Wiley, 2001.

Jaffe, Audrey. *Scenes of Sympathy: Identity and Representation in Victorian Fiction.* Ithaca, NY: Cornell University Press, 2000.

———. *Vanishing Points: Dickens, Narrative, and the Subject of Omniscience.* Berkeley: University of California Press, 1991.

James, Henry. *The Bostonians.* Edited by Charles R. Anderson. London: Penguin, 1984.

———. *Henry James: Letters.* Edited by Leon Edel. 4 vols. Cambridge, MA: Belknap Press of Harvard University Press, 1974–84.

———. *The Portrait of a Lady.* Edited by Robert D. Bamberg. New York: Norton, 1995.

———. *The Princess Casamassima.* Edited by Derek Brewer and Patricia Crick. London: Penguin, 1987.

———. *The Princess Casamassima.* New York Edition. Vol. 5. New York: Scribner's, 1908.

———. *Roderick Hudson.* New York: Penguin, 1986.

———. *The Sacred Fount.* London: Penguin, 1994.

Jefferson, Ann. *The Nouveau Roman and the Poetics of Fiction.* Cambridge: Cambridge University Press, 1980.

Juul, Jesper. *Video Games between Real Rules and Fictional Worlds.* Cambridge, MA: MIT Press, 2005.

Kantorowicz, Ernst H. *The King's Two Bodies: A Study in Mediaeval Political Theology.* Princeton, NJ: Princeton University Press, 1997.

Klein, Melanie. *The Selected Melanie Klein.* Edited by Juliet Mitchell. New York: Free Press, 1986.

Knight, Diana. *Flaubert's Characters.* Cambridge: Cambridge University Press, 1985.

———. "Whatever Happened to Bouvard and Pécuchet?" In *New Approaches in Flaubert Studies.* Edited by Tony Williams and Mary Orr. Lewiston, NY: E. Mellen Press, 1999.

Kortoxylon. *Phases of Fashion: and The Follies of the Age. A Satire*. London: Simpkin, Marshall, 1867.

Kripke, Saul A. *Wittgenstein on Rules and Private Language: An Elementary Exposition*. Cambridge, MA: Harvard University Press, 1982.

Lacan, Jacques. *Écrits: The First Complete Edition in English*. Translated by Bruce Fink. New York: Norton, 2006.

———. *The Ethics of Psychoanalysis*. New York: Norton, 1992.

Laplanche, J., and J.-B. Pontalis. *The Language of Psychoanalysis*. Translated by Donald Nicholson-Smith. New York: Norton, 1973.

Lerer, Seth. *Error and the Academic Self: The Scholarly Imagination, Medieval to Modern*. New York: Columbia University Press, 2002.

Lewes, G. H. *The Physiology of Common Life*. 2 vols. Edinburgh: William Blackwood and Sons, 1860.

———. "Realism in Art: Recent German Fiction." *Westminster Review* 14 (October 1858): 488–518.

———. "Sensation in the Spinal Cord." *Nature* 9 (December 4, 1873): 83–84.

Leys, Ruth. *From Sympathy to Reflex: Marshall Hall and His Opponents*. New York: Garland, 1990.

Litvak, Joseph. *Caught in the Act: Theatricality in the Nineteenth-Century Novel*. Berkeley: University of California Press, 1992.

———. *Strange Gourmets: Sophistication, Theory, and the Novel*. Durham, NC: Duke University Press, 1997.

Lubbock, Percy. *The Craft of Fiction*. New York: Peter Smith, 1947.

Lucey, Michael. *The Misfit of the Family: Balzac and the Social Forms of Sexuality*. Durham, NC: Duke University Press, 2003.

Lukács, Georg. *History and Class Consciousness: Studies in Marxist Dialectics*. Translated by Rodney Livingstone. Cambridge, MA: MIT Press, 1971.

———. *The Theory of the Novel*. Translated by Anna Bostock. Cambridge, MA: MIT Press, 1971.

Lynch, Deidre Shauna. *The Economy of Character: Novels, Market Culture, and the Business of Inner Meaning*. Chicago: University of Chicago Press, 1998.

Maraini, Dacia. *Searching for Emma: Gustave Flaubert and* Madame Bovary. Translated by Vincent J. Bertolini. Chicago: University of Chicago Press, 1998.

Marcus, Sharon. "Same Difference? Transnationalism, Comparative Literature, and Victorian Studies." *Victorian Studies* 45 (2003): 677-86.

Marx, Karl. *Capital*, Vol. 1. Edited by Frederick Engels. Translated by Samuel Moore and Edward Aveling. New York: International Publishers, 1967.

Mason, John E. *Gentlefolk in the Making: Studies in the History of English Courtesy Literature and Related Topics from 1531–1774*. New York: Octagon Books, 1971.

McCarthy, Mary. *The Group*. New York: Penguin, 1963.

McKeon, Michael. *Theory of the Novel: A Critical Anthology*. Baltimore, MD: Johns Hopkins University Press, 2000.

Menke, Richard. "Fiction as Vivisection: G. H. Lewes and George Eliot." *ELH* 67:2 (2000): 617–53.

Meredith, George. *The Egoist*. New York: Norton, 1979.

Mill, John Stuart. *On Liberty and Other Essays*. Oxford: Oxford University Press, 1998.

Miller, D. A. *Jane Austen, or the Secret of Style*. Princeton, NJ: Princeton University Press, 2003.

———. *Narrative and Its Discontents: Problems of Closure in the Traditional Novel*. Princeton, NJ: Princeton University Press, 1981.

————. *The Novel and the Police*. Berkeley: University of California Press, 1988.

Miller, J. Hillis. *Fiction and Repetition: Seven English Novels*. Cambridge: Harvard University Press, 1982.

Miller, Rowland S. *Embarrassment: Poise and Peril in Everyday Life*. New York: Guilford Press, 1996.

Minto. "Did Washington Eat Green Peas with a Knife?" *Magazine of American History with Notes and Queries* 16 (July–December 1886): 500.

Moretti, Franco. *The Way of the World: The* Bildungsroman *in European Culture*. London: Verso, 2000.

Mozley, Anne. "Dress." *Blackwood's Edinburgh Magazine* 97 (April 1865): 425–26.

————. "On Manners." *Blackwood's Edinburgh Magazine* 90 (August 1861): 154–65.

Muller, E. *La politesse française: Traite des bienséances et du savoir-vivre*. Paris: Garnier Frères, 1861.

Newton, Sarah E. *Learning to Behave: A Guide to American Conduct Books before 1900*. Westport, CT: Greenwood Press, 1994.

Nunn, Joan. *Fashion in Costume: 1200–2000*. London: Herbert Press, 2000.

O'Farrell, Mary Ann. "Provoking George Eliot." In *Compassion: The Culture and Politics of an Emotion*. Edited by Lauren Berlant. New York: Routledge, 2004.

————. *Telling Complexions: The Nineteenth-Century English Novel and the Blush*. Durham, NC: Duke University Press, 1997.

Pater, Walter. *Appreciations, with an Essay on Style*. Oxford: Blackwell, 1967.

————. *Selected Writings of Walter Pater*. Edited by Harold Bloom. New York: Columbia University Press, 1974.

Perrot, Philippe. *Fashioning the Bourgeoisie: A History of Clothing in the Nineteenth Century*. Translated by Richard Bienvenu. Princeton, NJ: Princeton University Press, 1994.

Petroski, Henry. *The Evolution of Useful Things: How Everyday Artifacts—From Forks and Pins to Paper Clips and Zippers—Came to Be as They Are*. New York: Vintage, 1994.

Phillips, Adam. *On Kissing, Tickling, and Being Bored: Psychoanalytic Essays on the Unexamined Life*. Cambridge, MA: Harvard University Press, 1993.

Porter, Dennis. "*Madame Bovary* and the Question of Pleasure." In *Flaubert and Postmodernism*. Edited by Naomi Schor and Henry F. Majewski. Lincoln: University of Nebraska Press, 1984.

Post, Emily. *Etiquette in Society, in Business, in Politics and at Home*. New York: Funk and Wagnalls, 1922.

Proust, Marcel. *Against Sainte-Beuve and Other Essays*. London: Penguin, 1988.

Pykett, Lyn. *The Sensation Novel from* The Woman in White *to* The Moonstone. Plymouth, U.K.: Northcote House, 1994.

Ramazani, Vaheed K. *The Free Indirect Mode: Flaubert and the Poetics of Irony*. Charlottesville: University Press of Virginia, 1988.

Ray, Gordon N. *Thackeray: The Uses of Adversity, 1811–1846*. New York: McGraw-Hill, 1955.

Reddy, William M. *The Navigation of Feeling: A Framework for the History of Emotions*. Cambridge: Cambridge University Press, 2001.

Renoir, Jean. *My Life and My Films*. Translated by Norman Denny. New York: Atheneum, 1974.

————. *La Règle du jeu: Nouveau découpage intégral*. Edited by Olivier Curchod. Paris: Librairie Générale Française, 1998.

Ricks, Christopher. *Keats and Embarrassment*. Oxford: Clarendon Press, 1984.

Rosa, Matthew Whiting. *The Silver-Fork School: Novels of Fashion Preceding* Vanity Fair. New York: Columbia University Press, 1936.

Rouleau, Th. G. *Manuel des bienséances: A l'usage de candidates aux brevets d'Ecole Primaire.* Quebec: Dussault Proulx, 1897.

Rowe, John Carlos. *The Theoretical Dimensions of Henry James.* Madison: University of Wisconsin Press, 1984.

Russell, Bertrand. *Power: A New Social Analysis.* London: Routledge, 2004.

Santner, Eric L. *On the Psychotheology of Everyday Life: Reflections on Freud and Rosenzweig.* Chicago: University of Chicago Press, 2001.

Schor, Hilary M. *Scheherazade in the Marketplace: Elizabeth Gaskell and the Victorian Novel.* Oxford: Oxford University Press, 1992.

Sedgwick, Eve Kosofsky. "Queer Performativity: Henry James's *The Art of the Novel.*" *GLQ* 1 (1993): 1–16.

Seltzer, Mark. *Henry James and the Art of Power.* Ithaca, NY: Cornell University Press, 1984.

Shaw, George Bernard. *The Doctor's Dilemma, Getting Married, and the Shewing-Up of Blanco Posnet.* New York: Brentano's, 1928.

Simmel, Georg. "Fashion." In *On Individuality and Social Forms.* Edited by Donald N. Levine. Chicago: University of Chicago Press, 1971.

———. "Sociability." In *On Individuality and Social Forms.* Edited by Donald N. Levine. Chicago: University of Chicago Press, 1971.

"A 'Slumming' Romance." *New York Times,* November 21, 1886, 12, in *Henry James: The Contemporary Reviews.* Edited by Kevin J. Hayes. Cambridge: Cambridge University Press, 1996.

Spacks, Patricia Meyer. *Gossip.* New York: Knopf, 1985.

Spencer, Herbert. "Manners and Fashion." In *Essays: Scientific, Political, and Speculative.* London: Willimas and Norgate, 1891.

Starkie, Enid. *Flaubert: The Making of the Master.* New York: Atheneum, 1967.

Stevens, Hugh. *Henry James and Sexuality.* Cambridge: Cambridge University Press, 1998.

Tanner, Tony. *Adultery and the Novel: Contract and Transgression.* Baltimore: Johns Hopkins University Press, 1981.

Terada, Rei. *Feeling in Theory: Emotion after the "Death of the Subject."* Cambridge, MA: Harvard University Press, 2001.

Thackeray, William Makepeace. *The Book of Snobs.* Cologne: Könemann, 1999.

———. *The History of Henry Esmond.* London: Penguin, 1985.

———. *Vanity Fair.* London: Penguin, 1985.

Tifft, Stephen. "*Drôle de Guerre:* Renoir, Farce, and the Fall of France." *Representations* 38 (Spring 1992): 131–65.

Timpanaro, Sebastiano. *The Freudian Slip: Psychoanalysis and Textual Criticism.* Translated by Kate Soper. London: Verso, 1985.

Tomkins, Silvan. *Shame and Its Sisters: A Silvan Tomkins Reader.* Edited by Eve Kosofsky Sedgwick and Adam Frank. Durham. NC: Duke University Press, 1998.

Trilling, Lionel. *The Liberal Imagination: Essays on Literature and Society.* Garden City, NY: Doubleday Anchor, 1953.

Valéry, Paul. *Analects.* Translated by Stuart Gilbert. Princeton, NJ: Princeton University Press, 1970.

Visser, Margaret. *The Rituals of Dinner: The Origins, Evolution, Eccentricities, and Meaning of Table Manners.* London: Penguin, 1991.

Warner, Michael. "The Mass Public and the Mass Subject." In *The Phantom Public Sphere.* Edited by Bruce Robbins. Minneapolis: University of Minnesota Press, 1993.

Watt, Ian. *The Rise of the Novel.* Berkeley: University of California Press, 1957.

Watts, Richard J. *Politeness.* Cambridge: Cambridge University Press, 2003.

Weiner, Jon. "Mike Davis Talks about the 'Heroes of Hell.'" *Radical History Review* 85 (2003): 227–37.

Wells, H. G. *The War of the Worlds.* New York: Tor Classics, 1988.

Welsh, Alexander. *George Eliot and Blackmail.* Cambridge, MA: Harvard University Press, 1985.

Whigham, Frank. *Ambition and Privilege: The Social Tropes of Elizabethan Courtesy Theory.* Berkeley: University of California Press, 1984.

Whitebook, Joel. *Perversion and Utopia: A Study in Psychoanalysis and Critical Theory.* Cambridge, MA: MIT Press, 1994.

Winnett, Susan. *Terrible Sociability: The Text of Manners in Laclos, Goethe, and James.* Stanford, CA: Stanford University Press, 1999.

Winnicott, D. W. *Home Is Where We Start From: Essays by a Psychoanalyst.* New York: Norton, 1986.

Wittgenstein, Ludwig. *Philosophical Investigations.* Translated by G. E. M. Anscombe. New York: Macmillan, 1953.

Woloch, Alex. *The One vs. the Many: Minor Characters and the Space of the Protagonist in the Novel.* Princeton, NJ: Princeton University Press, 2003.

Yates, Julian. *Error, Misuse, Failure: Object Lessons from the English Renaissance.* Minneapolis: University of Minnesota Press, 2003.

Žižek, Slavoj. *Looking Awry: An Introduction to Jacques Lacan through Popular Culture.* Cambridge, MA: MIT Press, 1992.

———. "Melancholy and the Act." *Critical Inquiry* 26 (2000): 657–82.

Zola, Émile. *Nana.* Translated by George Holden. London: Penguin, 1972.

Zupančič, Alenka. *The Shortest Shadow: Nietzsche's Philosophy of the Two.* Cambridge, MA: MIT Press, 2003.

Index